RELOCATING
YOUR
WORKPLACE

WADMAN   DALY

CRISP PUBLICATIONS, INC

Menlo Park, California

This is a Self-Help Book.

We have done our best to give the reader useful and accurate information, but we know that User situations vary, as do laws and procedures and interpretations of them. If you feel you need legal advice or other expert assistance, you should seek the services of an attorney, architect, or other competent professional.

TO LINDY, HUGH, GROVER AND MARY

Acknowledgements

For so many years a student at their knee, I am indebted in ways I can never repay to big brothers, ex-wife, colleagues, partners, associates, and clients, all wise and giving friends.

To Patti, Jay and Joyce who shared an earthquake and much else; to Hugh, Chris, Linda, Kyle and Sue who shortened the computer learning curve; to the library staffs of U.C., Berkeley, San Francisco State University, Stanford, Rice, the University of Houston and the cities of San Francisco and Houston for their guidance; to Phil and Mike for their faith; and to Saucy for pure inspiration, go my endless thanks.

Credits

Computer Compilation: Chris Waterson

Word Processing: Patti Seldner

Text Editor: Bev Manber

Cover Art: Harriet Yale Russell

Illustrations: Hugh Daly and the Author

Book Design: The Author

ABOUT THE AUTHOR

Wadman Daly is Chicago raised. After the obligatory schools and military service, he apprenticed at a New York industrial design studio, then went to Connecticut as a furniture maker, and to Bolivia with the Peace Corps. He returned to commercial interior design in the U.S in the early '70s, later entered commercial real estate brokerage and in 1990, in San Francisco, started his relocation counseling firm. For over thirty years, he has guided relocation projects for organizations in business, government and education, in virtually every type of commercial building, in cities across the U.S.

Mr.Daly is a graduate of Northwestern University and attended the Art Center School of Los Angeles, New York University Graduate School of Business Administration, and the University of Houston. In the fields of interior architecture and real estate, he has worked for Becker & Becker Associates, New York; Jarvis Putty Jarvis, Dallas; ISD, Incorporated, Houston; and Cushman & Wakefield, Houston and the San Francisco Peninsula. He has taught at the University level, and is a past member, or professional affiliate, of the AIA, CSI, IBD and ULI.

Mr. Daly is founder and President of **Business Relocation Counseling**, providing User/tenants with information about the physical environment of the workplace. For further information contact: **B R C, 11122 Claremont Ave N.E., Ste 25, Albuquerque, NM 87112; Tel. (505) 271-2857.**

ABOUT THE BOOK

For the first time in one reference, here are all the things the manager needs to know about the byzantine process of relocating to a building of any kind, anywhere.

This is a User's book!

No-punches-pulled observations on how you work with the Players: Architects, Brokers, Attorneys, Landlords and Public Officials.

Charts, graphs, and checklists. Detailed explanations of the Lease; Relocation Costs; Costs of Occupancy; Rents; Expenses; etc.

Evaluation Checklists for sites and buildings; Construction Checklists for the UPM (the User Project Manager); Move checklists for everyone in your organization.

DOING IT is a complete step by step instruction for the manager of the relocation process.

WHO SHOULD READ IT

This book is a must read for those who have ever felt frustrated trying to find and settle into an acceptable workplace. For large corporations and two-person shops, it is written for those who rent space for their organizations, who hire architects and lawyers, barter with landlords and try to understand real estate agents and brokers.

It should be studied by every businessowner, manager, or executive who has to deal with construction contractors, vendors and self-proclaimed experts in the building business, and be required reading for conscientious professionals.

READER COMMENTS

*" The comprehensive light you have shed on the entire business relocation process in **Relocating Your Workplace** is absolutely brilliant. Written in a clear, concise, easy to read style, and well seasoned with humor."* **Fred Croshaw**, *Real Estate Attorney, Houston, San Francisco*

" Being responsible for real estate development for a fast paced medical device manufacturer, I found that anyone in the trenches could use a dose of Wadman's approach." **Wm.Carey Chenoweth**, *Nellcor, Inc., Hayward, CA.*

*" The comprehensive checklists under **Doing It** are wonderful tools to evaluate, plan and execute a move. Detailed use of this will save hours of exasperation and stress, and many hundreds of thousands of dollars."* **Christopher J. Whyman**, *CEO, Eastern Realty Investment Management, Incorporated, Washington, D.C.*

" A definitive, easy to follow, comprehensive guide for businesses of all types considering relocation. In particular, the Chapter on "The Lawyer", is an invaluable tool for every lawyer handling real estate transactions." **Fred Caploe**, *Attorney, Richmond, California*

" As President of a large contract stationer, I've relocated a company and I know that the process can make otherwise normal businesspeople crazy and frustrated. This book can restore sanity to the process and may be the best expenditure you make while relocating your company !" **Steve Van Guelpen**, *Hayward, California*

*" **Relocating Your Workplace** is the basic book on business relocation."* **Robert L. Goldman**, *PhD, Management Consultant, San Francisco.*

CONTENTS

CONTENTS

INTRODUCTION

This book is about people and buildings

This book is about people and the buildings they work in today: the places where we spend half our waking hours - a third of our life. This is where we earn what we need for food and lodging, schools, kids, mortgages, vacations, health care, our future -life - where the light we see by and the air we breathe are products of the technology of our time, shared by tens and hundreds and thousands of others, human beings, fellow workers, and strangers who have become part of our extended family.

. . . And moving from one place to another

It is about the buildings of commerce and industry, the environment they create for us, and the nature and extent of our control over them. It is especially about that time in the life of an organization when a space has to be prepared to move into in order to begin life, or to continue it in an environment better suited to the changing needs of the organization.

This book is for building Users—Tenants and Buyers

This book is addressed to those who must occupy and use the workplace: the organization managers and entrepreneurs and executives who become responsible for acquiring it, through lease or purchase, and who are charged with making it suitable for human occupancy, if not transforming it into a stimulating and productive work environment. It is addressed to those who recognize that this is not a responsibility to be taken lightly, and that significant economic loss and worker dissatisfaction can result from haphazard planning and execution of it.

Readers will be buyers as well as tenants. Their focus is similar, if not identical, and they share many of the real estate investor's concerns over building quality, cost and long-term value. But you will find that the discussion invariably turns to the preoccupations of the non-equity-sharing tenant who is trying to find utility as well as value in America's commercial buildings.

Relocation is complicated and the building industry does not make it easier

The installation or relocation of a business, or any for-profit or not-for-profit organization, is a complex task. It is made so by the wide diversity of elements that make up the process and by a tradition-bound industry which, along with its principal protagonists, has only recently and reluctantly entered the Twentieth century. The business of the development, design and construction of commercial buildings is that industry. It is one that has grown like so many in these fast-moving times, with no more precedent than is provided by centuries of building dwellings and churches and great monuments. Its client, the productive forces of the world's economies, is already moving swiftly into the Twenty-first century, dragging with it, like a frightened and retarded child, a component that is critical to its success. There is no question of the importance of modern building facilities to the success of any enterprise.

Our emphasis is on high-density buildings

Because our bias is people and the way the workplace affects us, this text emphasizes the kinds of buildings and spaces where people density is liable to be greater than in those with concentrations of machinery and equipment. It focuses on offices and R&D buildings, light manufacturing and flex workspaces, even though much of the material will be applicable to factories, warehouses and special-use buildings.

The underlying purpose of all of these buildings is the same: to provide a workplace capable of safely sheltering productive resources, with the air and utilities that they need to function, and the undisturbed use of which is reasonably guaranteed over an extended period of time.

It seems like chaos, but you can get control

The interaction of the technical complexities of building with the distinctive attitudes and behavior patterns of the builder and his supporting cast of players has been the subject of much study and writing. It is an intricate dance that seems to defy choreography and give the appearance, if not the reality, of chaos, as the planning, design and construction of the workplace proceed. As witnesses to this process, as well as those who pay for it and suffer with its results, we fervently hope to avoid it when we can, and struggle to grasp and control it when it is thrust upon us.

This book is written to shed light and lend some sense of order to that process. It is written to serve as a working tool in your efforts to engage it, set it in motion and manage it. To that end, we have tried to present clear instructions and guidelines. But we feel that there is also an opportunity here for the alert and aggressive entrepreneur who, in the best sense of his mission, looks to go beyond managing a process designed and imposed by others - who looks for an opportunity to shape the process to his own goals and, ultimately, to draw from it more than it is designed to give. It is our firm belief that the latter is entirely possible in the process of acquiring, planning, designing, constructing and furnishing the Workplace.

We also believe that this admirable goal is achievable only if there are insights into the process that are not found in instructions or guidelines, or in textbooks written for the various disciplines involved in the process. For this reason, we have divided our book in two parts. Each bears on the subject in a complete way, from a different perspective.

Prepare yourself by understanding the process

In the first section, **Preparing Yourself**, we discuss the ideas, concepts, people, tools, skills, language, etc., that underlie and form the basis of the process of assembling the Workplace, and which are necessary to understanding how to achieve the one you seek. We provide some history because there is much and because to see where we have been is instructive to understanding where and how far we might expect to go. And we offer some views on the participants or players, their process, their language and the tools that they have developed over many years to achieve their—and your—goals.

Engage the process and make it work

The second section, **Doing It**, is set apart for easy and quick access. We lay out the process for the Reader to evaluate the workplace, find and acquire it, plan, design and construct it, and furnish and move into it. Because we have been through this process more than a few times ourselves, we know that the documents, charts, memos, graphs and memoranda, etc., that will be generated by you, or on behalf of your workplace project, will vastly exceed anything that we might write about it. But, since these documents are a critical part of your eventual success, we have devoted a substantial part of our presentation to their form and content. The intention is to provide you with firm guidelines, without restricting your ability to adapt to your own detailed requirements.

Nobody has ever done what you are about to do

What you are about to embark on, whether it means moving to the suite down the hall or into your own newly-acquired building, has never been done before. The ground you are about to set foot on, the process you will soon set in motion, is as new to those professionals and tradespeople who will assist you as it is to you and your staff. Those same professionals and tradespeople will try, in all good faith, to persuade you that they have been down this same path, have swum these same waters, and have overcome these same obstacles with great success. They have not been down the path you are about to lead them. They do not know where you are going or how they are going to help you get there. It is up to you to show them how. This book will help you do just that.

Our caveats

Professional real estate and facility managers, developers, brokers, architects, engineers and others who are technically trained in the great variety of disciplines associated with the creation of the workplace may be disappointed by our presentation. We are not writing for professional societies, for academia or even for those with whom we have worked closely for more than thirty years in this most demanding, challenging and so often frustrating field. There is little we have to add to the much admired skills of our peers, or to their dedication and vigilance in the interest of those to whom our labors are mutually dedicated: the users of our plans and our constructions and our buildings.

. . . And apologies

If our words fail to inspire or to inform and enlarge a body of knowledge, or if we seem too critical at times of the product or the effort of the professional workplace builder, we apologize. Our perspective is unabashedly warped. Our judgments are skewed to the belief that the workplace must be designed for human beings and must enhance their productive efforts, not remain forever an impediment to them.

PART I

PREPARING YOURSELF

An Introduction

There are not many activities in your business life that hold out the rewards of challenge, engagement and fulfillment quite like that of relocating the workplace. It is an adventure, with all the excitement and risks of one, but in familiar territory, on terrain you have walked, amid objects and faces you have seen. Preparation seems redundant because you know the places and the players. **Doing It** is what you came to this book for—not history or philosophy or characterizations of people with whom you have spent a business lifetime. And for that reason, half of this book is dedicated to just plain doing it.

For those who are less than confident about knowing this territory, and who have a nagging suspicion that there is more to do than follow a good checklist, the pages of **Preparing Yourself** are worth your time. *A Little Bit of History*, for example, suggests that our system of commercial building, literally and figuratively, has weak underpinnings indeed. If you glance at *Public Officials* in Chapter 3 after reading about *The Workplace*, you will realize that in this end of the century we are little better able to provide ourselves with a healthy working environment than we were at the beginning of it.

And if you are at all concerned with the cost of your relocation project, or feel that your Ph.D. in Financial Management will save any budget crisis, look over the roster of *The Players* in Chapter 3. Read about the legendary skills of those who make a good living at cleaning their clients' pockets.

If you are curious about the language of relocation, be assured that you are correct in thinking that it often bears little resemblance to English. A knowledge of its terms is as important to relocation as the tools and process we discuss, so we have placed a Glossary conveniently in the middle of our book--handy for *Preparing Yourself* as well as *Doing It*.

There is much more to be said about this adventure than will fit comfortably in this book. Things come to our mind that want for more detailed exposition, or that were excluded by seemingly arbitrary priorities or that appear in pieces scattered here and there like parts of some diabolical landlord's lease. So we ask that you read **Preparing Yourself** as you would a lease, with an eye to the margins and the spaces and the implied meanings.

As you read, move freely between **Preparing Yourself** and **Doing It** to get a sense of the total environment of this terrain, this new adventure.

Chapter 1

THE WORKPLACE

A LITTLE BIT OF HISTORY

It seems foolish to have to remind ourselves that the workplace is designed for people. But is it? Look around the next time you are in your office or place of work. Is it well lighted? Can you write, key and read your computer, and dial your phone without squinting or straining your eyes? Is the surface you walk and stand on during the day comfortable? Does it vibrate or make noise as you walk? Do you feel uncomfortable drafts of air, or damp, stagnant or smelly air? Are important workplace destinations, including the restrooms, within a reasonable distance, along well-marked, well-lighted and obstacle-free corridors? Do the colors and textures around you please you? Can you see outside light or an outdoor view from your workstation? Do you feel protected and safe from bumps, bruises or falls as you enter and move around your workplace? Are un-manned support spaces, like conference and storage rooms, fully equipped, well lighted and readily accessible? Have you been in other places that seem more user-friendly?

The chances are that your answer to the last question is a resounding *yes* and to the others mixed, if not largely negative. Do not be surprised. The Great American Workplace is not user-friendly, not easy to live and work in, and not particularly well-designed for the people who have to use it. Then, who or what is it designed for?

Are you ready?

Machines.

The industrial revolution re-shaped the farm-worker

The Workplace, as we know it, is largely a product of the nineteenth century. As the Industrial Revolution took hold, the building trades were pressed to adapt their limited technology to housing the burgeoning variety of equipment coming from the drawing boards of the great inventors of the era. Buildings had, first and foremost, to accommodate the then enormous size and weight of mechanical dinosaurs of every imaginable purpose— spinning jennies, carding machines, immense looms, forges and kilns of every variety, presses, casting and milling equipment, etc., and for the cumbersome steam-generating equipment that powered them.

The people who fed, attended and nursed these monsters were mobile and flexible; the machines were decidedly not. Machines were costly to build, long-lived, durable and productive. Workers were cheap, readily available, and neither durable nor dependable. Factories were designed and built so that the industrial worker would simply fit into interior spaces left over, once the machine was properly mounted and sufficient room was provided for the carts and drays that would haul raw materials and finished product to and from it. If the latter could move on a dirt floor or on a muddy one, or on a cloudy day in obscure light, so, certainly, could a worker.

Workers and managers alike were tucked into corners.

Straw bosses were accommodated in small enclosures on the factory floor, wherever these spaces could be made to fit into an unused portion of the interior. Superintendents and foremen and engineers were allowed minimal interior work spaces in lofts or crudely constructed mezzanines—where they continue to work today. Owners and partners, who were the entrepreneurs and decision-makers in the days before the corporate executive, sometimes allowed themselves a more human work environment in the form of an out-building. Very often this was a house already located on the premises, which had the luxuries of light, heat, a roof and a dry floor.

The concept of human amenity was not an operative part of the Nineteenth century notion of the workplace. The concept was toil—day labor in the biblical sense. Seen as more than a way to make a living, factory labor expiated one's sins. It was also worlds better than laboring in the fields. The factory meant relief from burning, bleaching suns and rain, and numbing chills and backs and limbs bent forever to the earth. It was enough that there were four walls and a roof. Light for the machines was an important consideration in the design of the factory building. That spoke volumes to the order of things in men's minds.

Primitive beginnings led to bad building habits in the Twentieth century

These early industrial buildings, forerunners of the commercial buildings we work in today, were constructed of masonry—rubble or stone or brick—with walls that were very thick at their base, to carry the weight of a high roof with its supporting trusses. The extra-high roof was necessary to span the machines below as well as the myriad belts and gears that fed them power. Penetration of these walls for eye-level windows was either impossible or considered impractical and very expensive. Thus, the source for outside light became the clerestory, a row of windows placed horizontally just below the roof line, or the ubiquitous factory skylight that Americans everywhere came to recognize by its sawtooth silhouette. The exterior-lighting design features of these buildings became a standard that carried over to the newer kinds of construction being introduced at the end of the century. The development of structural iron and steel allowed for the use of thinner curtain walls that kept the weather out and did not have to support anything. But, even though the new materials would permit the installation of windows that could provide an outside view as well as light, factory buildings of every kind continued to grow up without them—after all, we had the great leveler that made windows redundant—the electric light.

Twentieth century building gave us monuments instead of people places.

While machines were responsible for the creation of the Great American Workplace in the Nineteenth Century, with the birth of the American service worker and the introduction of the urban multi-story building before the turn of the century, one would think that the human being would now become the principal focus of building design attention. People—as entrepreneurs, workers, shoppers, clients and tradespersons—would be their exclusive occupants and users and, presumably, their reason for being human in scale and in understanding of human function and need. Curiously, this would not be the case.

As the increasing economic activity of the new cities crowded more people and more enterprises into them, buildable land became scarce and costly. Building structures grew upward "with the advent of the steel frame and the elevator, the two technological innovations that made great skyscrapers on the one hand possible and on the other hand practical," says Paul Goldberger in **Skyscraper**. Sometimes, they did so with a specific purpose in mind: to house a bank or a newspaper, or the offices of an important manufacturer. As often as not, they rose as monuments with the vague notion that they would eventually be filled with doctors and lawyers and sales offices. What we now know as speculative office building was aborning, but it was not yet an identifiable industry with an economic reason for being, or even a recognizable and approachable market.

As land values pushed buildings upward, the cost of steel mounted with each additional foot of building height. Mr. Goldberger focuses on the character of the urban landscape as it is enriched by noble examples of skyscraper architecture. He also draws our attention to the massive infill of buildings that "were becoming more machine-made, more vulnerable to standardization, [and] were cheaper and more practical to erect." These were the buildings that housed the preponderant number of urban workers. The economies instituted by their developers did not come without a price, in terms of their human occupants.

"By turning our environment over to the machine we have robbed the machine of the one promise it held out—that of enabling us to humanize more thoroughly the details of our existence".

So wrote architectural historian and critic Lewis Mumford in *Sticks and Stones*, his seminal critique of the contemporary urban American environment. He notes that the factory affected the environment of architecture in the early stages of industrial development, but that in its latest incarnation, the factory has become the environment. The early century workplace was miserable; it became the standard for all that followed. The commercial building of the early Twentieth century was simply

11

a Nineteenth century factory turned on end. The same principles applied in bringing it together—making certain that the foundation was strong and durable, that its walls and columns would hold it up, that its equipment (elevators, stairs, furnaces and boilers, etc.), would fit, and that its occupants would be reasonably sheltered against the vagaries of nature.

The question of what human beings would do in it was treated much as it was nearly a hundred years before: people were mobile and flexible and would make good use of available space. Toilets were an amenity and did not appear with great frequency. Water for drinking or cleaning and the waste pipes to carry it away were equally scarce. Electrical power for lighting and operating equipment was limited to a handful of outlets per floor. And the management of conditioned air was a circus performed daily by overcoated secretaries and office boys, who attempted to manipulate recalcitrant steam radiators, transoms and immense operable windows, while battling building janitors and engineers.

Questions of health, safety and security were not broached unless they clearly related to the security and safety of the owner's property. Bad light and foul air, inoperable elevators, blocked or non-existent stairs and exits, leaks, breaks and ruptures of all kinds were endemic in the early-century commercial building; these conditions are well-documented. Like all the other features of the developing Workplace, these conditions constituted a kind of standard upon which the contemporary workplace would be built.

After World War II, buildings got better

In the years following WW II, conditions of the workplace changed gradually. Structures became leaner, with fewer interior columns that were more evenly spaced. Fuel oil and forced air circulating through overhead ducts replaced steam and radiant heat. Cheaper electricity was distributed more generously. The advent of the fluorescent tube meant more light fixtures for the power dollar. If the lavatory was not on the same floor, it was only half a floor away. And there was something called the Uniform Building Code that attempted to establish and monitor rules for construction as it affected public health and safety.

. . . But not by much

Thus, the economics of building that forced the developer to explore new technology, and the community's gradually growing concern for the dangers inherent in the new workplace, combined to produce improvements in it. But these did not always represent improvements from the user viewpoint. As Mr. Mumford pointed out, new conditioned air systems meant the end of the operable window and fresh air in factories, stores and offices everywhere. Leaner structural systems meant noisy, vibrating surfaces underfoot, and reduced floor-loading capacity—a major headache for manufacturers and users of large office equipment.

In the period before the war—which happens to be a handy calendar marker for many things, like major building that stopped abruptly and then started up again years later—the floor size of a typical urban building was quite small. This meant that people could be close to exterior windows. Larger, more efficient floors, developed through postwar building technology, began to throw increasing numbers of workers into badly lighted interior spaces that were ostensibly intended for storage.

We could not figure out the light we need

The fluorescent lamp, which has become the light source of choice for commercial builders everywhere, gave us fits for decades, with its wavering, low-intensity light and noisy, cumbersome ballasts. Its performance has been greatly improved, but control of its color and of its luminaire and lens environment is still wildly variable.

. . . Or the air we breathe

The battle for control of the window and the radiator in the workplace was replaced by a more genteel conflict over control of the thermostat; the underlying difficulty could be seen as the same—too warm in some places, too chilly in others. We made great strides in gentrifying the air conditioning system and fewer in improving its efficiency and service.

It took a half-century to discover the debilitating human effects of air-borne or friable building asbestos, which can still be found in insulating materials and floor tiles. More recently, in its place, we have put fiberglass in the walls and ceilings, and synthetic fibers on the floor—with little more idea of their ultimate effects than we had of asbestos.

Three-quarters of the air-conditioning dollars spent in America's commercial buildings is said to be spent on the removal of offensive odors—mostly tobacco smoke and bathroom odors. The latter may have to be tolerated as long as we function the way we do, but it may be light years before OSHA and the Congress can find ways to restrain the menace of tobacco smoke.

But the tragedy of modern commercial building air is that it can still find ways to kill. Witness the deaths from Legionnaires disease in Philadelphia in 1976 and more recently in Richmond, California in 1990. These events, which very well may not have been the first of their kind, are waiting to repeat themselves in commercial buildings across the country that employ similar ducting systems to recirculate interior air.

Commercial buildings are built for people. We want to be able to assume as much if we buy or lease one, or a part of one. But are they? History is instructive in this regard, even though it fails to uncover why we seem so intent on replicating failed buildings and building systems. While the making of shelters is an activity almost as old as the human race, the evolution of the shelter as workplace—a structure designed to support and facilitate man in the performance of productive tasks—is comparatively new and very much in its developmental stages.

We need to understand this fact of modern workplace life as we look for a place to put our organization, its people and its equipment.

THE WORKPLACE AS FACILITY

In the parlance of the trades that deal closely with these matters, the workplace is known as a facility. The idea is that it is a structure built to shelter, support or facilitate some productive human activity. A gasoline station is a facility. Though it may only be productive of horrendous scores, the golf course is a facility; a campus and the buildings on it comprise the school facility. When you are asked what kind of facility you are in by those in the trades that deal closely with these matters, the appropriate response might be: "a store in the downtown mall," or "a suite in the 200 Broadway building," or "a plant in Dodds Business Park," etc.

Coast to coast and border to border, wherever Americans work they grow facilities (those assemblages of brick and mortar, steel and glass, walls and doors and all the spaces those things shelter and enclose), and the sundry utilities passing in and out of them (water, waste water, electricity, cooled and heated air, etc.) and all of the equipment necessary to keep them alive and functioning (elevators, switchboards, furnaces, pipes and tanks, chillers and fans and transformers) all whirring and buzzing and thumping to facilitate the Great American Workplace.

The shape of the Twenty-first century facility will be dictated by law.

The facility may be thought of in a variety of ways—by the way it is built, by its age, by its height, by its location in the urban landscape, by its design type, by the use to which it is put or for which it was intended, etc. In short, it may be considered and catalogued in almost as many ways as there are distinctive features to it. But there is a kind of characteristic that undeniably and most effectively sets workplace facilities apart from one another: the extent to which they may or may not meet the requirements of the law. These requirements will be discussed more fully later on; for now, keep in mind that building features required by law are not always readily visible, that they do change with some frequency, and that they cannot be ignored in favor of some more attractive building features.

Facility Types: Four different kinds

There are four distinct groups of workplace-facilities:

- ■ **Factory**

■ **Office**

■ **Retail**

■ **Institutional**

The distinctions between these categories have become increasingly blurred in recent years. In newer downtown office buildings, in urban and suburban shopping malls, and in office and industrial parks there is a seemingly healthy mix of these different kinds of organizational activity that survives and thrives on a sharing of site features, structure and vertical transportation, mechanical and electrical systems, and maintenance and security services. Administratively, they often share the same kind of treatment of their rent and their payments for utilities and operating expenses.

Manufacturing plants are looking less like factories

Factory facilities can be separated into two groups, each with a broad spectrum of building type. The special-use building might include steel mills, aircraft hangars, local lumberyards and nuclear power plants. The requirements of these types of facilities are beyond the scope of this book, except when parts of them, like offices, fit into the more general concern.

The generic factory building is designed for multiple use while it retains features peculiar to manufacturing—railroad sidings, loading docks, heavy duty power, etc— and generally located away from population centers. For the last ten or more years it has been a one or two story building, often built speculatively, capable of adaptation to light manufacture of virtually every type, as well as warehousing, research and development, laboratory and, in some circumstances, pure office use.

Offices can go anywhere—and often do

Office facilities are hardly capable of definition by building type since people have a penchant for fitting into out-of-the-way places. Thus, we find offices in old homes, factories, churches, warehouses, garages, etc. In the city, the office is generally identified by a multi-story structure of any age or architectural style, divided horizontally into floors roughly 15 feet apart; a spacing that may be indicated by the building's window lines.

Since modern architecture brought us round, triangular and trapezoidal buildings, and commercial real estate re-zoned itself into suburbs and farmlands, we can further identify the office facility as a building with three or more walls and a roof enclosing an interior space of one or more floors. It may have windows; it may not.

Today, the most outwardly distinguishing feature of the office and the factory facility today is the ubiquitous automobile. Its presence in lots, rows or stacks in a parking structure is often the only exterior indication that the adjacent building is subdivided into offices.

Stores follow crowds of people and cars

Retail facilities share the distinguishing characteristic of visibility that is enhanced by a more or less formal effort at store design that may or may not carry over to architectural design. Building age and structural type are not of decisive importance; location is. More than any other workplace, the retail facility is dependent on the vagaries of demographics and forced to respond to them to achieve success. The latter is hardly a visible characteristic, except as one assumes that the presence of a large store or group of stores is, by itself, an indicator of a strong local retail market.

Market and demographic dependency often place the retail facility in or adjacent to other facility types—downtown or in suburban centers. And, like the office, the retail facility is distinguished by the automobile and proximity to some kind of organized accommodation for it.

Civic buildings look more and more like offices and factories

Institutional facilities include structures dedicated to government, not-for-profit organizations and recreational and entertainment facilities. They are best distinguished by their intended use (hospitals, civic centers, schools and libraries, stadia, theaters, etc.) and by their unique and often complex building construction features. We will not address these requirements except as they include needs related to work-intense activities, such as administrative offices. Many of these are already located in high-density office buildings and are very much a part of our concerns here.

The Facility is designed around its major spaces

The chances are good that when the commercial building is on the drawing board, its developing stages have a strong sense of order that takes shape within the context of Public Areas, Service Areas, and User Areas. Keep these spatial distinctions in mind when you visualize any building that may interest you as a prospective workplace facility. Whether you plan to be tenants or sole occupants, to lease or to own your own facility, it will be important to your staff, your clients, suppliers and visitors that the facility is organized in a straightforward, easily comprehensible manner.

Public Areas start at the front door, wherever that may be

Public Areas include any entry space, foyer or entry level lobby, as well as the corridors that lead away from the entry into the interior of the building. Stairs, elevators, escalators, lavatories, atria, telephone booths and waiting lounges represent spaces which typically fall within the Public definition. Similar spaces and corridors that lead people towards building exits on upper or lower floors may also be public. Nothing in the notion of public, used in the context of the typical commercial building, implies an owner obligation to provide unlimited access to the general public to his/her building. As a matter of fact, owners and building tenants alike look to place restrictions on who is allowed to enter the multi-tenant workplace facility.

The no-front-door syndrome

How many times have you been in the building of an associate where you didn't use the front door and would not know how to locate it? How many commercial buildings have you been in that you would swear do not have a front door?

This disorienting phenomena is not something peculiar to older downtown office buildings. Over the years these buildings have been squeezed together until many have lost their identity. It has been designed into new buildings as well. In downtowns everywhere, the fierce competition among developers to raise the ultimate major world-class building that will attract more notice and more tenants than any other has pushed them, and their architects into distortions of architectural order that defy common sense. The no-front-door syndrome in business parks, malls and complexes in the suburbs is carried to the limits of confusion by well-intentioned architects and landscape architects and builder/developers who have private visions of recreating Harvard Square or a mountain village in southern Italy. The indescribable pleasures associated with discovering the mysteries of the latter have become confused with the effort to locate a particular business in a suburban rat-maze of hundreds with identical architectural trimmings.

As we enter a building or a complex of buildings, we are looking for a sense of the order of things that we consciously and unconsciously associate with the idea of a front door, a principal entry, an introduction to a set of architectural spaces that represent our workplace. Because it reasonably follows that if there is confusion over the location or, worse yet, the existence of it, there is a concomitant confusion about who we are and what we do.

Building services need to be centrally located

Service Areas are far less distinguishable than Public or User areas; they are designed to be used almost exclusively by the building owner and his/her technical and maintenance staff. They are generally scattered throughout the building behind locked and unmarked doors. These include mechanical rooms and janitor closets, furnace rooms, penthouse or rooftop areas set aside for elevator or air-handling equipment, electrical and utility rooms, elevator, escalator shafts and machine spaces, above-the-ceiling spaces anywhere and everywhere, and other spaces set aside for the owner operate and maintain the building. Where these service spaces can be clustered, they are referred to as core spaces. All of these spaces differ principally in that the owner can choose—as he/she usually does—to lock these off from access by the public or building tenants.

User spaces are private spaces

We are most interested in User Areas, and these happen to be the ones that represent the bulk of the space, or square footage, inside any commercial building. The principal characteristic of these areas is that they are capable of being locked off —made inaccessible to the public and, with certain rights withheld by that person or entity, to the owner as well. This concept of privacy and non-interference in the reasonable conduct of a legitimate business extends to things like noise and light as well as to human beings. If you look at a facility that has everything you wish for and is designed so that the outside world cannot be shut out completely when you need it to be—from the sight, smells and sounds of humans and other animals—you may wish to look elsewhere.

The way the Players see Facilities often defines them

There was a time when user distinctions between facility types was helpful: when manufacturing meant dirt, smoke, noise and a part of town across the tracks; when stores had lofty interior spaces and expensive fixtures; when institutional buildings meant granite and beaux arts architecture; and when an office could go anywhere the other three types would not.

Brokers, contractors, developers and architects followed these distinctions. In many ways they helped to institutionalize them by focusing their skills and interests on one or the other and creating departments, divisions and studios to deal with the requirements of each. The great commercial building boom of the seventies and eighties democratized these players, however, by making one building type as attractive as any other. Today, the trades related to the business of building make, first and foremost, a clear distinction between their residential and commercial activities. Then, they generally distinguish their interests along the lines indicated above.

The players distinguish between those building types they are familiar with and those they are not. The commercial real estate brokerage office, which may operate a residential division in a separate location if it is large enough, hires agents to handle commercial and industrial properties. In the commercial group, responsible for office leasing and sales, there may be a retail specialist. The industrial broker deals with factories, warehouses, R&D and flex buildings, raw land and the hybrid assortment of properties that do not fall comfortably within the office or retail definitions.

Through the eyes of contractors, developers and architects

Large building contractors and developers tend to separate their operations in the same fashion; first they create a strong separation between residential and commercial activities, and then divide them by type. The latter tends to be identified with builder skills and experience, as these things relate to *kinds of construction*, rather than to use. Thus, the developer/builder skilled in one- and two-story steel buildings may not venture into high-rise construction, but he will build for any user imaginable that might fit into his one- and two-story program.

Architects are less likely to exclude a building type from their practice, and are also less inclined to attempt the broad reach of other segments of the real estate industry. Some larger firms will establish a group or studio to handle projects in user-related fields, with special requirements like health care, laboratories and office buildings. They are strongly user-oriented problem-solvers and usually loathe to identify themselves exclusively with a building type, however, those who have a strong background in commercial building, will often exclude or minimize their residential practice.

THE FACILITY AS REAL ESTATE

The workplace-as-facility would not be much without the real property it sits on. Our lease on the 40th floor downtown and our option to buy a build-to-suit in the local business park are predicated on the nature and characteristics of the parcel of land that go with the building. These parcels are often called building sites. The economics of modern real estate call for maximizing the building site, which means placing the largest footprint on it that the law will allow.

If you walk or drive up to a building you like because of the pleasant space around it, do not assume that all or even most of what you see belongs to your building. Zoning laws in most areas provide for minimal setbacks from the curb line and for spaces between structures, where those are possible, as well as pedestrian and vehicular access and parking accommodations—but that is about all. As a tenant or owner of a property, you will have a shared right to use this portion of your facility, in much the same way as you have an exclusive right to the use of your premises—or the part of your new facility in which you will work; provided these rights are included in your lease or purchase agreement.

Site descriptions, property boundaries, easements and other meaningful information regarding the beginning and end of your rights to property you lease or buy is seldom offered to the prospective tenant. And, when it is provided—usually at lease signing—it is often woefully inadequate.

It is not unusual for pieces of a seemingly homogeneous commercial property to be held by more than one owner. A distant institution, unrelated to the landlord of your workplace, may own an adjacent parking lot or storage building that you use. Under his own agreement with the adjacent property owner, the landlord may have a legitimate claim to rent from you for its use, even though he may have no control over its disposition. If that ownership should change, for reasons unknown to you, what you thought were your rights to use of the property may also change and bring some drastic results to the operation of your business. These are the kinds of real estate facts that are of great importance to you. The landlord, in blissful ignorance of your concerns, will also find it inconvenient to mention them.

Similar considerations can extend to the ownership and ultimate disposition of property adjacent to or near that which interests you, and which might affect your concerns about views from your suite, or client or delivery access to your place of business. It may seem attractive now, but be wary of the unbuilt space around the structure being offered. There may be no knowledge of that owner's eventual intent, but the local zoning office can tell you what can be constructed legitimately there. If adjacent property is developed, a quiet survey of its occupants can be revealing. Background on its owners can be helpful in determining how it will be used and maintained.

When you inspect the appearance of a given site, it can often be misleading—fences and curbs that have no relation to property lines, parking accommodations that appear to be available for your use and are not, driveways and building entrances that are for the exclusive use of others, signage that is misleading, etc. Commercial landlords often convey this kind of information so shabbily that the site description worked up by their marketers and leasing agents does not correspond to the legal description included, by law, with your lease.

Shortcomings in these real estate aspects of your facility may be less than critical to you, as the user of part of a multi-tenant property; though it should not substitute for your due diligence, there is some security in being surrounded by other tenants with similar concerns. Deficiencies of this kind can mean much more if you lease or buy as an operator with heavy shipping and/or receiving needs, with heavy transient traffic, or need to accommodate your employees in a special way.

THE FACILITY AS BUILDING, STRUCTURE AND SYSTEM

The common denominator of the greatest number of buildings you will look at to house your facility will be steel-frame construction. This will not be readily apparent to you, nor need it interest you greatly, but it does have implications for how you use your building. If you live and work in or near virtually any American city—or any in the Western world—you will have seen a steel frame building under construction; the enormous beams and columns look like so much steel shelving going up in the sky. Structural components are dropped into it, or hung on it and become floor and walls. The hung aspect of the outside wall, which bears only its own weight, contributes to its being referred to as a curtain wall.

The curtain wall may also be the principal part of the building *envelope*. It is comprised of glazing units, meaning window glass, panels and mullions. The horizontal spacing of the mullion may determine the width of interior work space; vertical placement of it may become a window sill that affects how we use furniture on the inside of the exterior wall. When the Bauhaus architctural style reigned supreme, and the architectural practice of *revealing*—or articulating—structural elements, like a building floor, were carefully followed, one could easily see the relationship of floor to sill while standing outside the building. No more. Changes in architectural styles combined with further advances in construction technology have conspired to erase that possibility.

One of the latter advances has been the further development of poured concrete construction. This type of construction provides economy as well as greater fire safety, but also means bulkier beams and interior columns. For the user, this may mean a firmer feel to the deck underfoot, a slight reduction in floor space and the size of openings available for windows and more interior wall surfaces that resist drilling or fastening of any kind.

The true masonry skyscraper

In *The Skyscraper*, New York Times architectural critic Paul Goldberger says, "The Monadnock in Chicago, 1891, by Burnham and Root, is not a steel-frame building; it is the last of the great solid-masonry-walled structures, yet it is a skyscraper, for here the powerful brick walls rise to 16 stories, smooth and clean in a way that must have appeared startling to nineteenth-century eyes. The walls are thick and heavy at the bottom and then, as if to express the diminishing weight they bear as they rise, they taper to thinness."

Masonry may be defined as built-up construction that consists of building units made of materials like clay, glass, stone or concrete. The way masonry is used in a building is of particular interest to the building user. A masonry bearing wall was used to construct the Monadnock, as well as many other brick and stone buildings in older parts of our cities. There are not many of them left, so you will probably not run across one during a facility search; however, because of their innate strength and sculptural beauty, you may be seeking one, so we want to point out problems associated with them. These include problems related to the soundness of the structure and to the distribution of air, power, water and waste water within it. If these problems are solved to the User's—and the City's—satisfaction, and the interior space is designed to utilize the masonry structure in a cognizant way, an exceptionally attractive workplace can result.

Masonry, principally in the form of brick, is also used as a veneer on the outside of commercial buildings of steel frame construction. Even for the trained eye, these buildings can be hard to distinguish from the buildings described above. The telltale signs are usually building height—the Monadnock notwithstanding, bearing-wall buildings are generally much shorter than 16 stories—and the thickness of the wall at building entrances and window openings. Brick-veneer buildings can be tall, large in scale, have many more windows than their older cousins, and otherwise act like other curtain wall buildings with other kinds of materials on the face of them.

For the less pragmatic user, an historic building is recommended

Many of the larger masonry bearing-wall structures around the country have been recognized by, or are qualified to fall within the purview of, the National Historic Preservation Act. This status can be a boon to an owner or prospective buyer of such a structure; it also can be a costly aggravation to someone who is uninformed about it. The Act is administered by the National Park Service (NPS) of the Department of the Interior. NPS' Technical Services Division in Washington, D.C. can provide information. Assistance is also available through the appropriate state Historic Preservation Office or NPS regional office. Since tax incentives are connected with rehabilitation of historic structures, your accountant may also have information on the subject. The acceptability of changes they wish to make to an already registered historic building is of particular concern to those who have no interest in Historic Preservation.

Building Design Standards

Design standards are a concept that affects the workplace as facility, as well as our ability to evaluate and use it. In *Experiencing Architecture*, Steen Eiler Rasmussen explains that when we consider how a building is produced, we realize that it is fairly necessary to work with standard units. The timber shipped to the lumberyard must fit the structure which the mason or carpenter has built up on the site. The stonecutter's work from a distant quarry must square with all the rest. When it arrives, windows and doors must fit exactly the openings that have been prepared for them.

When we look closely at the building in which we work, and at the buildings our attorney or dentist or other associate work in, we see the modern expression of the age-old standards to which Mr. Rasmussen refers: all interior doors are three feet wide; all floor tiles are a foot square and ceiling tiles are two feet by four feet, except that a few are the same size as the floor tiles; the windows are all the same width and/or height, and all the light fixtures look the same everywhere. Under their paint or fabric finish, we can not easily see the width of the gypsum board wall panels, but the thickness of the walls never varies. Outside, the panels on the face of the building are finished in different textures and colors. Yet their articulation— or separation from one another—shows clearly that they have been manufactured to some specified standard size.

In their introduction to *Construction: Principles, Materials, & Methods*, the authors tell us more about standards:

> "The preparation of standards may be the effort of a group of manufacturers, professionals or tradesmen seeking simplification and efficiency or the assurance of a minimum level of quality. Standards may also be the work of a governmental agency or other group interested in establishing minimum levels of safety and performance. Hence standards take on a variety of forms depending on source and purpose."

One of the outcomes of standards is economy in building. Another is uniformity. The first is a blessing for the builder; the latter contributes to making each workplace look and act like any other, regardless of its use.

An important standard for your planning purposes is the bay.

The user of any commercial building is necessarily concerned with how well it can be laid out to suit his operations. The bay size is another architectural and construction standard that is important to know about in this regard. The bay is simply the space between columns of a building. It is hoped to be a uniform space and often, though not always, is. The columns, of course, are the vertical structural posts that carry the weight of whatever may be above—a roof or another floor of the building—down to the foundation below. Structural columns, and the bay they describe, are usually in the same place on each successive floor, marking the four corners of several imaginary rectangles on each floor. One rectangle will generally be large enough to plan several column-free workstations or other enclosures within it.

There are some exceptions to the seemingly endless possibilities of planning with the structural bay. Because it is structural and set in place for reasons that the engineers tell us are more important than the placement of furniture, the column can only be moved in the design stages of new construction or rehabilitation. Also, columns may not be equidistant from one another on the same floor or may vary in size, shape and quantity from floor to floor as the building changes in height and configuration. Imagine the variety in San Francisco's Pyramid Building!

Bauhaus bays are boring?

Twenty or more years ago, office building developers began to ask their architects and engineers for bay sizes that would be compatible with their tenant's operations, and for columns that would be more orderly in their placement than was the case in many pre-war buildings. Bauhaus architecture was much in vogue in the 60's, 70's and much of the 80's. Its modular concepts and severely rectilinear forms lent themselves well to the request. In this era, when many of the commercial buildings in current use were built, there was also an effort to relate window spacing to bay size. An ideal bay, for example, might be 40 feet deep and 25 feet wide at the window wall, providing for five window openings of equal size. These roughly five-feet wide windows—actually five feet less the width of the mullions separating them—defined one dimension of the interior space; the bay depth defined the other.

This highly mathematical and relatively uninteresting approach to architectural planning and design resulted in the highest possible efficiency in the utilization of interior space—the developer/builder's dream. It also resulted in increasingly boring skylines across the United States. Bauhaus architecture has largely been replaced as a preferred style, but it remains as a discipline and the architectural order of bay and module are still very much with us.

The Building is organized around its core

Every building has a *core*. Whether it is a one-story warehouse at the edge of town or a modern downtown skyscraper, every commercial building has to have a place to put a lavatory, incoming power lines, a janitor closet, a stair, elevator or air-handling machines. Rather than scatter these about, builders, developers and architects prefer the planning efficiency implied in grouping them. This grouping is called the core of the building and has a number of characteristics which are important to the user.

The core invariably involves the origination or terminus of some essential building service that is costly to relocate after construction begins, if not before. It may involve solid masonry walls which are structural in nature and cannot be penetrated. There may be more than one core location if two or more stairwells or elevator shafts are in place. The core can shift in location from floor to floor as banks of elevators are added or terminated. Important plumbing and electrical connections are buried in core walls that also contain air-handling ducts. When a building is in its planning stage, before construction, it is often possible for one or more of these core facilities to be shifted to accommodate user functions. The user is seldom made aware of these possibilities. The alteration of a core facility in an existing building can be extremely costly, and user planning must always proceed with caution when it gets close to core spaces.

The hung ceiling organizes the look of what is overhead

If the intelligence of a corporate operation lies in its computer center, its heart, lungs, digestive tract and nervous system are located above the ceiling. If something goes wrong in the workplace, the repair person called in to fix it will invariably disappear into the dark and menacing spaces above the ceiling to work his/her magic.

These spaces are formed by the contours of the underside of the floor or roof above. The space is shaped by the periodic intrusion into it of structural beams that run under a floor from one side of a bay to another at intervals of a few feet. In shorter buildings, such as single-story industrial, warehouse or R&D buildings, these beams are open-work trusses designed to perform the same support function with less material and less cost. In either case, the beam or truss will extend downward into the ceiling cavity for two or three feet. The metal grid for the ceiling of the space below is hung about two feet below the undersurface of the beam, creating a space about four to five feet deep. Our critical services go into this volume of space that is interrupted regularly by beams or trusses.

More about the building's black hole, the ceiling cavity

First, there is the question of what actually goes into the ceiling cavity. There seems to be general agreement among architects, developers and builders that water and waste pipe, electrical conduit, air-conditioning duct work, etc., should be placed there. These are unsightly and are, at all costs, to be hidden from view. "Also, the entire space above a suspended ceiling can be used as one huge return-air duct; this arrangement is called a plenum return." (*Mechanical & Electrical Equipment for Buildings*, 7th Edition, Stein/ Reynolds/ McGuiness.) It has become part of the professional canon that a membrane of sorts is required to seal the interior environment off from undesirable exchanges of odor, light, sound, etc. With its tightly engineered grid and tile system, the hung ceiling accomplishes the latter objective while it conceals unsightly hardware.

The hung ceiling and the ceiling cavity: whose are they?

When your building was built, it was as much the building owner's responsibility to put in lavatories and drinking fountains and the water pipes they require as it was to install stairs and elevators. If you are renting, he installed something called tenant improvements after you signed your lease. This provided your space with water pipes for your kitchen or coffee bar, electrical conduit for your power system, the lighting grid he established when he built the building, and a duct-system that would carry air to different parts of your space. He did the same thing for all of the other tenants in your building, and he has done this since the building was built.

All of these new and old pipes, tubes and cables crisscross over your head. Keeping them company are thousands of feet of low-voltage wire, installed over the years for telephone, security and sound systems. Some still function; most trail off into the ether. The collection is a grab-bag of old and not-so-old code regulations that govern things like pipe, wire, insulation and hanging mechanisms and the way they are installed. The regulations change periodically, leaving clear signs of the old way behind, in the ceiling.

When one of these components of the building's system of services fails, the results may range from a call from the landlord asking for permission to enter your space to make a repair above your ceiling, to a fire or flood that damages a part of your premises. It is a tribute to the tradespeople who install above-ceiling equipment and the building operators and engineers who maintain it that these results occur as infrequently as they do. When they happen, there is invariably a question as to whom and to what to lay the fault and, ultimately, the—often-times substantial—cost of repair. Does the landlord bear the damages resulting from the broken water pipe since it belongs to him? Does the responsibility fall on the tenant, three floors up, because his water clogged the pipe? Or is it your fault because after all,it happened over your head, within your premises?

In our risk-conscious world, this will probably be sorted out by insurance companies and lawyers. Whatever the result, there may be a costly interruption of work in your workplace which is not considered in the compensation formulas. This may be true when a repair person has to park a ladder over your desk for an hour while rummaging above the ceiling tile. How are you reimbursed for this down-time? How can you control it? When will the interruption recur and for how long on the next visit?

Imaginative architects stripped away the phony ceiling

In the sixties, architects began to explore possibilities of returning some handsome turn-of-the-century masonry buildings to workplace use. After making structural improvements, their attention turned to interior renovation and ways of revealing the rugged beams and brickwork detail overhead. Instead of blocking these features from view, they omitted the hung ceiling and exposed the underside of the floors above along with the service hardware—pipes and ducts, etc.—attached to them. Paint was applied to the latter in colors that matched their surroundings, made them festive or simply made them disappear. These innovative solutions were popularized and spread to every city in the country with buildings worthy of this kind of renovation. It may have inspired the development of the high-tech look of commercial building ceilings in more recent years.

We tried too hard to zip up our buildings and got TBS

Aside from benign considerations of the aesthetics of the workplace ceiling, the more serious matter of its function as part of a sealed workplace enclosure has come into question with the discovery of something called Tight Building Syndrome.

During the energy crisis of the late seventies, building owners and their architects, looking to stop expensive leaks and thwart OPEC's effectiveness, began tightening up commercial and industrial buildings. Walls, floors and windows were designed to much closer tolerances than before, powerful new sealants and adhesives were introduced and mechanical systems for joining different building parts were readjusted for minimal conditioned air transfer. This tight construction created thousands of new buildings across the country where the chemicals used in the construction itself could not escape or dissipate into the outside atmosphere. The results were immediately apparent; office workers suffered from various mild to severe afflictions brought on by irritating chemicals that had nowhere to go.

Bio-aerosols, considered among the most common contaminants in tight building syndrome, are microbes found in stagnant water. They are assumed to be responsible for the bacteria that caused the infamous outbreak of Legionnaires' disease in a Philadelphia, Pennsylvania, hotel in 1976, and a Richmond, California, office building in 1991.

As-Built Drawings

All things being equal, we want to find a facility for our operations where accidents are least likely to happen. That facility is liable to be the one that can provide the most complete information concerning its operations before you buy or sign a lease. This information often takes the form of as-built drawings—drawings made after construction or an installation is complete.

Building owners do not expect to be asked for details regarding above-ceiling installations. Nevertheless, you can request drawings showing the type, size, location, etc., of these installations. If they are made available, they will tell an interesting story to the architect or engineer who translates them for you. If they are not available—the building may be old, it may have had several owners, architects or builders and its services may have been installed incrementally over a long period of time—try to arrange for the preparation of as-built drawings. These drawings look like an engineer's or architect's drawing and show building details as they were built. They can be somewhat costly since they involve on-site measurements but this cost is fairly shared between Landlord and Tenant/Buyer. This expense should be examined in the light of the size of the transaction—the amount of space being taken and the term of the obligation—or the nature of the user operation and the importance of the ready availability of building information.

As-built drawings are better than insurance

As you can imagine, the usefulness of as-built drawings can go beyond the need to record above-the-ceiling information. They are a requisite for good space and workplace management; they should be complete in every respect.

Whether or not the as-built drawings of above-ceiling details are done, an inspection should be made of this area to determine the general condition of the existing work. Note construction trash, loosened or missing hanger-wires, etc., and installations that represent potential obstacles to the placement of your own equipment and wiring along with the presence, if any, of hazardous materials such as loose asbestos fireproofing.

The raised floor does under-foot what the dropped-ceiling does

No discussion of a ceiling can be complete without acknowledging the floor above— or below—it. In commercial facilities of any size, there is an opportunity to stuff things under the floor, just as we have been packing them in overhead for years. But the floor we refer to now is a false floor, built on top of the building floor. This is called a *raised floor*.

When the computer room became a fixture on the corporate landscape, the raised-floor was introduced to accommodate the extra cabling and air-conditioning needs of then-bulky computer systems. The raised floor consists of a series of modular metal frames that can be secured to one another to cover an area of virtually any shape or size. These are covered with hard-surfaced tiles to form a load-bearing floor that can carry people and machines. The tiles are removable; it is this feature that is most attractive to those who install, work with and repair equipment on the raised floor.

Since main-frame computers are shrinking in size, weight and heat generation, the raised floor is falling out of favor for that purpose—while rapidly becoming an attractive addition in other parts of the workplace. The on-line computer, the video display unit, the Limited Area Network all create strangling amounts of cable and wire which can be conveniently hidden—and accessed—by the raised floor. It does have some drawbacks, however.

The building industry and the raised-floor industry have not yet figured out how one can augment the other without adding cost to the whole. The raised floor that covers a very large area is expensive and it has to sit on top of a standard concrete building floor. Since it raises the working floor by one to two feet, it needs a ramp to make it accessible from other parts of the building floor; these can become quite long and space-consuming. And, there is the matter of closing down the overall room height when the space with the raised floor has a ceiling installed at building-standard height.

Finally, there is the unpleasant possibility that the newly created below-floors space will provide an excellent home for building vermin. In single-story construction for laboratories, clean rooms, R&D, light manufacturing and office use involving extensive computer usage, the raised floor can be effectively employed without many of the usual problems, because of the additional height that can be built into the facility at little extra cost to the tenant/buyer.

USER/TENANT SPACES

The bulk of building interior space is there to serve the User/Tenant. This space is constructed and finished with Tenant Improvements. The term is intended to mean improvements to the tenant's premises. It further implies that the spaces you lease are not ready for your use until tenant improvements have been completed. The improvements referred to have to do with things like carpets, walls, light fixtures and perhaps some partitions and doors, making the space habitable for your people and your operations.

The underlying concept of tenant improvements goes back to the early days of commercial building when big companies, vying to build monuments far larger than they could use, began to rent their empty spaces. The typical attitude of the landlord toward the notion of paying for improvements to these spaces was born in this era when the corporate landlord was king. If you wanted a carpet you bought it; if you wanted a wall with a door, you hired a carpenter to make it. The landlord gave you a key and turned on the light and the steam heat and you were ready to go to work. The reality of the tenant improvement concept has been altered and refined, but some would say that the underlying attitude has not changed.

In concept, tenant improvements are the obligation of the landlord to provide—just as a car salesman would tune up the auto you purchase, or a furniture dealer would assemble your new cabinet and make sure all the drawers work. The make-ready is part of the grand American tradition of closing the sale.

Tenant inducements come into play

After World War II, when builders became developers and the era of speculative building was born, a whole new set of ideas came into play based on product marketing and inducement of the tenant to rent. These ideas had to work hand-in-glove with the way buildings were built. It did no good to say that an improvement could be made for a large tenant, if the costs or other implications of its construction would be prohibitive. There had to be a system—a way of relating what a tenant legitimately needed—with a way it could be built without undesirable disruptions, within a reasonable cost framework.

The marketplace made the builder a carpet salesman

For a long time, building owners resisted the idea that walls and doors could come down and that new ones could be put back in their place. They were not prepared for the disruption caused by tearing out something that had not lived its full, useful life of twenty or thirty years. The concept of *turnover* was novel in the building business; tenants signed ten and twenty year leases and renewed them arguing over nothing more than the landlord's obligation to periodically provide fresh paint. When upstart companies came along to rent space, they took what they could find, the way they found it; they fit in. They adjusted themselves to their surroundings, whatever those may have been used for previously.

With the advent of the sheetrock wall, metal studs and cheaper roll-carpeting material made from the new synthetics, the cost picture brightened a little. Landlords softened in their adamant resistance to change. And competition helped; more aggressive and entrepreneurial builder/developers were willing to accommodate turnover. Equally aggressive contractors and tradesmen were eager to capitalize on the profitable non-seasonal work represented by this new field of tenant improvements. They found better and quicker ways to tear down and build out. Marriages between building owners and interior contractors took place, so that the latter could enjoy some stability, while the former reduced and controlled his costs; the marriage was so successful in some cases that building owners found themselves reaping profits from interior construction as well as rents.

A system has been developed to pay for improvements—with your money

The owner/developer has unarguable control over the selection of the materials and finishes that are used in his/her building. These are immediately visible in the floors, walls, ceiling, light fixtures, elevators, etc., of the building's Public Areas and Service Areas. But competition and good business sense suggest that in those spaces dedicated to User Areas, at least the appearance should be given that choices are being left to the client/occupant. Thus, in newly-constructed buildings, spaces still awaiting renters will appear raw, in their emptiness of all amenity. Building owners and their agents refer to such spaces as raw space—a cement floor underfoot, a similar slab overhead coated with rough looking fireproofing material and hung with the cables and ducts of service hardware. Partitions that separate user space from service space, like lavatories or public corridors, will be plastered but unfinished. All this is awaiting a User/Tenant who will give instructions as to how the complete space is to look.

The building owner/developer will collaborate with the User in developing the plans, drawings and specifications necessary to improve the User spaces for occupancy. These instructions, which may initially take the form of sketches and memoranda will eventually become a workletter and construction documents, which we shall discuss more fully later. All of the information gathered together to flesh out the picture of

33

what the User needs in the workplace facility will be used to estimate the cost of improvements.

You will be worn out hearing the word standard

The greater portion of these estimates will be based on standards similar to those we talked about earlier: standard doors and hardware, light fixtures, carpet, window covering, paint, ceiling, dry-wall construction, etc. Certain standards may already be developed for this building by the owner/developer, for such items as counter-tops, cabinets, sinks, water-heaters, shelving and other installations that could occur with some frequency in the building, and for which such standards would be a convenience for the landlord.

We hear a great deal of this word *standard*. It is used extensively by building owners and their agents to imply an elevated level of quality. The truth is that it simply refers to a level of cost. This level of cost is the lowest at which the landlord can buy something that works, meets minimum code requirements and meets the competition. Thus, the standard—unique to each landlord—is devised to measure and control the cost of tenant improvements, something that also happens to regulate the appearance and quality of them.

Costs are, now and forever, a mystery

When the commercial building developer approaches a lender with a proposal for developing a new building or refinancing or refurbishing an existing one, he submits a pro-forma statement of all the costs that may be incurred—not only during the initial construction, but also during the periodic outfitting of it for new tenants over the life of the building. A sum of money is established that represents the cost of the first such out-fitting, or tenant improvement, of all User spaces, as well as a similar, but lesser, sum for subsequent improvements. It is assumed that there will be some re-use of prior tenant finishes. Since there is no way to accurately estimate these future costs, or the number of times the developer will have to improve tenant spaces, a best estimate is provided for in the loan request. This number, usually expressed in dollars per square foot of space, becomes the basis for tenant improvement cost estimates and for construction draw-downs from the lender.

Cost overruns and ignorance can hurt

Since the building owner already has a resource for the money he needs to build User space, and these costs are built into rent, why should we be concerned about tenant improvement costs?

We want to be certain, first of all, that we are getting value—in the form of tenant improvements in this case—for our rent dollar. We do not want to see dollars that are ear-marked for our tenant improvements go somewhere else. If they are going to go somewhere else, we want to know that, so that we can ask that our rent be reduced accordingly. This is part of a process called *rent negotiation.* If we pay $10 in rent and our neighbor pays the same, and our neighbor is outfitted with a workspace fit for a king and we do not have carpet on the floor, we have not been treated unfairly—we have negotiated poorly.

The corollary of this idea of negotiating for rent, which includes the cost of tenant improvements, is that we have some idea of the value of things. When we finally get carpet to match our neighbor's, is it really the same? Or did we get economy grade while he got plush?

Your consent to the expense of your money may seem reasonable but . . .

The owner's obligation to prepare User/tenant space has always been more clearly defined by competition in the commercial building business than by any legal or moral concept of providing a specific level of finish or utility to the workplace. Thus, the User/tenant has little more to look to in out-fitting his workplace than what the owner is willing to provide, on the one hand, and what is customary in the marketplace at the time, on the other.

For the User/tenant, the most important part of being informed is being aware that a cost liability can be incurred in the preparing leased space. If costs connected with the preparation of your space exceed whatever sum the owner believes is reasonable to absorb, the excess will be passed on to you. Though it would seem reasonable that there is some prior notice to this effect, and that such notice would give you time to accept, reject or alter the work in question, it may not be forthcoming.

If the work and the excess costs are objectionable and represent a misunderstanding between the parties, the time to seek a remedy is before, not after, the work is done.

Detailed prior agreements can relieve tenant improvement cost worries

We mentioned earlier that the building owner will make estimates of tenant improvement costs using information about User needs. To the extent that these things are generic in nature—that is they can be satisfied by the installation of the owner's on-site standards for items like doors, ceilings, light fixtures, carpet, etc., and conform to the limits of the owner's budget with respect to quantities—they may be installed at little or no additional cost to the user.

If the tenant's needs, no matter how utilitarian, fall outside the owner's list of generic or standard items, or if the quantity needed to be installed is in excess of the owner's allowance for the item, they may be charged to the User at costs that seem excessive. There can be a number of understandable reasons for this—and some that are less so. In any case, this kind of unpleasant surprise can be relieved, if not entirely avoided, by establishing and agreeing to unit prices for tenant improvement items prior to execution of a lease or purchase agreement.

It must surely seem to every business person who seeks a workplace facility that the building owner has a decided advantage—not only in knowing what and how to budget for things like tenant improvements, but in being able, in seemingly arbitrary fashion, to set contractual limits to them. As a matter of fact, it is galling to most landlords that they cannot do this to the extent they would like; in most communities, competition is at work. Since all landlords firmly believe there is no building product that competes with their own, it is incumbent on the User/tenant/buyer to remind them regularly of the competition.

In **PART I—Chapter 4** we talk more about tenant improvements in the discussion of the workletter, a critical component of the lease agreement.

Chapter 2

THE RELOCATION PROCESS

Chapter 2   THE RELOCATION PROCESS

Our innate sense of order

The origins of this commonplace and seemingly innocent word, *process*, are in Latin, and *modus operandi*, a way or method of doing something, is often used to describe it. But among the great civilizations of the world, the efforts of Western man seem unique in developing a concept around *process*, to employ, manipulate and record it. The ancient societies of the Orient, the Middle East and of the Americas, older and further developed than ours in so many ways, were inventive, but their purposes and methodologies were different from our own.

In *The Discoverers*, historian Daniel J. Boorstin brings to us in rich detail, the story of Mans' unending search "to know his world and himself". He reveals that Western man may not have conceptualized *process* until the Eighteenth century. Edward Burnett Tylor suggests that the processes of living were important to the study of man and conceived the science of anthropology. And in 1776 Adam Smith published the *Wealth of Nations* and established the notion of economic well-being as the result of a process, not simply the possession of treasure. Today, the word and the concept are a routine part of our vocabulary and are necessary to our innate sense of the order of things.

The process has not delivered on its promise

It is difficult to imagine the history of building apart from process since so much of the vocabulary of the industry permeates that of the processes of other disciplines. Every mathematical or natural science, study of language, behavior or economics has its language of building blocks and foundations. Concepts and ideas have their floors and ceilings to indicate their outer limits, their furthest reaches; those of particular worth are often deemed to be the mortar of this or that discipline. It is little wonder, then, that we consider the business of building to be firmly rooted in orderly process, and we are surprised, perhaps shocked to discover that the process has not delivered on its promise. This is the conclusion we must reach when we look around our workplace and the great buildings and wondrous cities that house it, and find it so lacking. We find that the workplace does not fit us and what we do or the way we work, function and live. We discover that it has been designed to be pretty, cheap, impressive or economically viable, but it has not been designed for the people who must use it. And so we come around again to the recurring theme of this book.

EPDEX

We theorize that the orderly process for which the building business is historically noted is primarily and admirably suited for the construction of civic monuments. And monuments of whatever persuasion are hardly noted for being tolerant of human intrusion. Even with the arrival of the industrial revolution and the relocation of the worker out of the home and into a shared workplace, the planning, design and construction of the buildings that would house him/her was dictated by the needs of production machinery and/or by owners needing monuments. The modern diffusion and dispersion of the owner among corporations and real estate investors, banks and insurance companies has done little to alter this approach to building. Today, the message of the primacy of the User, even when it is advanced by the conscientious architect or interior designer, is often drowned in the interests of the monument builders.

To advance the cause of the User in this environment, we have chosen to acknowledge the traditional process, to admire its correctness and perseverance, and to only slightly alter its direction and its emphasis. To make it correct in contemporary commercial usage, we first give it an acronym: EPDEX, representing **Evaluation, Planning, Documenting** and **Execution**. This is the process of facility relocation we will discuss in this chapter, and which constitutes the whole of our instruction in PART II—**DOING IT**.

Evaluation, Planning, Documenting and Execution

Students of architecture and construction will recognize the latter three stages or steps as part of the textbook approach to any building project. They will have little quarrel, we think, with the addition at the beginning of the process of **Evaluation**. To place the latter in context for those unaccustomed to seeing an "evaluation" tacked on to the front of the building process, think of the traditional architect, designer, builder, developer, etc, who has a history of trying and discovering things that do and do not work. The building professional may be said to be in a constant process of evaluating and re-evaluating his/her work; such a step at the start of your project might seem redundant to that professional.

This is one of those places where we take a turn in direction and emphasis. Our User does not have the building professional's experience. More importantly, however, the User has a view of the objective of building that is quite different from that of the builder. It is that view that demands a careful look at the facility as the User experiences it, and not as the builder knows it. For those now starting an organization and seeking their first facility, we suggest that they evaluate the building in which they last worked in any capacity—the important thing being that we look at an existing structure, facility, accommodation, etc., closely, through new eyes, or eyes given a fresh vision.

Once the Evaluation is complete, we defer to the traditional approach or process beginning with **Planning**. This is a long step, which takes considerable time and effort, because we believe that the greatest value in the concept of process lies in our ability, before we make big investments, to see in great detail—providing we make the effort—where the process is going to take us. We have broken this step into three parts, which we call **Preliminary Planning, Further Planning,** and **Commitment Planning**. They are explained below in Planning. A review process is built into these steps along with the GO, NO/GO concept of decision making.

Documenting is the first formal step to follow Planning. As its name implies, documenting means putting the decisions made in Planning into writing and on the record. The relocation process involves a number of contracts and documents of great value and, significantly, of continuing importance to the User as Tenant. Tenant/user experience across the country has demonstrated clearly that workplace problems do not end with the signing of a lease or completion of tenant improvements, and that complete and accurate documentation is critical to solving these problems.

One of our claims for the EPDEX system is that, closely followed, it will yield an **Execution** step of surprising ease and painlessness. This is the time when your good planning and diligent homework will in truth pay off—when you can watch others perform, build, finish and perfect your new workplace, while you look forward to a quick return to productive organization life.

The circularity of the process

Like many of the processes of modern industrial production, EPDEX is linear, but circular. We envision, work towards achieving our vision, accomplish it and compare what we have achieved with our first vision. Our Want List, discussed in Planning, establishes—together with our Program, another early planning step—the facility goals we are trying to reach. These become our guideposts for satisfactory execution of the process and the criteria for measuring our facility accomplishment. The shape and contents of the new facility become the basis for the start of a totally new facility evaluation process, because, as we will note later, we are placing our dynamic organization inside a static structure that begins to deteriorate from the first moment of our occupancy.

EVALUATION

If the rationale for evaluating the workplace seems obvious, the means of accomplishing it are much less so. In fact, the dearth of hard data with which to accomplish an acceptable evaluation by the norms of most professionals who might do this kind of work is so great as to discourage the hardiest among them.

There is, first of all, no common statistical yardstick. Our warehouse foreman might be able to write an essay on the inadequacy of the loading dock; the office manager might write several critical lines on the elevator, the power poles and the fluorescent light fixtures. But each would be hard put to identify and measure the increase or decrease in productivity that results from their observations.

Much the same would be true of our efforts to evaluate the probable effect on our facility of changes in our industry, in our markets, in our competition, or from new taxes or zoning laws.

Neither do we have a meaningful statistical baseline, since each of our variables seems to perform independently of the other, with differing performance ranges. Our measurement of interior workplace temperature, for example, may be within a narrow range of a few degrees Fahrenheit or Centigrade, with every little variation required between work areas. Our measurement of interior workplace lighting would utilize a completely different vocabulary, with a variety of measurements that might be made in task areas with differing lighting requirements—to say nothing of the fact that heating and cooling and building lighting are interdependent, with the latter placing a significant load on the air handling system.

Then how can we justify the effort?

We have to be conscious of the fact that the quality of the workplace is of great importance to us and, also, that it is a living, breathing manufacture of a multitude of interacting parts, each rather complex in its own right. Each part must perform at a level that is at least passive and non-interfering, if not one that actually contributes to and enhances our work environment and our productivity.

Beyond this, we must recognize where we are, and we must try to imagine where we might expect to be, in the best of circumstances.

We are already working in a facility for which the die, as it were, has been cast. It may have been built for us, in which case we began, hopefully, with an optimal facility that has deteriorated only in the sense that our dynamic organization has outgrown it and its potential. Or, as is more apt to be the case, we have been working for some time in a facility that has been adapted, over many years, to serve more than a few users.

A periodic evaluation can help us determine how we might continue to adapt our less-than-optimal workplace to our present purposes. By properly anticipating space, utility and equipment demands, etc., we can make many adjustments in an existing facility which will prolong our stay in it.

An increasingly inefficient facility will affect our productivity

Over time these adjustments will come at increasing cost, not only in terms of construction, meeting code requirements and making utility upgrades, but in diminished facility and productivity results. The evaluation process will have extended our facility to its limits for us; it should also have a long-term focus, which enables us to plan for the future.

Our evaluation process emphasizes the long-term aspects of facility planning in two ways: by incorporating considerations that would normally fall outside the purview of a strict facility analysis, and by attempting to establish a baseline method of evaluation. These added emphases are necessary in the decision-making process.

In *Managing For Results*, Dr. Peter Drucker discusses decisions on matters of complexity and high risk in a way that bears directly on our discussion of facility evaluation (analysis) and decision-making. He says:

> "...Altogether in any analysis in which the results are likely to be the subject of hot discussion and strong opinions the accent should be on utmost simplicity of tools and techniques."

Facility analysis is full of hot discussion and strong opinions

No aspect of an organization's activity is laden with a greater diversity of elements than its workplace; very few receive less attention than the workplace does. One of the reasons for the latter is this disparity between important components, or factors, and the unresolved task presented to the decision-maker of sorting them out and establishing some priorities.

Another is the variety of sources that facility information can come from: a facility manager (or the individual charged with that function), an assortment of department heads and staff members, representatives of the real estate industry, architects, engineers and other consultants, etc. Each represents an impeccable resource. Each has its own language, format and presentation of intricately detailed material. Each has its own bias and agenda.

We cannot, nor do we want to, alter the behavior of these well-intentioned people. But to be required to sift through and make sense of all their material is more than Dr. Drucker had in mind.

The fact is, even with a substantial and concerted effort made towards information reduction and integration—such as that proposed here—the decision-maker will be faced with a great variety of considerations to balance before he can make a good facility decision.

Change Factors

PART II—**DOING IT** (see *Evaluation*) describes a group of change factors that includes a broad mix of considerations from light fixtures and thermostats to government regulation and markets. All of these factors can impinge on your workplace decision. Certainly some other factors, unique to your situation, should be included.

Only one group of factors, *deterioration*, concerns itself completely with the facility—that is, buildings and grounds and supporting utilities and equipment. It is the principal, if not exclusive, focus of this book. It may also be the only one that is not already evaluated on an ongoing, systematic and detailed basis in your organization.

The lead time for establishing an organization in a new facility—that is relocating it —will range from one to three years. The timing will depend to a certain extent on your organization's size and, more importantly, whether it is moving into new construction. This is mentioned in connection with facility evaluation because, provided the process begins now, ample opportunity can exist for grading existing quarters and establishing performance criteria before a move must be made.

Examine already existing review tools and procedures

The first step is to examine the evaluation procedures your organization has established for operating systems—production, or personnel, sales, finance, etc.— and structure a system to review and evaluate your facility along similar, if not identical, lines. If such a system, already in operation for other uses, requires a job description and/or performance criteria, develop the same system for the facility. If organization practice includes monthly or quarterly reviews or reports to department or division heads, follow this schedule for the facility evaluation.

The measurement or grading of facility performance should be rendered in the simplest meaningful way. The individual with the greatest familiarity with a component's use should write specific performance criteria—though not necessarily of a technical nature. The warehouse foreman should detail the critical elements of the loading dock or the storage racks; the paralegal should describe the essentials of his/her workstation since she or he spends long hours there; the salesman, computer programmer, secretary, administrative assistant and word processor, etc., should all be responsible for defining their facility needs.

These descriptions can recognize existing conditions, but they should emphasize the ideal. The ideal condition, defined as the one which contributes most to our individual or group productivity, will form our baseline for performance measurement. Productivity, as defined by your organization, is the reason for its being. Manufacturers, service companies, charitable organizations, stores and corporate headquarters all produce something which, in some way, is measurable in its output—from the auto leaving the factory door to the smile on the face of the nurse or the receptionist.

Our workplace is an elemental and critical part of that productivity. No one denies that fact, but almost everyone ignores it.

Are all of your workers dodos?

In his book *In Search of Excellence*, Tom Peters discusses the rational vs. social, "X" versus "Y" theories of management, "the opposing views that workers are lazy and need to be driven and, alternatively, that they are creative and should be given responsibility." He goes on to point out that many corporate leaders have successfully wedded the concepts, demonstrating that they are not "mutually exclusive" and showing us that facility evaluation is an area where a liberal application of the "Y" theory can achieve much.

Why? A part of the answer lies in another interesting anecdote in Mr. Peter's book. He describes the Hawthorne experiments "aimed at testing the effect of work conditions on productivity." A series of events showed some unintended results when, in the course of the experiments, "the lights were turned up; productivity went up; lights were turned down; productivity went up again."

Peters holds that the main point of the many interpretations placed on this experimental data is that "the simple act of paying positive attention to people has a great deal to do with productivity."

We suggest that the simple act of reaching out to the plant, shop, factory or office worker for information about what that person needs to work with can also have a great deal to do with productivity.

Measurement, and the much maligned subjective response

The subjective response is to be embraced, not only because it can minimize the need for expensive and time-consuming consultants, but because it can give us on-line, real-time accuracy and dependability. You pay high rents and exorbitant operating costs for a workplace environment that represents your most important tool, after your people, and which is chock full of important intangibles: light, sound, odor, warmth, privacy, etc.

Your people are the only ones who can effectively evaluate these things. Adjustments in our heating and lighting systems in everyday workplace life result from calls from occupants who have problems, not from daily visits by building engineers.

Periodic measurements of equipment performance can and should be made by qualified, technical persons. The results of their findings should be tempered by an understanding of the difference between measurements of equipment output—even those taken at the workstation—and the physiological response to that output, over time, of the workstation occupant. We should establish our facility performance criteria first with the occupant, then with the engineer.

The measurement or grading of facility performance should be rendered in the simplest useful way. We recommend a five-point scale: two grades for the satisfactory side of your evaluation, two grades for the unsatisfactory, and one in the middle. Give each grade a point value so that a simple numerical comparison may be made. (See our description of the *Measurement System*, in **PART II**, *Evaluation: Change Factors.*)

We want to rate the effect of the performance of a building component, as well as how efficiently—quickly or smoothly, etc.—it works. If our state-of-the-art air conditioning equipment is programmed to shut off at 7 PM and it is uncomfortably warm when we start to work at 8 PM, our rating of that equipment is justifiably at its lowest level. The net result of its installation and operation in our building at 8 PM that evening is that it does not work.

Do not debate with the experts

At all costs, we want to avoid debates and arguments with experts. Experts will insist on talking in their language of shed loads, trench headers and footlamberts. They will often fail to listen to or understand User language; when they do, they will translate our language back into their own arcane jargon and their own finely calibrated units of measure. Here's the rub—the latter will become the ultimate and unequivocal measure of User satisfaction.

It is incumbent on us, as Users, to disabuse our experts of the notion that our individual and collective response to our work environment is only measurable in a finite number of footlamberts, watts or cubic feet per minute, etc.

PLANNING

One thing our readers have in common is a level of understanding and skill in planning. We suspect there may even be a certain antipathy toward the word; it has been over-used and abused by authority figures from the time we were in school to our most recent assignments. In a business conversation, the word seems to endow its user with a sense of the kind of superiority that comes from predicting some future event.

"You see, when 'X' happens, this is what happens next; you have to plan for it."

Predictions of doom

What is also implied, but seldom openly admitted, is that what is going to happen if we do not plan for it will be awful: the roof will leak; the price will double; I'll lose my job, etc. A litany of uniformly unpleasant results automatically occur without a plan and the larger the enterprise, the more disastrous the prospective failure. "Murphy's Law" is invoked by everyone in the business of planning as a sardonic warning of the magnitude of one's punishment for a failure to plan. "It won't just cost you; it's going to cost eight times what you thought it would." Or, "if you don't figure out how to put that thing in right, you're going to kill somebody."

Given—and taken—with a chuckle, such predictions of doom have evolved as the classic rationale for planning in the world of commercial building, leaving aside and behind the notion that with planning, something good can be even better.

We like the latter idea and recommend it to you. The workplace may be OK, but it needs to get better. If a facility relocation is in order, it is not just a matter of getting from here to there with the least pain, it wants to be a matter of making a more successful workplace along the way. Planning can accomplish this, which is good to keep in mind when people begin to get a little tedious on the subject.

Easing into it

A great deal of any planning process consists of discovery, or finding out what is needed and what can be involved in getting it. We start the relocation process with the *Evaluation* of existing quarters that we described in the previous section. We start the *Planning* process with a Want List, which we discuss in **PART II—Chapter 4, Tools**; then we spend a lot of time easing into the business of discovery. We do this because getting information can be costly. If there is a possibility that relocation might not occur, for example, in accordance with Murphy's Law, we want to be able to extricate ourselves from the process with as little pain as possible. This means in addition to limiting our financial exposure, we protect ourselves and our colleagues from the disappointment of unfulfilled expectations and from unwanted commitments to outsiders—brokers, developers, architects, etc.—among other things.

Preliminary Planning

We are suggesting a process which is both deliberate and appropriately conservative. The steps in **Preliminary Planning** are intended to start the relocation process in earnest. Yet, you will see from our graph of planning responsibility below that when the first review point is reached, you are still exclusively in control of information, procedures and budget.

Level of Involvement	You Alone	With your Staff	With Staff & Outsiders
PRELIMINARY PLANNING	●		
FURTHER PLANNING		●	
COMMITMENT PLANNING			●

By you alone, we mean that the steps outlined in our **Preliminary Planning** section of **DOING IT** are those you can take in the privacy of your own office, in the company of nothing more than your own computer, files and telephone. Whether yours is a small organization or a large one, relocation is a process that has broad implications and often-times far-reaching and irretrievable consequences. Managing the impact of these in the beginning is an important part of the future success of your efforts.

Further Planning

Now you are ready to take steps to move your organization further down the path of discovery and preliminary decision-making, to pinpointing locations, resources and costs, etc. At the same time, this planning stage leaves you comfortably clear of most, if not all, of the budget-committing action that would eventually be required.

You will need the assistance of associates and/or staff as you collect more detailed information concerning your needs and the availability of outside resources. As a result of your review of **Preliminary Planning** about people, place and equipment you have thought, and reached some positive conclusions; now is the time to study these things in detail.

Commitment Planning

The final planning stage is labeled **Commitment Planning**. It is in this period of preparing for your eventual facility relocation that you will commit to certain outside resources and expenditures. For example, you may be calling on the services of a commercial real estate broker, an architect and a technical consultant at this time, but agreements will be made for a very few specific tasks that commit to payment for these limited services only; no formal commitments (such as a lease) will have been made to a landlord or developer. The graph below will give you an idea of approximately when, and to whom, principal financial commitments are made within the three stage relocation process.

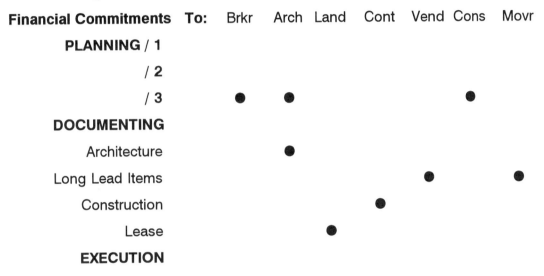

Financial Commitments To:	Brkr	Arch	Land	Cont	Vend	Cons	Movr
PLANNING / 1							
/ 2							
/ 3	●	●				●	
DOCUMENTING							
Architecture		●					
Long Lead Items					●		●
Construction				●			
Lease			●				
EXECUTION							

Reviews, checklists and keeping control

As you work your way through the **Planning** process, you will want to review your progress from time to time to see if the questions you continue to ask yourself and others are still focused on the goals you established earlier. Follow your own pace and your own sense of the process. To aid you in this periodic review, we have inserted our own checklist and scorecard following each of the first and second stages of planning. (See **PART II—Step P.**)

These are logical places to stop and catch a breath, as well as to review. It is the nature of the business of relocating the workplace that, once begun, it seeks to develop its own life, and to build and carry its own momentum. This is another way of saying that others will want to step in to advance your cause—something you should avoid, even when the help being offered comes, as it most often does, from well meaning and qualified sources. At least early on, think and plan alone; have emphatic and frequent changes of heart about the whole business, with no explanations asked or offered.

The checklists are intended as quick and broad indicators of progress and direction. They focus on the larger questions, which tend to define the need to move the facility and to identify the principal areas for caution and concern.

The Move-In Date

As part of your need description and want list at the very beginning of preliminary planning, you will indicate a date by which you would like to start work in new quarters. In spite of the complexity of the relocation process and the variety of greatly independent players involved in it, it is entirely reasonable to establish this date solely on the basis of User organization need.

We have already sounded warnings regarding the propensity of one or two or more of the key players to take your ball and run with it, to impress you with their needs and to make their priorities and their schedules yours. Their motives in doing this are as convoluted and complex as the industry itself. It could be that:

- They claim to have been subjected repeatedly to the impossible schedules of others and hope that your project is better planned

- They see your project as a godsend, which means that, given enough time, they could turn it into a handsome income-producer

- They are just a little unsure of how to do what you need done, and will require some discovery time of their own, preferably at your expense

- They have few key supervisory personnel and are spread thin

- They prefer to run similar projects concurrently to achieve project economies, coincidentally representing savings the User never sees, piecing yours in with others in the same geographic area, at the same stage of production, or using the same or similar materials from the same producer, etc;

- they may have a genuine concern for the time required to produce a good job.

Targeting the move-in date

Your first task is to establish and record a target date to accomplish your move-in, based on an optimum set of circumstances for your organization—circumstances that concern the timing of your personnel, markets, suppliers, internal planning, etc. In establishing this date, you may elect to recognize the so-called realities of building industry scheduling, depending on the known extent of your need for its services. However it is established, your target date should become as sacred as Christmas, Chanukah or Chinese New Years, and a fixture of equal importance on the calendar of everyone associated with your project.

As you progress with your planning, you will become more familiar with the relocation process and its possibilities and with the dates on which certain services, and/or products can be delivered. You will learn whether and how these dates can be made to work with your target date for move-in. You will be getting an increasingly clearer idea of the value of these services to you. At an appropriate point, perhaps toward the end of the **Planning** cycle, you will determine that an actual move-in can occur on a date at variance with the established target-date. Your calendar should be revised to reflect this different date, without deleting or otherwise altering your original target date.

The Players' view of your move-in date

Your organization may be in the unusual position of complete flexibility with respect to finding and moving into new quarters and, at least initially, may be able to follow the lead of other Players in establishing key dates. Even if this is not the case, it is worthwhile having an idea of building industry experience with the time it takes to do things.

If you were to say, for example, that your target move-in date would be a year from today, the building industry—the architect, developer, contractor, etc.—would adapt accordingly, and come up with a schedule which might look like the one below.

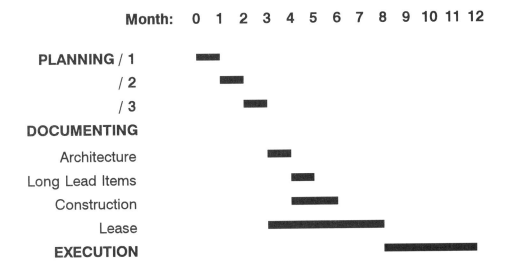

If you were to allow more—or less—time that time would be apportioned, roughly, in accordance with the schedule above. Note that each successive step overlaps the previous one, indicating that one or more activities can be going on at the same time. Reducing the total time frame tends to put heavier pressure on **Planning** activities, since these are often considered by the players to be of questionable value.

Similarly, when more time is allotted to a project, that additional time seldom goes, as it should, into planning.

The schedule outlined above might accommodate relocation to an existing structure of 3,000 to 5,000 square feet of retail space, 15,000 to 20,000 square feet of office space, and 100,000 square feet of warehouse space, where the ratio of office to warehouse space is roughly 1 to 5, 1 to 6 or less.

In addition to the nature and size of a commercial space, its level of quality or the extent of the detail work required of designers, builders, vendors, landlords, etc., will also work to extend or reduce every aspect of the schedule. In the example cited above, the retail space we refer to is well detailed by a competent designer, and involves some architectural, lighting and millwork design that is unique to the project. Office space is developed in a utilitarian manner, with modest design input; warehouse space deviates very little from the developer's standard for simple warehouse or flex space.

The User role is critical to timing

Typically, if you enquire of your architect, prospective landlord, contractor or technical consultants, etc., regarding a relocation in the size ranges above for these facility types, you could hear estimates ranging from 6 months or less to complete the project to 18 months or more. This depends largely on how each has factored the client's role into the work.

If they choose to ignore this role, or underestimate its impact, their prediction of the time required for their portion of the work will be comparatively brief. If they understand User organization processes and decision-making, and liberally factor these into their schedule, the latter may seem greatly overextended. This creates problems for contractors of every variety when the time comes to solicit work based on an ability to deliver within a specified time frame. The largest and most critical single element in any architect's or contractor's schedule is Client Decision Time.

Schedules, norms and guidelines

If you find that you do not fit within the parameters of the User organizations and schedule described in the previous model, or in others found in this book, remember that no one has ever done what your organization is about to do. Do not be alarmed. There is a schedule to fit your objectives and your plan, which has not had an opportunity to take shape.

It is critically important for your organization to fit its own schedule to its own unique requirements. It takes a little time for this to happen and we realize that norms and guidelines can be helpful in this connection. We shall discuss several of these, provided you remember they are not like one of your Mother's favorite recipes, to be enlarged or reduced proportionally with the same uniform and excellent results.

■ First, we should point out that the above model was not chosen at random. One year represents a very useful time-frame for delivering most small and mid-sized projects to completion. By size, we mean square-footage to be leased or occupied. Other project-completion estimates, by project size, are suggested below.

Size in Square Feet of Office Space

500	1000	2500	5000	10000	15000	20000	30000	50000	100000
3	6	9	9	12	12	12	15	15	18

Months to Complete

(These estimates are useful only for broad schedule guidelines.)

■ The proportion of time spent in each of the three relocation project stages, **Planning, Documents** and **Execution**, is approximately the same—one third, one third and one third—regardless of the project size. Generally, more time spent in **Planning** produces better overall results, increasing the possibility of shortening the other stages.

■ Increasing or decreasing the size of a project does not, by itself, increase or reduce the time required to complete it; changing the complexity of it will. In a smaller project, adding or deleting 75 square feet of space for an executive washroom or a major piece of laboratory equipment, etc., would represent a substantial schedule change; adding or subtracting 1,000 square feet of open work area would not.

■ Similarly, adding or subtracting any kind of User functions in the **Planning** stage may take minutes; in the **Documents** stage, the same changes may take hours; in the **Execution** stage they may take days.

■ Workspace plans that develop horizontally—on the same level in a building— are more simply accomplished in every stage of the relocation process than the same plan developed vertically over two or more levels. For example, a User organization that requires 30,000 square feet of space will—all other things being equal—complete its relocation more quickly by moving onto a single level, than by moving onto two floors of 15,000 square feet, or three floors of 10,000 feet each.

■ Time schedules may be affected by the degree of coordination between activities and Players, including the User. Players have a tendency to adjust schedules to fit *their*, rather than *your* priorities, and to throw carefully synchronized timetables out of whack.

- Labor, holidays and acts of God must be recognized by every relocation schedule. They are often referred to in professional service contracts, and are invariably a part of construction contracts. To determine probable effects on scheduling, Users need to be aware of labor conditions and generally recognized holidays in their community. And do not overlook the probability that major sporting events are frequently treated like national holidays.

- Architects and contractors can be excellent resources for scheduling information provided you recognize their biases and understand their particular experiences.

While the time schedule is important to the function of the construction manager, its utility as a working document for the User is often frustrated by its originator. The schedule most often seen by the User has been prepared by one of the professionals —broker, architect, landlord, developer, etc. It is limited to the activities, critical dates, and priorities that are important to the professional in question. If it is not all-inclusive, it fails as a working document and, after its novelty has worn off, it is ignored.

But a schedule/checklist prepared by User personnel for internal use, inclusive of all critical activities is of great value and should be employed by User staff throughout the project. Use the model schedule shown above, review **PART II—DOING IT**, note your organization's requirements and develop a schedule that fits your project needs.

Owning versus Leasing

An organization's space needs should not be analyzed purely as a cost of doing business. A wide variety of other opportunities exist for enterprises that spend substantial amounts of money on space rentals, without seeing any other benefit accrue than a yearly tax deduction.

In the early eighties, Tenants realized that landlords and developers from coast to coast were making money from the inflated rents and property values of their projects. Many of these same tenants chose to add the business of real estate to their investment portfolio by swapping their leases for equity. Although not all of these neophyte real estate developers came out ahead on their new investments, a new way of doing business in commercial building development was born. It promises to be with us for some time.

The disappearance of real estate investment tax credits, the deterioration of the depreciation allowance and other tax law changes in the intervening years have greatly altered the benefits landscape for the real estate investor. The IRS' view of the arms-length relationship between tenant/user paying rents to tenant/landlord has stiffened; they are known to be troubled by the project bustling with equity sharing tenants which always seem to show an operating loss.

These are not easy times for the tenant as investor. However, the ever-increasing numbers of businesses willing to buy and develop raw land or rehabilitate an existing structure for their own use still suggest tangible advantages to ownership. The currently depressed condition of the commercial real estate market everywhere is certainly a factor that is encouraging to prospective buyers. User/buyers with solid long-term goals realize that this is simply a good time to buy.

Other advantages may have more to do with what a User organization does, and how the workplace is an important production tool, and that greater control over its design, construction and operation is potentially profitable. The latter is of critical importance, and we suggest that you pursue any examination of opportunities for sharing in ownership of the workplace with an understanding of their implications for the investor organization as User.

On the face of it, the Investor and User roles are distinct and conflicting. As a tenant, it is incumbent on the User to extract maximum facility from the landlord at minimum dollar rental. As a landlord, the User must protect its equity investment in the same way, and to the same degree, that it does any other investment. The question arises as to whether there is some happy combination of these polar positions that might make sense for those who don't need to be at either extreme. To answer this question, we looked at the upside and the downside of five different options an organization might have as it searches for a place to do business, with the following results:

1. Leasing in an existing building

Leasing in an existing building provides the Lessee (User) with more knowns at the time new space is occupied than any other facility option provides. More so than in any other circumstances, the User is in a position to closely inspect both the facility and the terms of proposed leases in a number of competing locations.

However, the nature of the lease in an existing building signifies minimum tenant control over the potential variables in either lease or facility. Rental rates, maintenance and escalation costs, utilities and building features are fixed or relatively non-negotiable. Landlords may vary in their abatements and finish-to-suit clauses, however their basic price structure, like that of the building and mechanical systems, remains unchanged. Of course, there are no investor implications with this option.

2. Leasing in a planned building

The potential is the same as that of the first option. The significant difference is that building features will be new, up-to-date and, to a certain minimal extent, capable of adjustment to tenant need. If your lease is important enough to the developer, you may receive some attention when it comes to special requests for identification, parking, security, a prime location in the building, etc.

Caution is the byword here; both tangible base building features and building costs are unseen and untested. Proposed rental rates must be examined in the light of comparable projects with similar advantages. Descriptions of less obvious features like parking, air handling systems, security, maintenance, etc., should be clear and complete. The track record of the developer making the offer should be inspected carefully. Is there a history of quality construction at the rental rate asked, or one of build for quick re-sale? Is there a reputation for good maintenance or benign neglect? Regardless the size of the lease or the duration of the proposed tenancy, these and related questions should be probed.

3. Equity in a planned building

In this option, your organization enters into a joint venture with a developer on the basis of financial terms acceptable to you, for tenancy in a building that is planned, but not yet built. Your equity participation represents an opportunity for you to realize a gain from a share in the project's:

- Cash flow—positive or negative

- Depreciation

- Property value appreciation

In addition, your agreement may qualify you for an advantageous rental rate and certain considerations with respect to building design and construction, such as:

- Parking accommodations

- Shared building identification

- Interior finishes in public areas as well as your own premises

- Certain exterior architectural detail

- Availability of prime interior space

The characteristics of this option are substantially fixed regarding site location, building design and construction methods, financing, principal partners, etc. As a result they leave relatively little flexibility for the entrepreneurial User to negotiate financial terms or more significant tenant preferences than those mentioned.

The downside to the investor's risk is substantial in all of the areas mentioned above; if income stream and/or appreciation are important, market knowledge will be critical. Even in our presently depressed real estate markets, there are bright spots that produce well for their investors.

4. Equity in a development project

The characteristics of this option are similar to those described above. The significant difference for both the User/Investor and the Developer is that the often irrevocable decisions that affect site selection, building design, etc., have not yet been made. Thus, the User has an opportunity to affect all of the features mentioned above, plus:

- Building shell design

- Floor size and configuration

- Elevatoring and mechanical systems

- Interior structure for stairs, etc

- Electrical power and other building systems

Investor benefits may be heightened by increased User/Investor control over the design, construction and eventual maintenance of the project, plus an influence on the quality of other tenancy. Short-term financial risks may be softened by a User decision to make the project a long-term home.

Assuming the User/Investor has a dominant financial share in the project, financial risks noted in the previous options are magnified. Increased responsibility for the productivity of the project also means active participation in its maintenance, repair, utility costs control, etc., and the corresponding dedication of User personnel to these activities.

5. The User as Developer

This option suggests that it is perceived to be advantageous for the User to develop and build its own building. An assumption is made that there is in-house expertise in project financial planning, architecture and engineering, construction, leasing, building management, etc., or that these skills are readily and economically available. A *fee developer* might be used, for example.

A maximization of User control over all aspects of building financing, development, design, construction, etc., is a major benefit of this option, as is the realization of all of its short-term and long-term financial benefits.

The User as Developer must proceed cautiously. Many an attractive building project failed to meet its corporate profit center objectives because of unleasable tenant space, inadequate building management, an unrealistic valuation of project worth, poor planning, etc. A major real property investment may ultimately prove inappropriate for your portfolio. That is, when it is no longer a producing asset, commercial real estate can be a substantial drag on the cash-conscious entrepreneur.

In the final analysis

Ultimately the choice of lease vs. buy becomes one of User organization priority and interest. To the extent that it is affected by the upside potential of market conditions, the timing of such a choice is critical. But the timing of the real estate market bears little relation to that of any other industry, and may not fit the needs of your relocation.

When the choice becomes more purely one of getting the best and most productive facility, then the opportunities can get exciting and at the same time perilous. The design, development, ownership, maintenance, etc., of real property are demanding activities, unique unto themselves, and they are a challenge to the most astute of entrepreneurs.

DOCUMENTING

If **Planning** is what just about everybody knows how to do, **Documenting** the things we plan is something that just about everybody does not want to do. **Planning** gave us that wonderful feeling of anticipation of a future that we managed to look at not too closely—a little myopically, and perhaps with rose-colored glasses on at times. Now, while our expectations are up, we must face the task of putting to paper, in a very serious and deeply obligating way, the schemes and dreams that we have spent months, perhaps years developing. It is not an altogether pleasant task, nor is it an inexpensive one, but it is one which can provide us with a kind of deep satisfaction, knowing that when we are through this paper-making stage, we will have a solid foundation for realizing those dreams.

Documenting is a rather pompous term for creating a series of instructions, directed to different individuals and entities—and sometimes to the world—describing our needs, methods and intent. We call these instructions documents because for the most part they follow a form created by others; leases, permits, contracts, etc. Because they have legal status, they take on something of an official character.

In this latter sense, Documents differ from the Tools we talk about later in this book. The tools we use or devise to help us along the road to relocation are sometimes the official documents we labor over, and the latter sometimes become very valuable tools.

But our **Documenting** phase of the relocation process is more than just accumulating official paper. It is an activity, a series of events that moves our project along and involves people and their productive efforts in our behalf. Remember that this paper constitutes a set of instructions. As we move through **Documenting**, we will see a wide variety of Players begin to respond to those instructions until they are in full play in the **Execution** segment of the process.

In the pages that follow, we will talk about how to organize and move through the process of document preparation, and how to deal with the people and the issues involved. Please review **PART I—Chapter 4, THE TOOLS** for a discussion of a specific Document and its content.

Starting Up

As you approach the **Documenting** step, re-think the way you have been working through all of the Planning activity that brought you to this commitment to proceed with relocation. The ordered chaos created in your office—and perhaps at home as well—as you researched sites and collected tons of now not-so-useful data, must be replaced by another kind of order. Now your relocation project needs a discipline more in tune with that of your workplace; for a period of time it is going to be an integral part of your workplace activity.

From this point forward, you and your Project Team will be seeing much of people from outside your office; now is the period when the input of many of them will be most valuable. A first order of business will be to notify your employees and staff of your plans and intent. You may feel that the word has gotten around, that the rumor mill has already taken care of that item, or that your work with staff on the matter has obviated the need for a formal announcement. Whether it comes at this juncture, or earlier in your planning work, we suggest that this is a critical intersect in your plans for your organization's future. It must be given careful and deliberate consideration. There are no formal guidelines for such a notice, but whatever its nature or content, we see the distribution of a formal announcement of the rationale for the admittedly disruptive proceedings you are going through as requisite for the continued good health of your organization.

On the heels of your announcement of intent to your staff and employees, will come the hiring of a commercial real estate broker, and an architect or design professional. You have already used the services of people in these professions in a limited capacity. Now you must carefully evaluate their ability to continue to provide effective services, or proceed again with a carefully structured selection process. This temporary expansion of your staff will require adjustments for people and work habits, as well as for space and equipment.

This is war

During the **Planning** step, you had a taste of the telephone traffic generated by your limited contact with the outside world on this subject. That traffic will now multiply a hundred-fold. Beyond the additional team members mentioned above, will be a sizeable cadre of technicians, salespersons, representatives, agents, etc., who, with legitimate reason, will seek to enter and move about your premises to count, measure, inspect, verify and perform countless other important functions in behalf of your project. They must be accommodated, dealt with courteously and expeditiously, and assisted to a reasonable extent in accomplishing their mission, if you are going to get your money's worth out of them.

For a relocation project of virtually any size, we recommend a War Room and a communications center. The first is a modestly sized room (8 feet by 10 feet can be adequate) with a lockable door, a communications terminal, plenty of wall space for tack-up, a file cabinet, a work surface of desk size or larger and chairs for the User Project Manager (UPM). (See **PART I, Chapter 3** for a discussion of the UPM.) The room should accommodate meetings with two or three team members or contractors at a time. This dedicated work space would need to be supplemented periodically by a larger conference room with more spread space, and greater seating capacity.

The communications center need be no more than a single terminal, plus word-processing equipment, manned by a person whose sole or principal responsibilities include the administrative management of the project, and who is the focus for all written and verbal enquiries about it.

Working with your new team: differing priorities

In setting up for the work to be done in this stage of your relocation project, there are considerations which extend beyond the logistical; like the matter of notifying employees, these concern individual and organizational relationships, and the interaction of people with a wide variety of skills and motivations and priorities. You will want to review these, discuss them among your staff and develop, to the extent possible, a considered and uniform response to the circumstances and situations that will evolve as the project progresses.

Probably first among these circumstances is the situation in which members of the User group will often find themselves in the coming months: that of being totally surprised, at some moment, by the presence in their workplace of an unknown outsider and—ergo—an unauthorized person. The latter will have dropped by to count or measure something, and will be employed by any one of a number of advisors or contractors to the Relocation Team.

Organizations with an established security system of visitor ID will have already gone a long way to solving the understandable staff apprehension at this kind of encounter. Those without such a system in place will want to discuss simple and inexpensive means of dealing with this situation, short of shutting off a valued service or diminishing its effectiveness.

Another aspect of this encounter can lie in the nature of the questions—if any—put to the staff member by the visitor. Are they always simple, straightforward and uncomplicated? Chances are they are not, if the visitor is doing a good job of what he/she is about. So, do you muzzle the interrogator, brief employees on their responses to hypothetical questions or do you simply let the chips fall?

Probably some combination of these responses is worth considering. More important than anything else is the idea of open communication, constant dialogue and regular and frequent feedback—between organization leadership and staff and employees, and between the organization, usually in the form of the UPM, and the outsider.

Skeletons in your closet

Since we are always concerned with the integrity of your project and your control over it, we cannot overemphasize the need for unceasing vigilance in your relationships with those who are engaged to assist you. The nature of the facility relocation is that it invariably succeeds in investigating and studying the organization itself beyond a point of usefulness to the project at hand. In doing so, all kinds of skeletons are uncovered, very few of any use to the organization *or* the business at hand, and most of which succeed in feeding rumor mills and honing axes waiting to be ground.

Knowingly or otherwise, the individual responsible for exposing the skeleton and laying it at the doorstep of the most-likely-to-be-horrified staff member, will be an outside consultant or technician who feels constrained to be the white knight. The staff member, who cannot resist the unsolicited opportunity to be the bearer of bad news—who can?—spells out—perhaps with some embellishment—the gory details of the new-found skeleton for management which, diverted from the business at hand, is now in the unwanted position of having to prepare a response.

In the worst of circumstances, management, caught unaware and acting on the good faith belief that the information uncovered is dangerous to the health of the organization and persuaded that its source is impeccably professional, over-reacts—to the detriment of the project. In the best of circumstances, management recognizes the syndrome, quickly notes it for future, post-move-in reference, and rapidly and resolutely moves ahead with the project.

We mention this kind of occurrence because it can happen often during any sizeable relocation. It can be debilitating and costly, and although you cannot prevent it from happening, you can successfully defuse it. The latter is done in the same manner noted above regarding communication, dialogue, etc. By discussing, at your starting-up meeting, possibilities that will be present for outsiders to find damaging documents, have revealing conversations, observe conflicts, uncover costly discrepancies, etc., you can establish procedures for channeling these discoveries, and for interrupting them.

You can also have a similar dialogue with your service providers that channels their revelations to the most appropriate source and establishes reasonable limits to the extent of their helpfulness.

Handling documents

You, the Project Team and your User Project Manager will be concerned with handling a number of important documents throughout the project. Some will be generated by your group and some by others. Principal among these are the:

- Program

- Lease
- Bidding Documents
- Professional Contracts
- Vendor Contracts

Other records, forms, instructions, analyses, drawings, etc. are of significant importance. None have the impact of the above of being relied upon by others to fulfill their obligations to you.

The first three documents are discussed in some detail in **PART I—Chapter 4**, and the nature of professional and vendor services is dealt with in **Chapter 3**. The information below is presented to further clarify the purpose of these tools and to provide guidelines concerning their use and handling.

Handling the program

Perhaps because it has a lesser stature in legal terms, the **Program** is the least structured of the documents mentioned. It is also the one requiring perhaps the most vigilance in its preparation. By its nature, it is an internal document generated within the User organization to serve as a source of information concerning User needs. But because, in concept, it originated with the architectural profession, it most often takes a form developed and preferred by design practitioners. Thus, if the architect or design professional charged with compiling program data is computer literate, that document may consist of little more than a computer printout of space and personnel numbers. If the design professional is visually oriented, the program will be filled with complex balloon diagrams, etc., which may or may not be of value to the User. In many cases in which the preparation of a program is undertaken by such a service provider, the document becomes, upon completion, a very expensive shelf decoration.

A key characteristic of the program is that, in addition to developing critically needed facility information, it has a flexible format allowing for periodic or as-needed adjustments of that information. Computerized data input is ideal for this purpose; equally ideal is that changes may be made to the raw data on-site, in the User's workplace, since this is, obviously, where such changes will originate. A number of spreadsheet software programs are available capable of performing the kind of simple arithmetic calculations involved in the facility program; one or two of these is probably now in use in your business. Put your MIS person in touch with your design professional, if you are considering hiring one for that purpose, to work out the best way to keep program data and data manipulation in your office.

A corollary to the suggestion above, is that you establish the practice, as you wind your way through the relocation process, of reviewing facility requirements information, updating and changing as you see fit, rather than as the result of some artificially established review process. As raw data originates in your workplace, see that it flows in its most logical direction, from client to design professional, not the other way around.

Handling the lease agreement

One of the biggest User/tenant failings in attempts to deal with the lease agreement, not discussed in our treatment of the lease in **PART I—Chapter 4, TOOLS**, is that of managing the information that goes into it. It is also the natural result of a common oversight: a preoccupation with the forest to the point of ignoring the trees.

Whatever the origin of the lease document, a wide variety of information has gone into its preparation. It is also a composite, or layering, of information; some data is very current, others originated last month or last year, and still others hark back years, perhaps many years, before. Some are as simple and seemingly immutable as rental rates, suite sizes, insurance requirements, taxes, parking slots, and street addresses. Others represent once common practices, or are the result of an understanding of circumstances of the marketplace that may have changed dramatically in the months and years since they became a part of the lease you are now reading.

Some of this information is of incidental importance, but other—in reality most of that contained in the typical lease agreement—affects the User pocketbook in some way. Rents should reflect current market rates; taxes, current law; insurance rates, current practice; suite sizes, current measurements; etc. A whole range of other lease considerations may be called into question on the basis of how well they reflect the law, real estate practice and market conditions. Landlords are as aware of this as they are to the fact that most tenants will not make an effort to probe beyond what they read in their lease, or to reinforce themselves with updated information when they are negotiating a lease agreement.

Start a Lease Data File Now

There is usually ample time, during the planning of the relocation, to start an informal collection of useful data and to incorporate this into a Lease File. As you perform the due diligence necessary to start you on the road to a relocation decision, you will collect news articles from local newspapers that will enlighten your site search. This same information will also contribute to your ability to negotiate a tight lease. Local classified ads will provide a range of commercial rent rates and availabilities which, though they may not fit your requirements, can help describe the local leasing picture. News articles concerning area real estate developments appear on a weekly basis in most urban area newspapers. Most of this news will be devoted to residential construction, which can be of interest in terms of the level of demand for architectural and construction services, but commercial development of any kind will be reported diligently. The latter can be of as much interest in its absence from the news as in its descriptions of ongoing or projected commercial projects.

On the regional/national scene, weekly business newspapers like *Northeast/New England Real Estate News, San Francisco Business Journal, Houston Business Journal,* and like-named publications originating in other major urban centers will carry detailed information on commercial real estate transactions of every kind. Whether or not it is specific to your need, all of this information can be useful in defining leasing trends in areas in which you are interested. Nationally, monthlies and bi-weeklies like *National Real Estate Investor* and *Commercial Property News* carry news of major commercial development projects, and also publish an area or city focus with each issue which reviews developments in the targeted area in some detail. *Black's Guide* is another annual or semi-annual—depending on where you are located—that is useful for locating specific buildings as well as professional service providers in the major urban areas it services. These and any of the other periodicals devoted to business and real estate news inform, through their advertising as well as their editorial content. They provide information which, compiled along with your notes from conversations with fellow business-persons and service providers, etc., can make your Lease File a formidable resource, and reduce your need to accept outdated and costly lease language.

Handling construction bidding documents

Our discussion in **PART I, Chapter 4, TOOLS**, describes the components and use of bidding documents. These are the domain of the architect hired by you as the User, or by the owner of the property you will be renting. Since these documents control the construction of your premises, you will want to be apprised of what is in them. In most circumstances, you will be asked to formally approve and sign all or a portion of them before construction begins. If, under the terms of your lease, the landlord is responsible for providing architectural services, this matter of tenant signature can create an awkward situation. Technically, the architect has an obligation to protect documents developed for his/her client—the landlord in this instance—from the scrutiny of others. As the landlord's tenant, you have a special privilege in this regard; as far as the landlord/architect team is concerned, that privilege may be quite limited. It may only extend as far as the partition plan and list of finishes, etc., which comprise what is euphemistically called your work—that for which you had some direct input and for which your signature is requested. But, as with everything else in this business of workplace relocation, every transaction, piece of paper, and drawing is attached to every other. Similarly, for almost every partition relocated or built, there is a corresponding impact on other structures, as well as mechanical, electrical and plumbing systems. These systems directly affect your workplace. You should receive the tangible assurance, in the form of drawn and written instructions to the contractor, that appropriate adjustments to them will be made.

Risk protection: bonds and insurance

Traditionally, the architect has managed the negotiation with the contractor or builder concerning the protection required during, and after, the performance of work for the Owner—the *owner* in this usage being synonymous with *client*. This made much sense in the salad days of construction, when the building contractor was king and had limitless assets. Now, even though these matters are dealt with in an orderly fashion in the AIA contract forms, (see the discussion of **Bidding documents in PART I—Chapter 4**), it is every Owner/User to him/herself, and woe be to the one who fails to pay close attention to risk coverage. Thus, any readers who are assuming responsibility for the construction of their premises should consult with their own insurance manager or attorney on types and amounts of recommended coverage.

The General Conditions of the AIA contract for construction provide for a performance bond and labor and material bond to be furnished to the Owner by the Contractor. In the event of a Contractor default, or the inability of that party to complete the work for any reason, the surety, or bonding company, would become responsible for its completion under the original terms of contract. If the bond so specifies, the bonding company would also become responsible for removing any liens placed against the work by subcontractors, vendors, suppliers, etc. Once the bonding company assumes its responsibilities for the construction contract, it also takes on the right to complete the specified work in whatever way it sees fit, and to receive whatever payments for it are still outstanding. If you happen to be the luckless User whose Contractor falls by the wayside in mid-contract, and one who has also taken pains to select that contractor carefully, being left with a surety company of unknown resources and skills may be disconcerting. It is even less reassuring to remember that bonding companies are liable to be selected for their rates rather than for their building skills. For this reason, it is wise for the concerned User to know what those skills are and/or be able to take steps, before contract commitments are made, to assure a continuity of good work performance should the bonding company be required to take over.

Liability for personal injury to persons hired for the work, tradespersons, subcontractors, etc., and to those unrelated to it, the general public, and for damage to property other than the work being contracted is normally insured in agreed-upon amounts by the contractor. All-risk insurance is generally provided for the full insurable value of the work by the Owner, but an arrangement can be made to allow the contractor to purchase the agreed amount of insurance on the account of the owner.

Bonding and insurance levels are determined by the principals to the construction contract, except in jurisdictions where minimum legal limits are established. Where they exist, statewide bonding limits, established to protect public agencies as much as the User-at-large from unscrupulous contractors, do little to reassure the User. Often, by establishing artificial ceilings, they work to keep competent independent contractors away from projects they can handle more efficiently and less expensively than the big guys. Here, again, the User is well advised to inform him/herself about the details of project insurance and bonding. The cost involved will be borne by the User whether it is paid directly or is passed through in fees or overhead charges.

In your handling of bidding documents, and/or construction documents prepared for a negotiated contract, you will arrive at a point where some evaluation and comparison must be made concerning construction costs. Watch carefully for amounts of overhead and profit and the ways these are applied to your contract. Wherever you can, put caps and limits on the effects of percentages.

Professional and vendor contracts

In the discussion of the Request for Proposal in **PART I, Chapter 4**, we point out the need for a kind of uniformity and consistency that is often provided by the organization's purchase order. The contracts you develop with professional service providers and major equipment vendors have a similar thread of uniformity. Even though they deal with a greatly disparate group of organizations, products, services and idiosyncrasies, they can all receive your package of relocation project documents for starters. This information, consisting of relocation goals, organization background, facility requirements, etc., will be more than most require to perform their particular service; having it will save them much time in answering future questions. Perhaps more importantly, its certified presence in the contractors hands will reduce the potential for future disputes over so-called inadequate or missing information.

Another way of simplifying the laborious task of ordering this alphabet soup of equipment, furniture and esoteric services is to request an appropriate description of the product or service in question from the provider. It may come greatly embellished, but the editing of the provider's material and the adding of needed detail may be much simpler than starting from scratch. It will certainly gain points for you with the happy provider, and these could even translate into dollar savings and improved performance.

EXECUTION

This is the easy part of **DOING IT**. This is the part you can sit back and enjoy and watch while it all comes together as a result of your thorough planning and documenting of what needs to be done.

But it is also the part that keeps you on edge, wondering if you planned and documented everything, if you have it all organized properly, if it really will get finished on time. This is the part that brings knots to the stomach, and that hyped-up feeling that comes when the adrenalin is flowing because the workmen have already begun to swarm through those premises-to-be, to execute your orders.

The Pre-Construction Conference

Before the workmen start swarming, you will want to bring together at one meeting the Landlord's representative, your Design Professional and your Contractor, key subcontractors, (Mechanical, Electrical and Plumbing, etc.) and vendor representatives (telecommunications, furniture systems, major equipment, etc.) and anyone else who will have a critical role in the completion of the project. The purpose of this meeting is two-fold:

- To introduce key players to one another on a peer basis, and to give them an opportunity to dialogue about the upcoming work

- To discuss common issues and concerns, and establish guidelines regarding the conduct of the work

The first thing to bear in mind about this conference is that few, if any, of its participants *want* to be there. For the most part, you are bringing together a collection of independent and iconoclastic personalities who disdain the boardroom and the white-collar environment, and who admire performance skills over verbal skills. Each of these consummate professionals has a deep and abiding faith in his/her knowledge of what needs to be done and ability to do it. They harbor one concern, that someone or something will get in the way of their doing it, and one fear, about getting paid.

But there is a grudging recognition among this group of the skills and needs of others, the need they all share, for example, to be able to work quickly and safely in a confined space with limited resources. And many of them recognize the need their wage-paying clients have to keep project schedules and budgets under control.

It is in this climate that you will arrange your pre-construction conference and your first concern will be that each invitee appears with the manager or work supervisor assigned to your project. The next is that you have an agenda and some important information to share which will make the work of contractors and providers move more quickly and thus more profitably for them.

The following suggestions for topics that might be reviewed at this meeting are predicated on some of the information and decisions discussed in our previous segments on **Planning** and **Documenting**.

- **Introductions**

  Make sure everyone brings business cards to exchange

- **Chain of Command**

  Identify User, Landlord and Contractor representatives. Depending on the Workletter agreement and final contractual arrangements, the landlord's role in construction may be passive, except with respect to a contractor's interface with Landlord's building and property. Ask the landlord's representative to spell out rules for moving about his property, hours, delivery, off-loading, elevator usage, protection measures and devices that are required, etc. Remind all that the User will respect the contractor-worker-sub relationship and will communicate with workers only through their managers or supervisors. (Identify mutually agreeable exceptions to this.) Assure all that the material to be discussed and the agreements to be reached will have the sole purpose of making the work go faster and more efficiently, and thus be more profitable for everyone. (Wait for applause here.)

- **Unions**

  If you are in an open shop community, identify contractors who operate union shops and/or will have union personnel on your project. Identify union practices that should be observed to maintain harmony at all levels throughout your project. If you are in a closed shop area, ask the General Contractor (GC) or the union representative to clarify critical union practices for the benefit of vendors and other services.

- **Schedules**

  Review the entire Execution Work Schedule with anticipated start and completion dates for each trade or discipline. Uncover and discuss any conflicts or problems. Ask the GC to explain proposed schedules for the building trades, partitions, walls, floors, ceilings, etc. User and vendor representatives should provide scheduled dates for delivery and installation of telecommunications and other major systems and equipment. Discuss and identify Holidays and other scheduled non-working days. Provide each representative with a copy of the schedule you have just reviewed. Review and discuss the Workletter guidelines for Tenant Delay and Landlord Delay in the work, if appropriate. If the project is to take several months or more, repeats of this meeting of key project personnel should be scheduled to review the progress of the work and to make any suggested procedural changes.

■ **Change Orders**

Ask the Design Professional to explain the acceptable procedures for initiating changes in the work. For example, materials substitutions of any kind, even when they do not involve an increase in cost, normally require the written approval of the User/Tenant.

■ **Permits and Approvals**

Discuss and identify required permits for work, who will be responsible for getting them, who will accompany inspectors on their rounds, and how and in what form inspector feedback will be generated and distributed for action and response. Discuss any experiences with local inspectors, or their Departments, that might provide insight to the project team. The UPM should inform all of the results of his/her due diligence with local regulating agencies.

■ **Safety**

Understanding that each discipline, trade and contractor has its own established safety precautions, review and discuss those of particular importance in connection with this project. If appropriate, provide assurances regarding the presence or absence of hazardous or toxic materials on the building site; discuss procedures for managing same during the construction process. The User representative should share the results of his/her due diligence in this area, since the rules of the game change with great frequency.

■ **Site Visit**

For contractors, sub-contractors, vendors, etc., who have not as yet visited the work site—your new location—provide each with the information needed to arrange such a visit prior to the start of their work.

■ **Security**

The Landlord and the Contractor should review security procedures related to building and grounds during the construction and make-ready process. A sealed and secured area should be provided on site for building materials— which User dollars are paying for. A limited access or secured area for contractor tools and personal belongings should be provided when individual worker parking is distant. Hours and means of access to the site should be established.

■ **Housekeeping**

Telephone and command post locations should be identified. The User representative should have an on-site telephone, as well as the various contractors. A protocol should be established for checking for and returning telephone messages. For those who do not have them, consideration should be given to the leasing of beepers for key personnel for the duration of the project. Guidelines should be established regarding work-site clean-up and maintenance. Entries, corridors and work areas should be unobstructed by tools or equipment. Power and light cords should be strung off the floor, on-site toilet and lavatory facilities provided, as well as operable and safe elevators, etc. Uniform Building Code (UBC) and/or municipal ordinances relating to on-site working conditions should be spelled out, and a means of policing their observance should be established.

The alert and savvy User can also use the pre-construction conference to generate enthusiasm about the project and develop a camaraderie among its team members that can contribute greatly to its on-time success.

Monitoring construction: the User's site inspection

The User's purpose in making site inspections during construction or during an installation of any kind is threefold:

(1)   To report to the responsible contractor any observed circumstance or installation that appears in need of change or correction

(2)   To allow a change or correction to be made with minimum impact on the work and its budget

(3)   To provide a record of the observation for reconciliation of matters of responsibility for the occurrence

The User's site inspection provides the party initiating the project, paying for it and reaping the results of it—however well or poorly achieved—an opportunity to control those results. It is an unassignable responsibility that, oddly enough, is often given over entirely to others with the explanation that the User lacks expertise.

You probably wonder what you can possibly contribute to the overall success of your project, simply by walking through it and observing the work being done. After all, you were never trained as an architect, engineer or contractor. And aren't they the only ones who can understand what is going on? Wrong!

As construction work proceeds, very often the pros are not as alert to the implications of what is happening as a lay-observer, fortified with a strong sense of self-interest. You are intimate with the details of planning, the why of all the instructions drawn by the architect, you have had to learn the language of drawings and specifications and to critique it. You have been through the landlord's building with a fine tooth comb and have acquainted yourself with codes and ordinances and regulatory agencies—all because you wanted to save yourself and your organization some expensive surprises. By now, you are eminently qualified to walk the concrete slab that will soon be divided by your walls and covered with your carpet.

Some guidelines for the User's site inspection

Here are some suggestions to follow as you observe the work of your team executing the plans and documents of your facility relocation:

- Sometime prior to the start of work at your site, assuming that you have not had a meaningful experience with commercial construction before, ask your contractor or design professional to take you on a brief tour through a similar site under construction in your general area. Such a tour would valuably increase your level of recognition of parts and processes, and would reduce the time the professional normally spends in on-the-job client education.

- Describe your plan for personal observation of the work to your design professional and your contractor; request their cooperation. Reassure them that your efforts will supplement their own monitoring activities, will not be redundant and will not be interfering in nature. Discuss the ground rules for on-site communication with workers and with supervisors or managers— minimal in both cases. Let them know that you plan to be invisible at the work site.

- Arrange regular, informal meetings with the contractor's Project Manager to inform him/her of your observations, including any deficiencies noted, to pass on any new data, measurements or any changes in the work or schedule required by the User, etc., and to receive feedback on the contractor's observations concerning progress of the work. These meetings should be supplemented by a schedule of regular telephonic contact so that important new information is not delayed.

- Develop a simple format for written confirmation of your periodic observations directed to the Contractor's Project Manager and/or any other responsible persons involved in the work. These confirmations should be prepared and delivered to the recipient as expeditiously as possible after verbal transmittal. For example, if you telephone your contractor to report an installation being made in error, confirm that report in writing no later than the following day. Before you start your site visits, discuss the purpose in doing this which is, simply, to control the effects of mistakes.

■ Before your first working site tour, pay a get-acquainted visit to familiarize yourself with its general environment: access and parking, entry, stairs and elevators, general lighting conditions, etc. Be sure to carry a heavy-duty lantern in your car for the black-as-pitch interior space that never gets a drop-lite.

Check in with the job superintendent, confirm your identification and get a hard-hat. Let him know what you will be doing and where you will be on the site, and for about how long—this constitutes a regular routine. Get a feel for potential danger areas, heavy dirt and debris areas, and for the kind of optional shoes and other clothing you might want to carry for future visits. A long cloth lab coat kept at the site can be handy for both men and women from the User organization.)

■ The best site visiting hours are before 8 AM or after 3:30 PM: in the morning, if you want to watch people at work, and in the late afternoon if you want to see what has been done today and want some relative quiet while you observe.

■ Schedule your visits with a specific installation in mind; partitions, ceiling, AC ducts, electrical conduit, etc. Practice visual occlusion: observe what is on your list for that visit, and put everything else out of sight. A construction site of the simplest variety is a visually confusing place for anyone. For most people who are charged with walking the site, including professionals, distractions can dilute the effectiveness of a tour—you spent two hours getting there in tough traffic, so you want lots of focus.)

■ There are degrees of urgency in reporting your observations and seeking corrections. Of course, the first among these is observance of an endangering condition: fire, flood, collapse, etc.; these should be reported immediately to the party best suited to provide the remedy needed.

The next order of urgency has to do with things like how much something costs, the probable difficulty involved in making a change, the probability that subsequent work may make correction more difficult, where the error, if any, originated, etc. The best rule to follow is to report the deficiency immediately, in the context of the routine established between you and your contractor.

■ Get User organization technicians, department heads, executives, lenders, union representatives, etc., involved in periodic site visits. Provided these visits can be planned to occur under escort and in a non-disruptive way, much can be gained from widened participation in the development of the process.

A few things not to do during the User site inspection

We also suggest that you observe a few don'ts in connection with the User site inspection or walk-through.

>**Don't** hang around the site.
>
>**Don't** kibitz.
>
>**Don't** give instructions.
>
>**Don't** arrange or tidy.
>
>**Don't** pick things up.
>
>**Don't** get in the way.
>
>**Don't** be careless.
>
>**Don't** get alarmed or mad
>
>**Don't** be a pompous know-it-all.

Vendor follow-up

Much of what has been said above can apply to tracking the production and delivery of vendors. The single outstanding difference is that we cannot, except in the most unusual circumstances, walk through their premises and inspect the work in progress, as we can that of the construction contractor.

But, applying the principles involved in the construction-site inspection noted above, we can make some adjustments that might be applicable to the off-site vendor and still give both the User and the vendor the benefit of the periodic progress check.

First, consider that there is probably no major office or factory system or piece of equipment that can be expected to arrive and be installed in off-the-shelf condition. Even the ubiquitous office copying machine requires checking and adjusting for floor loading, power, ventilation, operating and maintenance space, general lighting conditions, etc. And these comprise conditions for which standards usually must be met for equipment warranties to be effective. Without being more complex, other equipment can still involve a level of customization for your unique requirements that calls for vigilance and attention to these considerations:

- At, or before the time the order is placed, determine those components of the finished assembly that are being manufactured by the prime vendor/manufacturer and those being sub-contracted by others.

- Determine what parts are scheduled for assembly on your premises, where they will come from, and who is contracted to do the assembly.

- In the event of a delay in the timely shipment of a component to your manufacturer or your site, you may be able to speed its shipment by a well-placed follow-up call, or by suggesting a substitute.

■ If it seems appropriate to do so by, virtue of the size or nature of the equipment, arrange for off-site testing of it, either in your presence or with written test results based on previously agreed criteria, forwarded for your conditional approval.

■ Determine major manufacturing stages and manufacturer's shipping priorities. This means knowing, in capsule fashion, how the manufacturer works, who and what they depend on, and what their current backlog is.

■ Determine the kind of handling and routing the equipment or assembly will get once it leaves the factory door and starts its journey to your site. Will it go directly to the site or to an intermediate storage location? And who is to pay for the latter?

■ Become familiar with the names, at least, of key vendor personnel—the ones who make things happen. All vendors want you to follow their rules for customer service—usually of the don't call us, we'll call you variety. Yet, many fail to follow their own rules and will yield to aggressive buyers who are pursue the interests of the customer organization.

Schedule your follow up and follow it

Once you have accumulated all this information about each major piece of equipment to be a part of your new installation, you will be ready to prepare a schedule of follow-up activity. Schedule one or more calls to the producer at each major intersection in the life of your order. Reported delays should not become occasions for handwringing and castigation, but for planning alternatives— alternative schedules, routes, suppliers or assemblers, or alternative sources for the item in question. Intersperse telephone calls with fax transmissions and keep records of all follow-up efforts.

For critical production or telecommunication equipment, consider sources for backup equipment—leasing, for example—as soon as your order is placed; have a date established on which to trigger that alternative. For extremely time-sensitive installations, consider writing liquidated damage clauses into purchase contracts. These provide for payment to the User/Customer of an agreed-upon fixed sum for each day—or other period of time—of delay in the installation of a piece of equipment beyond the agreed upon delivery date. Since this becomes a kind of insurance for which the manufacturer will add some premium to the estimated cost of the installation, you will want to use some discretion in applying this liquidated-damage language to your equipment contracts.

Changing the address and telephone number

The organization's address and telephone number will probably change, unless you are moving down the hall or to another floor in the same building. Confirmation of the address is simple if you are moving to another established location in the city. However, you should request confirmation of the Landlord and/or the local Post Office in writing before you commit yourself to the many thousands of dollars involved in new printed materials. A move to a new construction site may require a visit to the city Planning and/or Zoning Department for a correct address designation. Then, check with the P.O. to see that they have the same information. When you get your new address, get the full nine-digit Zip-code number. The Post Office will make this mandatory, soon.

Even before you do any of this confirming, consider what your options might be and make some creative choices. If your building lies at an intersection with the possibility of a choice between two street names, think of which you might prefer. If you are the first tenant on an empty floor, exercise what prerogative you can to take a suite number that sounds good or looks well on your letterhead.

Something of the same kind of option exists with respect to the assignment of your organization's new telephone number(s). These are provided by the utility that gives you your dial tone. It will usually come from the phone company switch located closest to your new address. Except in urban areas of the highest density, batches of numbers are available for the telephone company to choose your number from at any given switch or prefix location. If you leave it to the telephone company, they will give you the next number to be crossed off their list. But they also understand the importance of certain number sequences to all businesses and will cooperate in the search for one closer to your needs. If the prefix number does not work for you, enquire about the additional operating costs involved, if any, in moving your connection to the next closest telephone company switch. Once you have settled on this choice, be prepared to stick with it. It is easy for the utility to change it for reasons of *their* own, but considerably less so for you to get them to do it.

It should be obvious that address and telephone changes that will give you some degree of flexibility in choice are going to require a significant amount of time to arrange. On the other hand, be prepared to be given a narrow window of time within which to make these arrangements.

Converting printed material: cars, trucks and baseball caps

Not all decisions concerning the ordering of new stationery have to wait for final Post Office and Telephone Company edicts to be issued. Early on, you will wish to consider the opportunity provided by the relocation for a re-design of your printed matter. If you have more than a passing concern about the visual impact of this material—from corporate logo to mailing labels and everything in between—we suggest that you contact a qualified graphics designer. Like the architect and the interior designer, this person has special training and qualifications, and we urge you to be informed about these in selecting one. For example, printing, computer graphics and desk-top publishing houses may offer a competently and economically produced product, without any trace of design.

Whether there is redesign or simply insertions of the appropriate new address and telephone number(s), you may want to look at reprinting or changing over:

Calling cards	**Billheads**
Memo pads	**Catalogs**
Brochures	**Advertising layouts**
Rubber stamps	**Postage meters**
Portable signs	**Letterheads**
Envelopes	**Order forms**
Cars and trucks	**Advertising Specialties**
Uniforms	**Directories**

The advertising specialties category is the one that includes all those gimcracks that you have had printed with the company's name and passed out to friends and customers over the years—like pens and pencils, calendars, paper weights, T-shirts and caps, etc. You can not recall all the stuff that is out there, but you might take advantage of the organization's move to print and distribute some more.

A competent graphic design service can mean a savings for you

One or two color printing of most cards and letterheads can be accomplished in most urban areas in a matter of days, but ten days to two weeks is a good planning period. Four-color work, advertising specialties, uniforms, portable signs, etc., could require four to eight weeks of lead time.

If you are already printing catalogs and brochures, which can require many months of preparation for a total revision, you will be the best informed about necessary lead times. If you are embarking on these for the first time, be careful in planning the insertion of telephone and address information, so that it can be easily corrected when necessary. Be prepared to accept whatever schedule your printer gives you.

The utilization of graphic design services in connection with any of the above can, depending on the number of different pieces and the amount of detail work required, add a few days or several weeks to your delivery schedule for printed matter. On the other hand, a competent professional design service can work to shorten overall lead times by coordinating and integrating designs and printing media. This may seem like a simple bit of business. It is decidedly not.

Organizing for packers and movers

Perhaps your staff has already recognized what a wonderful opportunity the planned move presents for a giant house cleaning—not of the broom and mop variety, but of the paper-shredding kind.

Since most relocations are closely tied to an organizational regrouping, in turn associated with revised and updated procedures, the move does more than present an opportunity; it almost demands a rejuvenation of internal operations. Thus, we suggest that the rethinking and retraining required by the physical change of location begin in the existing one, as soon as possible after the final GO,NO/GO decision has been made. This process can become an integral part of packing for the move, lending that otherwise onerous task a more positive, even exciting purpose.

After its people, the organization's physical move typically involves the transfer of:

- Files
- Furniture & Equipment
- Accessories (e.g., staplers, art, clocks, appliances, etc.)

Each of these categories has two further distinctions for moving purposes: they are items which are

- Shared
- Dedicated

Dedicated files, furniture, equipment and accessories are those normally in use on a daily or other regular basis by an individual, usually at that person's workstation. They may or may not be that person's personal property. The responsibility for culling through, labeling and organizing these items for the move belongs to their dedicated User.

Shared files, furniture, equipment and accessories are those normally used by more than one or a few individuals and are usually found in central file areas, data processing centers, conference rooms, assembly areas, kitchens, etc., outside of the individual workstation. These items are invariably the property of the organization. The responsibility for organizing these items, and labeling and preparing them for the move, is assigned by the organization to the individual normally responsible for their day-to-day maintenance.

Responsibilities for moving lie with those who have a stake in it

Depending on how the Mover is equipped, file cabinets might be picked up, contents and all, and shipped, or as is more common, they might require unloading and repacking in labeled cartons before being trucked away. The latter should be done by the User personnel identified above.

If the normally responsible individual is not being transferred, the moving task should be assigned to the person inheriting the vacated job responsibility. From the point of view of efficiency, fairness and, very importantly, security, move responsibilities should lie with persons who have a stake in it and who will be at the new location to help reorganize. If, as often happens, there is no immediate assignment to fill the empty shoes, this caution should extend to your selection of a substitute.

Color-coded, self-adhesive labeling is commonplace among commercial movers today. This should be accomplished by User personnel in accordance with Mover instructions. They are less used to good mapping, however, and the User must defend against finding heavy furniture or equipment placed in the right room, on the wrong wall. Advise your Mover that User personnel will securely tape a clearly drawn furniture layout on the door of each room and will hold the mover responsible for placement of items in accordance with the layout. A move-in punch-list, performed by the UPM prior to the departure of mover personnel, can use these drawings to verify the correct placement of furniture and equipment.

Refinishing & Repair: another way to achieve a new look

As the costs of your relocation project go on their, hopefully anticipated, upward spiral, you may want to think about refinishing old, but still very useable, furniture.

All-metal pieces, like filing cabinets, can be electrostatically refinished on-site, usually in a matter of days. A week to ten days lead time should suffice for this work, which is also relatively inexpensive. The quality of the finish is directly proportional to the expense, however; if something more than a cosmetic change is sought, longer lead times and greater expense must be considered—including that of emptying pieces so they may be refinished at an off-site location.

Upholstery and reupholstery can be an effective route to achieving a new look at a fraction of the cost of new furniture or work station panels. Lead time for this work will be affected first by the local availability of the fabric you choose. Shops that handle this kind of work will typically have a narrow selection on hand—usually not in the quantity you need—but will have routinely available resources, some of which will have quick order arrangements with their suppliers. Allow ten days to two weeks for your fabric to arrive, and from four to ten or twelve weeks for completion of your order. Work station panels will not usually require the time involved in reupholstering workstation or executive seating. Comparing delivery times for new furniture, the rehabilitated item can take as long or longer, but the low cost of the latter may more than reward your patience.

Use local fabricators as well as refinishers

Metal refinishing and reupholstery can be accomplished in most areas with greater confidence by using a wider variety of local sources than can the refinishing of wood pieces. Here again, the replacement costs for items like large wood conference tables can be so great that local refinishing and repair is recommended and—where period design detail is not as great a concern as functionality—local custom fabrication is a worthy consideration. But if you can't get your wood seating fixed, replace it with durable, and dependable, new wood furniture. Local fabricators can be less than reliable resources for seating.

In a quality workshop, allow from eight to ten weeks for the repair and refinishing of major wood furniture pieces, and longer if exotic hardwoods or veneers are involved. For planning purposes, furniture repair, reupholstery and/or refinishing can be equated to the lead time required for new items, all of which clearly fall into the category of long-lead items.

Chapter 3

THE PLAYERS

Chapter 3   **THE PLAYERS**

Their Roles

Like the Four Horsemen—not of the Apocalypse, spreading famine, death and disease—but of the fabled Notre Dame football backfield of the 30's, combining their superior strength and skills to overwhelm all opposition, so are the principal Players in the making of the Workplace: the Developer/Landlord, the Architect, the Contractor/Builder, and the real estate Broker. Their history is deep, their talents are unique and finely honed, and their importance in satisfying our facility needs is almost beyond question.

Almost, because successful commercial facilities have certainly been raised without their special skills. But these Players are so critical to the success of any workplace facility project, that it is difficult to imagine circumstances that suggest that such a project should proceed without the assistance of one or another. Why, then, would we hesitate to recommend their involvement in your project?

Why is it that these invariably healthy, intelligent, and attractive men and women, whose achievements on the playing field are requisite to their profession, and about which there is a never-ending supply of stories for the telling, find it so difficult to leave their less attractive playing field attitudes behind them ? Why is it that, taken as a group or individually, they are so difficult to communicate with, so hard to manage, much less lead, and so seemingly arrogant and often downright unpleasant? Because our description of the attributes of this aggressive team of "hard-ball players"—as they so often like to refer to themselves—is acknowledged by most to be mildly stated. And if this is the case, who needs the grief? What is it about what they do that makes each so important to your facility search?

This Chapter tries to find some answers. It examines each of the Players involved in the relocation process, where they come from, how they work, and what skills and resources they can conribute to your project. As for why they are the way they are, that question remains for you and others to determine. Suffice to say that the business of modern commercial building is fraught with risk and danger for all the Players. It may require some of those playing-field skills, and a dollop of arrogance as well.

THE DEVELOPER

The achievements of mankind from the beginnings of built history have been most eloquently expressed in constructions—Abu Simbel, Timor, Teotihuacan, Machu Picchu—by those responsible for raising them. Kings, pharaohs, prophets, emperors and Great Incas may have been our first developers: men of vision, energy, and overwhelming ambition, with the wealth, position and intelligence to persuade those around them to undertake seemingly impossible tasks.

Were these visionaries—men so persuaded of their own infallibility that they allowed themselves to be deified—the progenitors of our modern captains of industry and skyscraping monument-builders? Were they the antecedents of the Zeckendorfs and Tishmans, the Dowlings, Galbreaths and Hines of mid-twentieth century America? If so, the metamorphosis has been less dramatic than might have been hoped after 20-odd centuries of growth in the development of man and his knowledge of the world around him.

Just plain real estate men

Variously known as land speculators, town jobbers and just plain real estate men, the Nineteenth century American developers looked from border to border and saw one great tract of real estate to be bought and sold. Land and buildings were things to speculate in for a short time, or to invest in at longer range. Whatever functions these units might perform, there was only one that really mattered—that they return a profit.

In 1957, *Architectural Forum*, America's class monthly of architectural criticism at the time, looked down their long nose at the "breed" of real estate men who presumed to know not only what a building should look like and how much land it should take, but to have a better grip on these things than any architect. The latter was considered a "mere technician, and not a very practical one at that".

Coming as they did, from America's most prestigious architectural magazine of the day, these instructive remarks were ironic. They are also pertinent and accurate descriptions of much of the atmosphere of the real estate business today. The motivations, the characters and their attitudes have changed little in the intervening period, though there have been changes in the business of building buildings that its protagonists prefer to think of as *refinements*.

The making of commercial buildings is no longer the sole dominion of private wealth, nor should it be. The developer we encounter today is more likely to be a large organization than an individual practitioner, even in areas where land is cheaper and buildings more modest in size. The development process is complex and costly. The credibility of those in charge of the investment represented by even a modest-sized commercial building is of critical importance to their investors and lenders. And it is of equal importance to those in search of a workplace, who are thinking of buying or leasing one.

The developer is an enormous risk-taker

The developer must be able to respond to mega-dollar risks, the responsibility for which can fall beyond the reach of a project-financing agreement. The discovery of previously unknown toxic materials on a building site may be one such hazard. The loss of a major tenant/occupant and the failure of an already completed project upon which the developer depends for leveraging credit, can be others. Forces at play, both within the development project and totally unrelated to it, can jeopardize its completion and success.

The developer, large or small, local, regional or national, has typically financed its activity on a project-by-project basis using long-term, non-recourse financing whenever and wherever it might be found. The project may refer to an office building of any size, an industrial park with rows of similarly finished warehouses or light-manufacturing facilities, a retail mall or strip and other such viable commercial structure that can be defined as a unit of real estate.

Lenders and investors like to be able to identify the project easily, and to clearly separate its management and accounting functions from those of similar projects the developer may be involved with. This suits the developer who, with its non-recourse financing, has limited its financial responsibility to the value of the site, building(s) and improvements, etc., that comprise the project. Thus, the developer operating on a national scale may lose, or default on, a large building project in one or two cities, while continuing to maintain very profitable operations in others, or in other areas of the same city.

Permanent financing does not assure tenant peace and tranquility

It is important for those who tenant in one of these projects to be aware of the nature and source of its financing, to avoid disruption of the workplace. Contrary to the popularly held opinion that a large project is, by its very nature, capable of sustaining itself, the experience of such projects in the late 80s and early 90s suggest that the largest of them can fall. In a very real sense, the developer acquires a significant partner when a bank, insurance company or other lender is invited to participate in a project. Upon the abdication, for whatever reason, of the developer who is the acknowledged real estate professional, the passive partner becomes, at least temporarily, a real estate operator. But the lender may very well not have the professional skills, or the interest, to operate as such.

The result of this developer withdrawal for the occupant is, at best, a kind of benign decay of its facility until a new professional operator/owner is found or, at worst, a decline leading to collapse of critical building services, and the building project itself.

Sometimes the term developer seems synonymous with "landlord"

When a project is in its development stages, before steel has been put in place, the developer and its marketing group will tout the various exciting features of the incipient project to prospective buyers, tenants and users. An important part of the sales pitch will consist of reassurances concerning the developer's skills in managing and operating properties; an impression is often given that those skills will be available through the life of the project. Typically, the developer's presentations and literature do nothing to dispel this notion, nor do they remind the innocent prospect that the business of the developer is the realization of profit from real estate, and the turnover, or sale, of it as often as possible. In other words, in less time than it takes for your lease to grow whiskers, you may have a new landlord.

Wise tenants/buyers of commercial properties no longer look to sincere entrepreneurs, trustworthy development organizations or their staff to assure them of the reliability of future services, without having the detail of those services meticulously spelled out in their contract to buy or lease.

THE BROKER

In 1917, in California, an unsuccessful attempt was made to license persons acting as agents in real estate transactions. Opponents of such licensing claimed that it would be an unreasonable interference with a citizen's right to engage in a legitimate occupation. They were successful in quashing the attempt. It was a time when life was good for the now-and-then land hustler. But two years later, in 1919, the California legislature passed a real estate licensing law, the legitimacy of which was later upheld by the Supreme Court. Life was still good to the land hustler who was willing to stay with the trade and get respectable. In that same year Oregon, Michigan and Tennessee passed similar laws. Today all fifty states and the District of Columbia have real estate licensing laws on their books.

Buyer beware

As the only person, other than the principals in a transaction, who is liable to be intimate with the details of both sides of it, the broker was often in a unique position to take advantage—and often did. At a time when the term *conflict of interest* was not yet on the books, the broker was able to act as buyer and seller without the risks inherent in either position. By participating in the formulation of an offer by the selling party that might be unfairly low, then persuading a buyer to accept an inflated price, the broker who was practiced in his trade, could pocket an attractive difference. There were no laws broken by this practice. *Caveat emptor* was the operative phrase of the real estate business, just as it was in every commercial activity involving the trading of a commodity. A seller always had the right to bypass the broker and go directly to a prospective buyer. The deal might or might not be fair to both parties, but it would, at least, cut out the broker's commission.

In turn of the century American real estate, however, the broker had to deal increasingly with the innocent and vulnerable public in the sale of homesteads. The experienced hustler was quick to realize how much easier it was to make money off the ignorant layman. Popular literature and film are rife with stories of the eager pioneer leaving urban squalor at the urging of a hawker of worthless land somewhere, only to find misery in the hostile plains or the desert rock. They are stories, often told with a touch of humor and a wink at the hustler, or a sense of irony when the sucker struck oil or made millions running cattle. But the fact remained that buying and selling real estate for John Doe in America was a gamble, with big property owners and brokers holding all the cards.

The John Does of America looked around and discovered they were an army

We would like to think that it was the strength of the righteous army of John and Jane Does that successfully got the attention of its legislators, and not just the hucksters and charlatans who could afford to pay to legitimize a lucrative practice.

Whatever the roots of real estate licensing, the various state laws were, and remain, flawed. The biggest complaint, of course, is leveled by those who wish to be a part of the industry and find themselves blocked by the controlling legislation—legislation which, they claim, protects and provides unfair advantage to existing practitioners. Licensing in any industry tends to have a similar effect. For those inside and outside of the industry, licensing laws restrict and restrain practitioners without addressing their qualifications. Thus, while legislation tends to limit damage by fraudulent acts, it does little to protect the vulnerable from injury through the simple ignorance of the practitioner. Additionally, most legislation fails to distinguish between the vastly different practices of real estate.

These last two complaints about the licensing laws on the books in most states are worth exploring, since the reader and prospective buyer or tenant should be aware of the effect of the law, if any, on the practice of commercial real estate brokerage.

The practice of real estate brokerage is many faceted

Many of those outside of the real estate industry, and some of those inside it as well, assume that the practice of real estate is monolithic, regardless of the type of property or transaction involved. This is an error that can have serious consequences. The industry has evolved, grown, splintered and reformed itself into evermore refined specialties, shaped around its market and the unique requirements of its components. Some of these components are product-related as is indicated by the terms used to distinguish the two major areas of real estate activity, residential and commercial.

Others have their origins in transaction-type, since many segments of the market are interested only in the return on their investment in real estate. The latter may buy and sell government instruments, shares in a Real Estate Investment Trust (REIT) or participate in a syndication of real property, residential or commercial.

The residential market is composed of a variety of product-types: existing and new, single and multi-family, condominium, apartment, etc. It is also composed of a set of renters or buyers whose attitudes are established by the complex set of motivations found in anyone searching for a home.

The commercial market is composed of altogether different product types: offices and warehouses, factories, stores, restaurants and other kinds of places where people go when they leave their home and go to work, shop, or get their teeth fixed. And it is composed of people who have a very different set of motivations for buying or renting their workspace than they have for acquiring their home.

Search for the Broker who specializes

These distinctions would appear to be obvious. Many of those who will seek commercial properties to buy or rent will take the time to search for a broker who specializes in the type of property in which they are interested. This interest will probably focus heavily on the financial characteristics of the property in question, and how it can be seen to serve the commercial interests of the tenant/buyer.

The commercial user may look to the real estate broker to generate information on area demographics, perhaps relating to market formations or labor availability; on building types and structures; on local planning and zoning regulations; on costs-of-occupancy and rent rate structures and tenant improvement costs, among a multitude of other data. This information is unrelated to the concerns of the home-buyer and thus, information that normally does not fall within the purview of the residential real estate broker.

Yet the state, in its infinite wisdom, requires the same limited course work, and the same answers to the same questions in its licensing exam for all brokers, leaving the User with the impression that they all perform the same services, regardless of the nature or needs of the User. This impression is reinforced by the disproportionately large numbers of residential brokers in any community—backed by their well-organized industry groups—in comparison with the much smaller cadre of rather poorly organized brokers who specialize in commercial properties.

Residential real estate brokers perform a complex and badly needed set of services for their homeowner clients. Appropriately, they are licensed to perform these services as a protection for themselves and the communities they serve. Commercial real estate brokers perform a different set of services for a very different kind of client; there are questions as to whether licensing in its present form is of any value to them or to their clients.

The singular focus of the Commercial Broker: the Sale

The background, education and training of the commercial real estate broker have traditionally been left to the vicissitudes of the industry and its individual practitioners. The novice to the trade must be articulate, positive, self-confident and eminently presentable. Academic credentials and even a lack of general business experience are likely to take a back seat in evaluating individual potential, if the broker-aspirant possesses those magical qualities that make for the successful salesperson. This is because the first order of business for the practitioner of real estate brokerage is making the sale—in the jargon of the trade, "selling the exclusive", closing the deal.

Real estate transactions routinely involve high-dollar values and take place, with frustrating infrequency, in a competitive and volatile marketplace. The emphasis on selling abilities dominates the brokerage house, although not necessarily to the exclusion of skills critical to the transaction.

Every commercial real estate broker needs a grasp of real estate finance, the law of contracts, architectural planning and construction, even if it is as rudimentary as the level required by most licensing law. Happily for the User, strong competition has always existed among young entrepreneurs for the opportunity to be part of the excitement of real estate deal making and, especially, to achieve the mega-dollar earning levels reputed to be part of it. In recent years this has generated an influx into the trade of individuals well-trained in at least one of the areas, other than sales, mentioned above. This training may be uneven—a broker with an MBA here, another with a degree in accounting there, etc. The User is well-advised to make no assumptions about training levels and to question each commercial broker with respect to his/her particular skills and capabilities.

The Broker is a knowledgeable middleman

Unlike the developer/landlord, architect or constructor, the broker does not plan, finance, design or build. In modern times, as a knowledgeable intermediary with indisputable marketing skills, his/her principal function has been to serve as a salaried or commissioned agent of the developer/ landlord in the marketing or leasing of a commercial property.

In this role, the broker is on the other side of the table from the User. At the same time, the broker can be of use to the User by providing information and assistance that will encourage the transaction to go forward. Thus, if the completion of the real estate transaction is endangered by lack of attention to the prospective tenant/buyer/user's needs, the alert broker will often make an effort to attend to those needs, in the interest of earning his/her own reward—compensation—at its closing.

The broker is of more meaningful assistance to the User when the former is unencumbered with landlord relationships, and can focus his/her talents and experience on the User's needs. Working directly for the User, the broker provides a variety of critical information gathering and analysis functions that no one else in the flow of the facility acquisition process can offer.

The brokerage house can be full of useful information

The brokerage house can be an unequalled repository for detailed demographic data surrounding commercial sites in the area that the broker operates. Property and space availability, current market rates for rents and sales, specific site and building development histories, comparable transaction information, tax rates, building operating costs, typical tenant improvement costs and tenant improvement allowance, comparable lease and workletter language, etc., are a part of the professional broker's arsenal of resources, unavailable to the tenant/buyer/user through any other single source.

The Right to Represent Agreement

The Broker has traditionally made these services available through a right-to-represent agreement, usually prepared in brief letter form by the broker. This is executed by the User and, in turn, is presented by the broker to competing property owners, as evidence of an exclusive right to payment of their commission.

The commission represents a percentage of the total dollar value of the transaction. It is established in negotiation between the property owner and the broker. The law provides for free-market action with respect to this commission—it cannot be fixed in any way. Thus, it is not unusual for the amount of it to vary from one competing seller/landlord to another, or for a broker to hold two or more commission agreements providing for different—i.e., more or less attractive—terms of payment for the same transaction.

Broker commissions. Who pays?

In the sale of commercial property, brokerage commissions will usually be paid at closing by the seller. In tenant/user transactions, broker commissions are paid by the landlord at closing or in accordance with some formula based on tenant occupancy. Commissions also become a part of rent, in accordance with a landlord budget that recognizes this expense as a routine cost of doing business. Thus, when a rent of X dollars is proposed to the tenant/user, the figure includes an appropriately scheduled, or amortized, portion of all brokerage commissions. This is considered to be a convenient arrangement for the tenant in that an unwelcome expense can be deferred, if not avoided entirely.

Free, like the flowers in the atrium

In spite of the fact that the User is paying for them in rent, many Tenant/Users share the impression that the brokerage services they have enjoyed have come at no cost. They are somehow free, like the flowers, furniture and artwork in the lobby—a munificent gesture of goodwill, volunteered at the expense of the property owner/landlord. While this impression prevails, there is a reluctance on the part of the User/tenant to question the amount, kind and quality of brokerage services. It is a resignation to another of the vagaries of the real estate industry, that leaves the tenant without a sense of control over direction or expense.

Another way of skinning the commission-cat

In recent years, a trend toward direct hiring of the broker by the Tenant/User under more practical circumstances has gathered momentum. This is especially common among larger user organizations with recurring needs to lease space in multiple locations. It is a simple, good-sense procedure that can also have application for smaller organizations, with non-recurring needs. It begins with a realistic and detailed statement by the User of the services to be required of the broker, which the latter can assist in preparing.

A fee is structured by the broker for the work outlined in the User's request-for-proposal. It is negotiated with an understanding of the ultimate responsibility of the User for the broker's compensation. The burden on the User of this agreement is eased by a collateral agreement, between User and broker, to seek reimbursement of the broker's fee by the property owner/landlord who is successful in selling or leasing to the User.

So long as that fee does not exceed the amount budgeted by the property owner for broker commissions, the property owner/landlord can reasonably be expected to make such a reimbursement. If the landlord's budgeted commissions exceed the agreed-upon fee, the User can ask that the excess be directed toward a reduction in rent, or tenant improvements, or additional broker payments, etc., at User discretion. Such an arrangement shifts control of the real estate transaction to the principal with whom it belongs, the party whose funds are ultimately driving it—the User— but not without placing a burden of careful planning on that principal.

And Users have obligations to Brokers

It has long been a complaint of the commercial brokerage community that Users are capricious in their demands on broker services. They abuse the up-front nature of them, a traditional part of the broker sell, and use them as crutches for their own lack of planning. Our reader is not guilty of this, of course, but be aware that you may encounter increasing numbers of savvy commercial brokers, trained in their MBA programs to use their time wisely and get paid for it, whether the latter comes as part of the traditional pay package or not. The responsibility for the pay ultimately falls on your desk, as will the need to plan carefully to get the most out of your broker dollars.

Different landlords, property owners, brokerage houses and brokers in different communities will have varying opinions concerning the workability for each of the idea of fee-paid, direct broker hire; all will have some concern about the application of local law to it. It may be argued, for example, that the law will not support the payment of a real estate commission to an unlicensed principal in a transaction. (It is a hallowed tradition of the industry that real estate law is freely interpreted by its key players, for the benefit of the User, of course, and usually in support of the argument of one player or another.) You would want to verify such a conclusion with your own legal counsel or the responsible agency in your area.

The Department of Real Estate in the State of California addressed this question in their *Real Estate Bulletin for Spring,* 1976:

> *It is not a violation of the Real Estate Law or any of the general laws of the state if a licensee rebates a portion of his commission to a principal in the transaction. Section 10137 of the Real Estate Law makes it unlawful for a real estate broker to compensate any person who is not licensed as a broker or a salesman **for performing any acts for which a real estate license is required.** [Emphasis theirs] A principal in a real estate transaction is not performing acts for which a license is required. Hence, there is no violation of the law if the fee paid by the licensee is simply a refund or a reduced commission.*

The mystique of the commercial building industry, long nurtured by its protagonists —developers, landlords, brokers and others—has been giving way to pragmatic concerns for values delivered to the User. Archaic practices that fail to add value to the transaction, like some of those involved with the payment of broker commissions, are being seriously questioned and, in some cases, abandoned. The functions performed by the real estate broker are too important to the User and to the property owner to be jeopardized by traditions of doubtful worth.

THE DESIGN PROFESSIONALS

O Beautiful for spacious skies, for amber waves of grain, has there ever been another place on earth where so many people of wealth and power have paid for and put up with so much architecture they detested as within thy blessed borders today?

Thus begins Thomas Wolfe's popular polemic on modern architecture, *From Bauhaus to Our House*, a clever monologue on the excesses of architects and architecture in America. Ten years later Professor of Architecture, Robert Gutman writes in *Architectural Practice: A Critical View* (Princeton Architectural Press) of the suspicions of architects' motives held by Users of buildings and urban environments: "The profession is looked upon as venal and selfish. Architects are perceived as people who are mainly interested in advancing, often on the basis of spurious arguments, the economic interest of building owners and developers; and therefore, indirectly the wealth of professionals themselves. The public's trust in the fidelity of the profession is being undermined."

In 1992, Joel Warren Barna wrote, in *The See-Through Years* (Rice University Press), of the decade of the '80s in Texas, where all of the glib excesses of modern architecture and urban planning and real estate development came together. He wondered if the "motley collection" of "see-through buildings"—many by America's "anointed" architects—justify the hundreds of billions spent on them.

Probably no professionals or tradespeople, with the possible exception of doctors and lawyers, are so alternately glorified and vilified as are architects. Certainly no professional is as given to introspection and self-castigation.

The history of the architect: the story of the master-builder.

In the beginning, vision, concept, structure and art were a unity. The skills necessary to evoke them were sometimes found in one exceptional human, but more often among many, in a community of closely-knit and inseparable talents. Thus, it was, we are led to believe, among the artisans responsible for the great cathedrals of Middle Europe, during the Dark Ages. Stonecarvers, engineers and architects, skilled in erecting the fortifications of medieval Europe, pooled their resources to solve the problems of immense heights and slender columns and walls, with results of astonishing beauty.

94

As the list of uses to which buildings would be put was gradually enlarged, growing beyond the spiritual and monumental, and becoming more diverse and secular in their purpose, the differentiation of tasks among those responsible for their construction became more clearly defined. The ancient Greek master-builder, or archi-tect, became still more remote from the trade and crafts people of building. The ranks of the patrons were swollen by visionary statesmen, merchants and bankers.

Vitruvius built for the gods, Bramante for the Sforzas and the Medici. The architects of the Renaissance were students of line, form and space, and the architectural orders and ornament of the Greeks and Romans. Their clients busied themselves making war, and accumulating and dispensing the spoils therefrom.

In this respect, little has changed

The Italian princes of commerce of the Sixteenth century became the captains of industry of turn-of-the-century America, and the villas and pallazi of Tuscany, the mammoth halls of commerce of New York and Chicago. The Rockefellers, Morgans and Vanderbilts exerted the same prerogatives as their Sixteenth century predecessors, exhorting their architects to reproduce their monumental visions of power and grandeur in mortar and stone.

And one imagines that they did so on a very personal basis, delivering their instructions to a cowed or defiant architect in a well-appointed Manhattan, Lake Forest or San Simeon drawing room. The between-the-wars world of architecture was as painted by Ayn Rand in *Fountainhead*, brash, exuberant, creative, full of giddy climbs, dreadful falls and super-inflated egos.

As the curtain fell on a wildly eventful first half of the twentieth century in America, the nature of the client-architect relationship was undergoing a not-so-subtle change. The client half of it was losing its identity in the amorphous nature of the Great American Corporation. The patron of the architectural project was now a client spokesperson responsible to, and fronting for, a confusing array of executives, board members, trustees, and stockholders. The departure of the iron-fisted sponsor of an architecture that must reflect his most outrageous whim was welcome, but in his place came the committee, and the arbiters of corporate taste, about which Arthur Drexler in *Transformations in Modern Architecture* had this to say:

> *What was called "bad taste" is now seen to be ripe with "meaning". Those who actually have bad taste think they have its opposite, but "good taste" is a quality or condition no serious architect would now claim for his own work, lest it be misunderstood as representing "middle-class values", which middle-class intellectuals disdain.*

An industry emotionally clinging to the Nineteenth century

The impact of this evolution of the architects' clients was to bring about some overdue changes in attitude and practice that were not altogether welcome to the fiercely iconoclastic practitioner of the ancient art of architecture. Even today, 58 percent of the architectural firms in the U.S. employ fewer than five people and only 7 percent employ more than twenty. This is an industry with an intellectual capacity for the twentieth fifth century, emotionally clinging to the nineteenth. It is not an industry that was readily able to deal with the corporate mentality, a condition that every architect had to understand meant clumsy, oafish, dull and insensitive, that is, middle-class. But the practitioner's Edwardian sense of nobility of purpose, and capacity for rising above the masses has been responsible for some exciting architectural experiences in the second half of the twentieth century. And the architect has, in large part, however grudgingly, begun to adjust his/her practice to that of the corporate sponsor.

For an understanding of how the architect works, we need to look outside the practitioners' sphere of professional activity as well as inside it; that is, we need to know something of the community's demands on it, as well as those derived from the customs and practice of architecture.

The architect's handiwork is very much in the public domain

We use it and, not to over-dramatize, we risk our lives in and around it. Thus, there is a community concern for construction of virtually any kind. This concern has resolved itself in the form of permits and licenses that are required of people who design and build structures. Licensing laws applicable in some form or other to the practice of architecture are on the books in fifty states. Like most such laws, they exist for the two-fold purpose of protecting the public and the trained professional from the unscrupulous practices of the untrained. Like all such laws they fall short of achieving their intended purpose for either. There are many reasons for this; most of them can be described by likening the effectiveness of the architect's license to that of the automobile driver or the physician. The license is necessarily limited in its capacity to protect against damage to persons or property, unintended or otherwise.

Design is the area in which the architect's license makes no pretense to protection of any kind. The art of architecture is ephemeral and elusive. It defies, as one has reason to suppose it always will, any bureaucratic attempt to define it, much less to test for it.

Crossing lines and joining hands

Many years ago, licensing exams in states that had them were protective and exclusionary in nature. Architects did not cross state lines, and responsible clients did not invite them to do so. It was bad manners and showed a lack of respect for the local practitioner, even if that party had never designed a building of the type required. Bolder clients who invited the architect from out-of-state had to make sure that their choice had a license for their state, employed someone with such a license, could obtain one in sufficient time to start the project, or could join forces with a locally licensed practitioner.

None of these choices represented very happy ones for the client or the architect. Compounding the difficulties inherent in the parochial nature of state licensing were the inequities in the exams themselves. Some state exams were tough, some were easy. Some states admitted practitioners who were licensed in certain states, but not in others. The demands of the post-war building boom were clearly too much for this archaic and highly protectionist system.

Through much hard work over many years on the part of state licensing boards, educators and concerned professionals, a testing system was devised that could be applicable to the practice of architecture in any state willing to accept it—as most, eventually, were. The exam, administered yearly by the National Council of Architectural Review Boards (NCARB), is reputed to be even-handed, though about as tough as the most difficult of the state exams for which it is now a substitute. The institution of this uniform licensing procedure should be of interest to the User who attempts to evaluate an architect or architectural practice. In states where earlier licensing practices may be suspected of being weak, the year of a practitioner's license—pre- or post-NCARB—may be indicative of a level of testing if not of proficiency. Since all states did not join NCARB at the same time, a call to the office of your own state Architectural Review Board can establish the year in which licensees began to be admitted to architectural practice based on the NCARB exam or, as in California, based on a revised state examining procedure.

Your first conversation with an architect may be the most important one

The typical architectural assignment—and, of course, there is no such animal— begins with one or more conversations between the architect and the User to introduce the nature of the project on the one hand, and the nature of architectural services on the other. It is unusual for fees or charges to be attached to these kinds of exploratory dialogue. They represent an opportunity for the architect to comprehend the work that could be involved, to marshall his/her resources, and to begin to define fees for the work he might do.

For the User, initial meetings with the architect are ideal occasions for picking-brains in the best sense of the term: for more accurately defining user organization needs, for establishing the nature if not the particulars about project costs, and for finding out what it takes to be a good client for architectural services. At some point in this User/architect dialogue a statement of need and a request for a proposal of services will emerge. The RFP is prepared in a written format preferred by the User. It contains information about the proposed project and the User organization, that will help the architect prepare and return a cost-effective proposal for services. This is more fully discussed in **PART I—Chapter 4, The TOOLS.**

The architect responds with a written proposal

Except in the smallest of projects and the simplest of architectural procedures, the architect's response to the RFP will be in writing. It will include a statement of the work to be done and the fees to be charged. This proposal may constitute a contract for the architect; it may be accompanied by a contract form such as an AIA document; it may call for a contract to be drawn up by the user/client. In the case of the landlord architect, the practitioner hired by the owner of the property the user is buying or leasing, the contract may take the form of a work authorization. Since the latter can carry serious financial implications for the user, it should be examined carefully.

The Design Professional's five-step approach.

Most practitioners in the building design professions—that is architects and interior designers—approach their work in the same fashion, if not with precisely the same language or emphasis. The five-step, or-phase, approach to their work has evolved from years of design practice:

(1)   Following the formalization of a contract for services, they will put together a written statement of facility needs, called a *program*, based on a study of the user organization operations.

(2)   This will be followed by the presentation to the User of one or more planning and design ideas in schematic or outline form.

(3)   On the basis of the presentation, the ideas most preferred by the client will be fully developed.

(4)   By this time, schedules and budgets will have been reviewed and approved. The design professional will prepare the documents necessary to construct and to purchase materials, furniture and furnishings, and equipment.

(5)   When all contracts have been let, the design professional will observe, follow and guide the various processes, including construction, to completion.

The above synopsis is derived from the traditional five-phase process of the design profession, outlined in the AIA Standard Form of Agreement Between Owner and Architect. The User organization that plans to invest more than a few thousand dollars in its facility project is encouraged to review this and other pertinent AIA contract documents, like the Standard Form of Agreement for Interior Design

Services, before hiring, or even interviewing design professionals for its project. These forms are available through the nearest office of the American Institute of Architects.

Things the architect can do, but does not plan to.

A sometimes amazing laundry list, called *Additional Services*, is found in every design professional's proposal or contract, as well as in the AIA contract documents. This list circumscribes the professional's services, and develops his/her intent more succinctly than any other phrase, sentence or paragraph. We recommend that you review this list carefully. When using an AIA contract document, be sure to study the fine print in *Owners' Responsibilities*.

The User organization's role in the facility planning, design and construction process is seldom made clear, beyond the need that everyone has to collect money from their patron, periodically and frequently. The real role is actually acknowledged by most to be an actively participatory one, in which the party dispensing funds is in control. The mechanism for this control consists of an understanding with the design professional, preferably reduced to writing, that certain steps taken without the express approval of the User will not be paid for by the User.

The Interior Designer and the art of interior architecture

Many of our readers will not be concerned with building buildings or even with substantial alteration of one as they try to assemble their new workplace. Their planning and space preparation needs may be handled very adequately by an interior designer. In certain kinds of commercial construction, most often retail stores and restaurants, the visual effect of the interior designer's work can have greater impact than that of the architect. Certainly it is the designer's work that is felt most personally and intimately in any furnished space.

Naturally entwined with architecture

Traditionally, the decorative arts have been considered a branch of architecture, says Sherrill Whiton in *Interior Design and Decoration*. In fact, Mr. Whiton, who through his valuable texts has informed generations of interior designers of pre- and post-World War II vintage, preempts the architect altogether by placing the decorator-designer squarely in the caves at Lascaux: "Period decoration as a profession has existed for 20,000 years, since early artists painted the murals in the caves at Altamira and Lascaux."

Having captured the artistic high-ground for decorators, Mr. Whiton had an easy time corralling and branding some substantial names from the history of western art: "Giotto, Massachio and many others decorated chapels throughout Italy. . . . The Sistine Chapel is not especially noted for the beauty of its architecture but for the decorations by Perugino, Ghirlandaio, Botticelli and . . . Michelangelo's ceiling."

We do not argue with these historic presumptions of Mr. Whiton, or of the interior design profession. It is clear that man has always seen fit to introduce elements of utility and comfort and beauty to his personal surroundings and tried to bring these surroundings into human scale. It is also clear that the preoccupation of architecture has been elsewhere, with the bolder and more heroic concerns of its client, perhaps, that leave voids literally and figuratively inside their buildings—not voids without purpose or use, certainly, but empty spaces, nevertheless, which will be adapted at the appropriate time.

The Architect and Interior Designer often collaborate

The view and approach of the architect and the interior designer to the same project are quite different, though complementary. The architect builds from the ground-up and the outside-in; the interior designer, from the inside-out. The principal concern of the architect is the context in which the building is to be placed; the concern of the interior designer is the usage by its occupants. This distinction does not deny the dictum that architects be conscious of and informed about building interior usage, or that interior designers be aware of architectural intent. Each is often found in the other's territory. Architects are known to select wall fabric, paint colors, drapes or blinds, etc., in the absence of a competent interior designer. Interior designers are known to design moldings, soffits, interior stairways, etc., in the absence of a competent architect.

In the best of circumstances, the two will be on the same job, virtually at the same time, and their efforts will mesh with and support one another. We find frequent examples, in buildings where the two are known to have been present, of a level of sensitivity on the part of each that makes the result appear the product of a single drawing board.

And they often compete

Designers and architects are often found in competition with one another for the same project. There are several reasons for this, beyond the obvious one—that each is looking for new business. Many firms in each area augment their staff with practitioners in the other. Architectural firms of any size will almost invariably employ one or more interior designers. Interior design firms, usually smaller on the average than their architectural counterparts, will have a staff architect or, as is more often the case, an arrangement with a local architect that makes that person's services available as needed. The intent of all of these practitioners is to leave the impression with the prospective client that every aspect of its need for architectural and interior design services can be met by their firm.

Often a commercial facilities project will give the appearance of being a pure interiors job. This is intended to suggest that the work in question requires little more than the specification of loose furniture and furnishings and may come about at the inference of the User who is attempting to minimize the scope of the work involved. The interior designer cites the nature of the work in question as being, obviously, in his/her domain. Perhaps the project requires the movement of a couple of interior partitions, however, and the architect points out that this work will involve electrical and plumbing utilities in the wall, and the relocation and possibly substantial reworking of overhead lighting and air-conditioning duct work. The architect thus cites the nature of the work in question as being, very obviously, in the architect's domain.

In cases like these, there is an unfortunate tendency on the part of professionals in both areas to emphasize the important of their own particular service, to the detriment of the understanding by the prospective Client/User of what kind of service is really needed.

Let's look at what each does, and what each does best

If we can recognize the distinctions pointed out above between a professional preoccupied with structures and all that those imply, and one whose chief pre-occupation is the things that people need to live and work with, we can begin to get a sense of what each can contribute to the project.

The architect is critical in matters concerning the location and construction of floors, walls and ceilings, and other components of the building that are essential to its function. Notwithstanding the competence of others in this area, including the user who may have some appropriate technical training, there is the matter of permits that are often required for interior renovation, as well as building construction. The issuance of these may be dependent on the submission of drawings and specifications bearing the stamp of a registered architect.

The academic training of the architect is largely theoretical, cerebral, intellectual, logical and major-issue oriented. For every student admitted to a Bachelor or Master's program in Architecture, there is an incipient I.M. Pei or Edmund Bacon studying the nature of the built environment and the urban fabric, buildings as mass, form and volume, the site and building planning processes, building codes, structures and building technology, etc. It is training which, at its best, is eminently suitable for the likes of the Messrs. Pei and Bacon, and marginally suited to the layout of work-station furniture and the selection of upholstery fabrics.

The interior designer is critical in the selection of the materials, colors and finishes of architectural interiors, and the specification of furniture and furnishings. In the pantheon of professionals involved in the facility planning and design process, no other is as likely to be as qualified to deal with matters of interior light, form, color, pattern and texture. No other will have as firm a grasp on the myriad of products available for use in the commercial interior.

The training of the interior designer is much more difficult to characterize than that of the architect (who must follow a curricula formed, in large part, by the eventual need of the student for a license to practice). It may involve training beyond the secondary school level, where a number of colleges and universities offer majors in the subject, some in their Schools of Architecture or Environmental Design, or it can involve a widely varied collection of adult-education or correspondence school courses. Only a dozen states have licensing requirements—installed in recent years—for the interior designer. This means that most practitioners in these states are "grandfathered", the majority having been in practice before passage of the licensing laws. In three-quarters of the states, they are not licensed at all.

Industry organizations

Qualification, accreditation and licensing of interior design practitioners is very much a concern, however, of the industry groups principally responsible for organizing and representing them: the American Society of Interior Designers (ASID), the Institute of Business Designers (IBD) and the American Institute of Architects (AIA).

In the early-70s the latter established an AIA Associate membership for practitioners of interior architecture, and the three groups, together with responsible educators in the field, succeeded in organizing a National Council for Interior Design Qualification (NCIDQ). The NCIDQ, much like its big brother, the NCARB, administers an exam each year to qualified aspirants who are then awarded a certificate of achievement and registered with the Council.

It should be emphasized that none of the industry organizations noted above, each of which provides a valuable service to its membership, is charged with the licensing of practitioners; membership in their respective organizations is not a requirement for practice. They represent a reliable resource for the names of practitioners in any given area, and can be called on by the user who seeks information about their professional qualifications. AIA membership, including its interior architecture component, suggests, as one might expect, an emphasis on the architectural aspects of any given project; the IBD membership consists largely of commercial interior designers, space planners and furniture specifiers; and ASID membership cuts across all lines, with an emphasis on residential design.

DESIGN PROFESSIONAL SELECTION

Approach is a shop-worn, but useful, cliche. The designer's approach to his/her work is something we might check against an established model, like the five-step process we outlined earlier. A significant deviation from this model may be acceptable, but the variance should raise some questions with the User that the professional ought to be prepared to address. But what of the quality of the work to be done in accordance with the approach described? Is the work in phases (1) through (5) to be done at the best level possible? Or at a good, or at a professional level, and what do these words mean?

These are questions that are seldom, if ever, addressed except in the vaguest of terms, either by the design professional or by those who pay for services. Is the design professional who is capable of articulating User organization needs in phase (1) assumed to be able to prepare an equally lucid space plan in phase (2)? Is the excellent technical competence shown in a practitioner's construction documents indicative of a sensitivity to design issues? Are all design professionals required to work at the same level of proficiency and competence? By whom?

The Great Divider

The greatest separation of talents among design professionals seems to come in the area of *appearance design*. This term is intended to make a distinction between design that makes things *work* right, like a good space layout, and design that makes things *look* right, like floor and wall finishes, fabrics and art, etc. The first has a conceptual and aesthetic element, but deals chiefly with things that can be measured and arranged in a tangible and functional way. The other does not serve a measurable, work-a-day purpose, except that it determines the light, sound, color, form and textural content of everything in the workplace.

These two aspects of design are really inseparable, but the distinction is useful when evaluating the many design professionals who are adequate in preparing functional layouts, and seem to be at sea with intangible aesthetics. As we noted earlier, this is one area in which the design activity can be logically broken into parts; it is often approached this way by firms whose staff is comprised of architects and interior designers.

To judge design skills, look at some design work

In attempting to judge this area of the design professional's capability, it is useful to visit already built installations of his/her work to see first hand the results of past assignments. In fairness to both designer and User/client, this method of evaluation has the disadvantage of a solution seen with only glancing familiarity with the problem. There is also the matter of housekeeping which, if not well-attended to, can make a good design solution suffer. Viewing the work of two or more professionals will provide something of a level playing field in this regard.

The hazards of sensory overload are always present in any evaluation of the work of design professionals, whether the presentation medium consists of site visits, slide, video or multi-media presentations, or some combination thereof. To be useful to the User/client and fair to the presenter, they should be approached with an informed and critical level of understanding that has established some criteria for evaluation. These criteria should refer, not to the professional's portfolio, which may be extraordinary and include examples from critically acclaimed projects done for clients of unmatched size and repute, but to the specifics of the project at hand. They should refer to the need, for example, for

- A good space plan, which is seen best in plan form
- An effective use of task and ambient light, best seen on-site
- A competent handling of interior—windowless—spaces, best seen on site
- An efficient wire and cable management system, which should be seen in diagram form
- An effective budget control plan, which is a paper exercise

Each of these User-project-based criteria for evaluation should be developed by the User representative who is most familiar with the need; each should be identified with the environment or medium in which they are most efficiently and effectively seen. The latter can be accomplished with the assistance of the proposing design professional.

The Design Professional seen as predator

As a relocation project enters its Planning stages, there is a natural self-protecting mechanism that appears among User representatives; this mechanism often evolves into a mild paranoia. The design professional, who is and should be seen as a resource, is suddenly viewed as a predator. Doors are locked, barriers go up, telephone communication goes down and the User, in a futile effort to free him/herself, becomes a prisoner of indecision and ignorance. Each contact with the professional is seen as a sign of weakening, encouragement, favoritism or worse yet, as a loss of stature, position, face. This condition, which can last a long time where a variety of unforeseen circumstances delay the project start, is not a happy one. It is known to have contributed to the reputation that this birthing stage has for being one of the least pleasant of all—this should not, and need not, be.

We suggest that there are many unanswered questions concerning your project—the answers to some of which you had hoped to find in these pages—that can be put to your persistent design professional. They may concern the cost of workstations, permit procedures, the number of square feet on the third floor, or some arcane aspect of building systems or structure. They may be such good, tough questions that they make your pesky professional think twice about wanting to call again. Or they may get you some good informative answers. Either way, you have made your valuable telephone time pay off, without stress.

How does one react to design presentations ?

When the time comes to sum up your response to a slide presentation or a visit to a project executed by a design professional, there is always the hope that whatever the feedback may lack in sophistication it will make up for in useful content. To say that design is *subjective*, and to leave it at that, is to say nothing at all. To say "I know what I like", with respect to the intangible matters of esthetics, is to risk entering into a dialogue of unfortunate comparisons—food, cars, music, etc.—and to risk losing the advantage you can gain from an expression of informed judgment. And to form a committee of individuals who express themselves this way is to make the selection of a design, or a design professional, a noisier process, without improving its clarity, accuracy or usefulness.

There are many ways of expressing oneself subjectively—and how else are we to do it—about design that can contribute to helpful dialogue about it. It is the dialogue, the exchange of thoughtful commentary among User representatives that is needed to select the design professional most appropriate to the task, and to draw from that person or organization the design most appropriate to the User's needs. Design,"good"," bad" or otherwise, is the consequence of a great deal of study and effort on the part of the designer. To give it its due, we can discuss what we "know" about it, or we can look to be counselled by someone who has had similar preparation. For example, a local design professional who is non-competing and has no axe to grind, might be invited, for a limited time and at modest expense, to tell us what to look for and how to look for it—to relate the objectives of our facility design needs to what we see in neighboring workplaces that we like, or in photographs, magazines or brochures from the design professionals soliciting our work.

Effective design can emanate from the simplest of instructions and directions given by the User. The size of spaces which are not to be determined in strict accordance with their usage, can be described as wanting to be "large", "big", "not-over large", "comfortable", "un-ostentatious", etc. Desired light levels and/or the emotional quality of a space can be identified similarly as "high", "low", "warm", "cool", "sparkling", etc. These and other descriptive adjectives will often provide the competent designer with all that is needed to develop the desired aesthetic. These same kinds of descriptions can flesh out instructions given to design professionals competing for your work. And they can be incorporated effectively into your design evaluation dialogue.

Evaluating the products of their work

In **PART I—Chapter 4, TOOLS**, we discuss the products of the design professional's work—program, space-plan, construction documents, etc. We explore how these have been developed through professional practice over the years, to describe the needs of the project and the work to be done with the greatest possible clarity. Casually observed, these documents may look the same in format and content from one design studio to another; in fact, they will vary in the care and attention to detail with which they are done. These last characteristics are of critical importance to the success of the client's work. They are characteristics that can be evaluated by the alert user before the design professional is hired.

A few key documents should be identified by the user as important to a review of professional qualifications. These should include a typical program, a typical set of construction documents including sheets on mechanical, electrical and plumbing (MEP) work, written specifications, and a typical completed punch list. Preferably, the samples shown would represent actual work done by the design professional on a recent project, and would be accompanied by some explanation as to the methodology behind them. Such a request is best made in writing; it should include a brief statement concerning its purpose, specifics regarding the documents requested, and an acknowledgement of their confidential nature. The User might expect some editing of materials submitted for this purpose, but most design professionals are willing to share with and educate prospective clients in this way.

Look for easy to understand language: visual and written

Be prepared, once the design professional's sample documents are in hand, to evaluate them with a sharp eye to how they fit your project, your needs, your planning and design emphasis, your budget, etc. If you are planning to open a fashion boutique in the local mall, and the designer soliciting your project sends photographs of condominium projects and construction drawings for the offices of an insurance company, be aware that there is already a big gap between your needs and this candidate's experience.

Look at the verbal/written content of construction documents from the point of view of the young tradesperson who will execute the instructions contained there. Are they written in clear, simple, direct and understandable English? Even abbreviations and code symbols should be spelled out on the same sheet, or in the same document, in ways that are clear to you, the untrained. Check the accuracy of information from one document to another. Construction documents are, for the most part, translations of program information that has, in turn, been translated from the client's description of User need.

The Design Professionals and risk protection

There is an observation worth noting here with respect to warranties against damages arising from the traumatic incidents that almost invariably accompany a relocation project of any size. Risk protection is available in the form of the aptly named Errors and Omissions (E&O) insurance, which is written by a limited number of major carriers to protect professional architects, engineers and others from the hazards of their profession. These are understandably enormous, and the continuous rising cost of insuring themselves against "acts of negligence" has caused many architects to forego the protection. This creates a dilemma for both architect and User/client, since the latter has a right to some kind of recourse for a project that sours, and the former a right to be judged professionally on the basis of something other than his/her insurability. Nevertheless, the question of E&O insurance is one that should be asked at the outset, in conversations between you and the architect soliciting your work. Should your choice of design professional be very clear except for the matter of insurance, you might consider an equitable plan for sharing some of its cost with the professional involved.

But there is very little that E&O insurance can do about—not the calamitous event —the occurrence(s) the user organization has the right to fear most—those that might shut it down, however briefly, and/or damage the effectiveness of its operation.

The precautions to take against these occurrences come with the hiring of the design professional, and the avoidance of "constructive ignorance" of professional practice recommended by some. The latter calls on the not unreasonable notion of the superiority of the practitioner and concludes, and here is where a leap of faith comes in, that all practitioners will not only act responsibly, ethically, in a professional manner, etc., but will, as a result, do a good job. Notwithstanding a huge leap of faith on the part of the User, the good job may not get done without a close examination of the professional, before the job begins. In the long run, the expensive E&O insurance may turn out to be much less meaningful in avoiding disaster than that person's competence.

Select with a great deal of gentle scrutiny

The hiring of the design professional can and should be treated like that of any other professional advisor or consultant, any responsible executive or manager in your organization, or any partner in your firm—that is, with a great deal of gentle scrutiny.

You must have an idea of what you want to accomplish. Look for guidelines for doing that in this book. Write a goal statement and review it with your associates. Couch your description of need for professional services in your own language, or the vernacular of your business. The design professional will happily translate it into the language of architecture.

THE ENGINEER AND TECHNICAL CONSULTANTS

The history books tell us that the first engineer known by name and achievement is Imhotep, builder of the famous stepped pyramid at Saqqarah, near Memphis, in 2550 BC. Many other structures of this era, some enduring to this day, testify to the skill, imagination and daring of other engineers, builders and architects. Reference is made to the many treatises from antiquity that serve to provide a picture of engineering education and practice in classical times. One in particular, Vitruvius' *De Architectural*, was published in Rome in the first century after Christ. Thus, two thousand years ago the battle was joined between engineers and architects over the credit turf.

Who came first? Which discipline is it that bears responsibility for mankind's most magnificent structures? Even Vitruvius, writing about building materials, construction methods and hydraulics, as well as classical forms and ornament, does not give us much help. Was he an architect? Or was he an engineer writing about architecture?

Is there cause for debate here?

The siting and massing of buildings, the planning and design of their interior and exterior spaces, and the detailing of their ornament became the domain of the builder/architect whose sensibilities lay with place, form and volume. Considerations of structure, and those physical elements essential to support and human safety, were of concern to the architect. But another set of sensibilities were necessary to explore and perfect their possibilities. The latter belonged to the builder/engineer. Each epitomized the dual and oftentimes conflicting aspirations of their client for grace and monumentality on the one hand, and strength and durability on the other. But the latter set of qualities were those the client knew no building could survive without.

In the best of circumstances, there was a seamless outcome to the collaborative effort between architect and engineer, for each understood the responsibilities and limits of the other. This was true over 500 years ago at Chartres, and Cologne, but perhaps no less so than in the last quarter of the 20th century at Chicago's Sears Tower, where, with a notably less aesthetic result, architect and engineer came together again to master the problems of height, wind and gravity.

This idea of the seamlessness of the collaboration is an important one for the User. We are all concerned with the quality, utility and appearance of our surroundings. But we also have concerns about our personal safety which, especially when they extend to the safety of others, can be over-riding ones. And when we select the building in which we will work, we want to feel that it will be, above all, safe. So the building design and construction industry, and the community, through its various regulations, see to it that the engineer's skills are included in every construction destined for human occupancy.

Anonymity

Perhaps the most outstanding characteristic of this profession is that of its anonymity. The engineer is just not very visible to the man-on-the-street, or to the User. Although this practitioner will play a large role in building design, often being called into a project at its conceptual stage, he/she is most often used to verify design data that has been proven in many other similar—though never identical—circumstances. Buildings that appear to differ a great deal to the un-trained eye, for example, may be seen to be exceptionally alike under their skin or inside their envelope. (It is something of a commentary on the originality of American commercial building design that under the stylist's facades, so much of it is the same. And the excuse for this sameness is most often laid at the feet of safety, a rarely questioned companion of *cheap*.)

In these more typical instances, then, the engineer will be called upon by the architect, for whom she is often a staff professional, to specify a structure appropriate to the architectural design. If the engineer finds a structural problem with the design, this is worked out to the architect's satisfaction; the engineer is satisfied when the requirements of the structure are met.

Since the relocation project is usually concerned with the interiors of buildings and does not frequently involve itself with structure and matters of building safety, there are few occasions for the User, or User architect, to call upon the Engineer's expertise. Thus, the User should stay alert to such a call when it does occur. The reason for this is that the engineer, at a safe distance from your project and from any knowledge of what it involves, often becomes the whipping boy for its problems. The landlord's favorite excuse for not doing something, when the cost or other unpleasant aspect of the task looms large, is that "the engineers won't allow it".

This is not an altogether unwarranted reaction. In the mind of the landlord, the relocation of new tenants into the her building is always fraught with danger: the danger of the tenant request for altered columns, floor structure, core spaces, exterior walls, glass or, god forbid, an interior stairway. Faced with the implications of these requests, including the possibility that some of them are frivolous in nature, the landlord falls behind the first available line of defence—the black-hatted, never-identified engineer.

Structural modifications: how to accomplish them

The savvy User, faced in turn with the likelihood of this kind of building-owner response to an expression of User need for some structural modifications, can approach the matter in one of several ways:

- Buffalo the landlord into believing that your tenancy will be lost unless your requests are met.
- Offer to pay any price for the professional engineer's services necessary to determine the feasibility and cost of the proposed alterations.
- Offer to meet with the landlord's engineer to discuss your proposals.
- Hire a competent engineer, preferably one with high positive visibility in the local engineering community, to discuss your proposals with you and to provide you with a preliminary opinion about their implications and feasibility. Armed with this opinion and a positive attitude, discuss your requests with the landlord, or prospective landlord.

The first suggestion falls into that category we call perpetuating the adversarial relationship and is not a good approach to take. The second and third suggestions somewhat diminish the confrontational aspects of the discussion but have other dangers. The first among these is the cost of professional services. Engineers' wages are not yet as stratospheric as those of medical doctors and lawyers, but the amount of work entailed in a seemingly simple request can be staggering. The removal of a column or relocation of one or more in a multi-story building has repercussions throughout the entire structure. In a new building where all engineering data are available, the engineer must sort through the various permutations and combinations of this information to arrive at your answer.

The answer itself may be relatively simple and its construction not overly complicated, but the fees expended in arriving there can be substantial. If the building you are looking at is more than fifteen years old, when its engineering data was less likely to have been computerized, the task of ferreting out the answers you seek can be more costly yet. The landlord and the landlord's engineer are fully aware of all this, which might seem on the surface to be an advantage, with one outstanding exception; the landlord simply does not want the answers you are looking for, and will so instruct the engineer in his/her employ.

Due diligence and a positive attitude

The last suggestion is recommended when you seek to propose any kind of alteration to the building you wish to occupy. Before its owner is aware of your desires, it is wise to get some professional assistance, do your due diligence, and put yourself in a position of knowledge and understanding of both the building and its owner. As noted above, the instances of tenant need for substantial alterations to a rented structure are few. In these cases, the User is well advised to take the extra step of looking at the overall implications of User need for such changes, and the ways their impact can be lessened or even turned to an advantage for other tenants or the landlord. Many of them, for example, might be couched in terms of improvements to landlord property, enhancing its utility and its value. The extent to which the tenant prepares his/her argument and succeeds in persuading a landlord of this point of view may be the extent to which the landlord will accept the costs of improvements, or a share of them.

The call for the engineer may well be a call to a wide variety of technical experience and training. Many architects, though by no means all, are graduates of schools with accredited architectural engineering programs. These practitioners will enter the field with a combination of skills in building design and building structures. Architectural firms may employ one or more structural engineers or contract this kind of work out to independent engineering firms who, in turn, employ a wider variety of engineering specialties. These may include the traditional fields of structural, civil, mechanical, and electrical engineering, as well as those with degrees in a variety of environmental studies, such as seismic or earthquake engineering and industrial waste management studies, etc.

Macrocosms & Microcosms

The common thread among these technical specialties is their unvarying concern with the macrocosm, or larger nature of structures and the built environment. The engineers mentioned above are not likely to get exercised about things falling off shelves, or light fixtures, electrical plugs and water taps that do not work, whatever the reason. For concerns with the interior of the built environment, we look to other kinds of engineers and technical specialists, some of whom will be found within the ranks of the broad-based engineering firm; many of whom will be working independently, as consultants to other related professionals, like architects. These specialties include acoustics, lighting, industrial engineering, human engineering, and heating and air conditioning, all of which are represented in college level degree programs; many are controlled by state licensing law.

They are not always easy to find. Often the best place to start your enquiry is with a highly visible local architectural or engineering firm. One of these may have the specialist you seek, or be less likely to demur in referring you to one. Another excellent source of this kind of information is the nearest chapter of the American Institute of Architects which in many locations has periodic joint meetings with local members of the national engineering societies.

THE CONTRACTOR

If, in the eyes of the User, all landlords, developers, brokers, architects, designers, etc., appear intimidating, the building trades contractor must loom as nothing less than life-threatening. Characteristically, this person is male—women are entering the building trades and succeeding, for the most part, by assuming the behavioral traits of their male counterparts—and athletic. He is engaged in a physically demanding activity not greatly different in its skill requirements than the sports activity the contractor may have been proficient in at a younger age. This sports analogy is fundamental to an understanding of the individual who, along with his/her colleagues, is directly responsible in ways no other Player is for the ultimate physical reality of the workplace.

Along with the manual skills and hand-and-eye coordination required in virtually all of the trades, there is a competitive attitude and a camaraderie associated with them that is uniquely expressive of the work-a-day world of the American male. Nowhere else in that world does the modern American male feel so confident in the superiority of his skills, so much a part of an established tradition, and so important to his place on a superior "team" as he does in the building trades. This should not be hard to believe for any one who has spent more than a few minutes watching any of them perform.

The ballet of carpenters and bricklayers

Competent trades-persons can mesmerize any audience with their deftness and precision. Bricklayers, whose parent trade of masonry draws on literally thousands of years of practice, embody the rhythms of the symphony conductor as they eye their row, select and examine a candidate masonry unit—like a brick—measure, throw, lay, tap, and score their mortar lines in accordance with the architect's instructions. Bricklayers and their admirers enjoyed a particularly productive revival in the late 1960s and 1970s as brick veneer (so-called because the full brick is laid, or veneered, to an already structured wall) was rediscovered and specified for commercial buildings of every type and size across America.

Carpenters, whose equally ancient and respected skills guide a project from the chaos of the mud-filled foundation excavation to the fine furniture finish found on the boardroom millwork, are a similar study in rhythm, strength and economy of motion. The much-feared and fearless ironworker epitomizes the skill and daring of the construction worker. Guiding steel beams and immense cauldrons of concrete, or rigging the fragile construction crane perched, for all the world like its namesake, atop some sky-bound steel skeleton, the ironworker challenges gravity and fate.

The world of the Contractor

This, then, is the world of the contractor. The construction site is his school and training ground, his club and locker-room, his office, church and library. Small wonder that he is less than comfortable in your workplace or your conference room, trying to speak in the quiet measured tones to which you are accustomed, and which do not work in the open air filled with diesel engines and clanging steel and terse, shouted commands. His presence, usually a large one, fills the modest space of your office and his manner, groomed to the demands of the construction site, appears gruff and unfriendly. This is the scenario for a meeting of two vastly different segments of American industry which contains the seeds of growth, renewal and confrontation.

You and the Contractor

Understanding and learning to manage the scenario just sketched is an important part of your preparation for the construction aspects of your relocation project, but by no means the most critical. There is, first, the notion that you must come into contact with this important Player at all, especially when your landlord or developer, and your architect, appear to have assumed such broad responsibilities. It is wise to remind yourself that you, the User, are paying for that person's very expensive services and will be the one using his/her very important product.

For this reason, the same quality of due diligence with respect to checking the Contractor's background, experience, staff, methodology and treatment of labor and material costs, etc., must be pursued as with the other service providers you choose. Following are some guidelines, observations and common pitfalls .

The spots have changed, but the nature of the beast is still the same.

Our description of the contractor is liable to be a less than complete rendering of the person who fills this role today. While the background, experience and manner may be as pictured, this individual can also have advanced degrees as well as considerable practice in boardroom dress and behavior, or may have hired someone who does. As so often happens, the dressing up, in language as well as costume, does not always signify a better opportunity for good communication.

The General Contractor (GC) is the Player we most often refer to when we speak of a contractor. The GC used to be notorious for armies of laborers, and yards full of trucks and cranes, but this is seldom the case today. Instead, he operates from a small office with an estimator, a computer and an army of subcontractors. This arrangement has subtle but meaningful implications for the User.

The contemporary GC has greater flexibility, but less discretion

With greater independence from the burden of owned or mortgaged equipment and permanent payroll, the GC can cover a wide range of project types over a vast geographic area with greater efficiency than ever before. However, the GC has relinquished much of his control over project delivery and quality to his subcontractors. The GC has become a general in lower case only.

The User must first evaluate the GC's choice of project managers, and then his choice of sub-contractors. After the boardroom parley, the GC will fade, if not disappear altogether, in favor of an associate or employee he designates as the manager of your project. Once construction on your work begins, this person is in a position of unusual authority, becoming, as he/she does, both the general contractor's and your on-site representative. This designated manager should get your closest scrutiny before construction contracts are complete. Your right to request the removal and replacement of that person, at any time and without reservation, should be a part of those contracts.

A wide variety of sub-contractors are involved with even the smallest construction contract. Their competence and the overall quality of their performance, including their ability to interface well with your staff and other contractors on the job are critical to you. You should have the same right to examination and approval of those to be hired as you would those whom you hire directly.

Contractors will usually only hedge on two aspects of your work: time and costs. But at this they are expert beyond belief. They will vastly over-estimate the cost of a project initially, under-price it to get the work, then grossly overcharge for it in all the places where contract loopholes allow. Their treatment of time follows basically the same principles: an initial over-estimate by several weeks or months of the total time to complete a project, followed by a "tight" schedule to meet or better the competition and win the award of contract, followed in turn by a number of schedule revisions (read "extensions") required to adjust to "unexpected delays".

The User must understand that there are often legitimate reasons for these aberrations. He or she must also know when and how to call the contractor to task for those that make no sense.

The Contractor and the Developer/Owner/Landlord

A sense of confusion often seems to attend any attempt to understand the roles and responsibilities of the construction contractor, vis-a-vis the developer or the Owner/Landlord. This occurs most often in the leasing of commercial facilities, frequently as a result of poor communication between the professionals involved— landlord, developer, contractor, architect, etc.—and the User, who does not yet know what questions to ask.

In the leasing of commercial facilities, the owner of those facilities controls all matters relating to their construction and their outfitting for tenants. In new construction, the owner/operator role is filled by the developer who conceived and financed the project, and hired an architect to design it and a general contractor to build it. The contract between the developer and the GC normally covers all aspects of the initial construction of the facility. It may exclude construction needed to prepare leased space for tenants. The reasons for this exclusion tend to follow the variable logic of the industry: the developer and/or the construction lender are not interested in the open-ended, longer-term contract required by tenant construction; the parties involved do not want to complicate or delay the base building construction; the developer does not want to jeopardize leasing opportunities, etc.

But the aggressive contractor will not be put off in this regard. The opportunity to add the hefty piece of business represented by tenant work is valuable; he let the developer know that the base-building contract has been made more attractive precisely because of this additional opportunity. The savvy developer, who may wish to protect a long-standing relationship with, or even a financial interest in, this base-building contractor, offers an often-practiced solution to their mutual problem. Without altering their exclusionary contract, the developer and the contractor make it appear to any enquiring tenant that the developer is obligated to the contractor to have the latter perform any tenant improvement work in the developer's building.

The Punch and Judy Effect

This is accomplished in a casual but convincing way, through statements to the prospective tenant like: "This is Mr. X, our contractor. He does all the tenant work in our building" or, "We understand that you are moving into Mr. Y's building. We do all the tenant work there, so give us a call when you're ready".

This otherwise innocent charade leaves the User with a number of erroneous and potentially harmful impressions of the landlord or developer/tenant/contractor relationship. One is that the User/Tenant is "locked in" to a contractor and to all that implies—the contractor's schedule, prices, personnel, etc. Another impression is that the developer is, in effect, the general contractor—ready to assume all responsibility for the timely, etc., completion of the tenant's work. And still another is the impression that the developer is fully competent to estimate and execute the tenant construction work.

In these circumstances, tenant attempts to get definitive answers to the hard questions he/she may pose concerning the timing and costs of the construction of tenant premises are often rewarded with vague answers. The developer, having no contractual agreement with the contractor in the matter of tenant improvements, does not want to quote prices and delivery dates he cannot control—nor does he want to appear to be lacking control. Frequently when the developer shares in the revenues from the tenant construction work, even greater confusion and conflict is apparent.

The contractor, caught in ambiguous circumstances—at least partially of his own creation—finds himself dealing with the User, at times as a principal and at other times as a sub-contractor to the developer. Since these two Players are well-practiced in their roles, and have found ways to make them productive, the User has the task of threading his way through the tenant-improvements minefield.

The Construction Manager

The User can accomplish this in one of several ways. One is through the introduction to the project team of a professional construction manager.

Historically, this functionary is a stepchild of the GC's project manager (PM). Chosen for his allegiance to the GC, the PM is usually selected from among his principal tradesmen. It is the PM's job to run a trouble-free project that keeps GC costs down. This responsibility includes reasonable efforts to keep the User/Tenant happy. But there are a number of shortcomings built into the role that are troublesome for Users who seek strict control over the management of their construction project. Foremost among these is the potential for a conflict between the interests of the contractor, from whom the PM draws his paycheck, and those of the User/Tenant. Another is the shear weight of the job of on-site-supervision, which allows little time for the subtler tasks of scheduling and budgeting. Still another is the highly variable level of familiarity the PM might have with the more esoteric trades.

For projects of the most routine variety, involving standard building construction items, and traditional and standard mechanical, electrical, plumbing, and telecommunications fixtures, the contractor's project manager is usually adequate to the task. Requirements of the job that go substantially beyond this level will need more expert supervision.

The Construction Manager is a third party construction professional whose skills now constitute an academic specialty in the engineering schools of many colleges and universities across the country. Though the universities do not endow their graduates with immunity to conflict-of-interest situations, their construction management graduates, working independently of the GC, can be effective in controlling costs and managing schedules. On the job, they interface between the User/Tenant and the GC, and/or his PM. They have achieved a wide level of acceptance in the construction industry, among construction lenders, and by large corporate Users. Since they do represent an added cost to the User, their value must be measured carefully in terms of project cost and User risk in working with other traditional industry resources.

The User Project Manager (UPM): the Player on your side

Other resources for the responsibility of project supervision include personnel from the User architect's office, qualified personnel from a manufacturer or equipment contractor, and personnel from the User staff.

Many of the problems of relocation, even those involving complex equipment or systems, originate with a lack of attention to some basic concepts of work management. Thus, the User who is confident of their abilities will find that her own team is adequate to the task, and that on that team there is an individual suitable for the post of User Project Manager (UPM). User selection of this person is extremely important, but the qualifications for it are deceptively simple. For example:

- There are no gender-related qualifications for the job.
- There are no hierarchical (as in corporate hierarchy) or seniority qualifications for the job. This position may be filled by someone of low or high organizational rank.
- There is no requirement for previous experience, either with construction or with other matters related to a relocation. Such experience should not prejudice the candidate's selection, since it does not necessarily enhance it;
- The position requires ample amounts of: physical and mental energy, a strong sense of logic and order, familiarity with User operations, self-confidence (an innate refusal to be intimidated), good communication skills and imagination. The latter implies an ability to visualize the implications of alternative solutions; a great many of these will be suggested as the project progresses.
- A willingness and ability to absorb new material and understand new processes quickly.
- Comfort in working with numbers and simple arithmetic calculations.

Implied in any estimate of the success of these qualifications is the full support of User management and the cooperation of User employees and staff. Management demonstrates their support most effectively by relieving the UPM of operating responsibilities for the duration of the project.

Collaboration is critical between the UPM and staff persons with special skills and responsibilities—Operations Managers, MIS Managers, Laboratory Directors, Shipping and Warehouse Managers, switchboard operators, mail clerks and others whose organization functions involve systems and equipment with a strong connection to facilities. This collaboration, between the User representative (the UPM)—who is totally dedicated to User goals and purposes—working with these in-house specialists—totally familiar with User technical requirements—can obviate the need for all but the most highly specialized technicians from outside the organization.

The principal charge of the UPM is to guide his/her organization into new quarters as painlessly as possible. The tasks to be undertaken to achieve that goal are numerous and varied:

- Coordinate in-house information gathering and analysis
- Prepare and maintain schedules
- Manage project budgets
- Coordinate the activities of outside personnel
- Hire, fire and pay outside personnel
- Provide continuous progress updates for organization management, etc.
- Become a flash expert in a number of fields: Architecture; structural engineering; building construction; furniture design and manufacture; equipment design and manufacture; personnel administration, purchasing and accounting; real estate law and real estate; government regulatory systems; negotiations; the psychology of conflict; etc.

These tasks and the parallel need for instant learning combine with a process whose demands do not recognize your schedule—contractors like to confer around six, A.M. or P.M.—or sympathize with it. They simply want full-time attention. For this reason any organization that becomes involved in a facility relocation should appoint someone within that organization to assume these temporary responsibilities fulltime.

There is a similar need for administrative assistance to the project. A large volume of telephone traffic is generated as the project cranks into its Documenting and Execution stages; the requirement for the creation of paper is substantial. These needs can sometimes be met by assigning an individual who concurrently carries other responsibilities, provided the organization gives priority to the relocation project.

With both the temporary, full time UPM and the full or part-time administrative assistant, the User needs to have control over the project and its finances. Whatever extensive assignments are given to outside service providers, there will always be a need for hands-on vigilance from within the User organization. It is best that that vigilance not be spasmodic or occasional, but focused and constant for the duration of the project.

Subcontractors

Much, if not all, of the above discussion is applicable to the many sub-contractors who work in the construction of the workplace. Of this substantial list, those of most critical importance to the User are the:

- mechanical—or HVAC—contractor
- electrical contractor
- plumbing contractor

■ telecom cabling contractor

Interestingly, the characteristic that each of the above have in common is the independent nature of their relationship to the general contractor. It is common practice for the latter to do little more than hire one of each of these specialists and give him room to do his work. Basing the hiring on the specialist's price, availability, and, perhaps, degree of personal familiarity, the GC in these instances may provide little of the added value for which, theoretically, he is reimbursed. This prompts us to recommend exceptional vigilance to the User, who is often asked to provide a kind of rubber-stamp approval of these sub-contractors.

With other key contractors, there is a higher expectation of GC control and direction. Carpenters, dry-wall contractors, ceiling contractors, landscape contractors, painters, cabinet-makers (usually doing millwork in shops away from the construction site) require the GC's close coordination and supervision.

Floor-covering contractors represent the kind of specialists whose expertise and on-the-job performance derive little from the presence of the GC. Those responsible for floor finishes need to have direct contact with the User who, with the User's design consultant, will specify the particular qualities desired and approve the product's material, construction, texture and color, type of installation, cost, etc. This kind of detail is too often lost when it is translated through the GC. And the GC must add his overhead and profit to a material cost which looms large in every tenant installation.

Substantial economies can usually be realized by purchasing this commodity directly from a reputable manufacturer (or dealer), but its installation must be carefully coordinated with your GC.

VENDORS

In recent times the vendor has become a notable presence among contractors dealing with Workplace requirements. The reasons for this boil down to technological advances in product design. In spite of our earlier comments about the retarded condition of the building industry as a whole, which we shall let stand, those who design and manufacture the component parts of our commercial buildings have, for the most part, continued to develop more innovative, efficient and economical solutions to the problems of building. The evolution of the industry tends to be epochal. Twenty-five years is not a long time in its history, but significant advances in the last quarter century have touched virtually every area of building technology. Many of these have resulted from the direct application of computer technology to building operation, maintenance and security. This has contributed to the rise in popularity of the *smart-building* description.

Many other products and materials have benefited from the application, at their origin, of CADD and other sophisticated software systems: building structural components, sheathing and fascia panels, building insulation (including the demise of asbestos), fastening systems of all kinds, mechanical and electrical systems and hardware, the systems part of glazing (glass manufacturers are still in their pinched-glass, carnival-mirror rut), water heating equipment, floor coverings, cabling and power distribution equipment, etc. Even the sheet-rock mechanic now routinely uses a sophisticated laser beam to locate and level the supporting track for the interior ceiling grid.

Manufacturers are in the construction business

The increasingly complex technology of these advanced products has placed an understandably greater burden on those responsible for their installation and maintenance. Where these functions were traditionally handled by the building trade contractors, they are being assumed more and more by manufacturers. Building products once delivered to the contractor FOB the manufacturer's front door or through a series of unmotivated dealers and distributors, are now shipped to the building site and installed by persons for whom the manufacturer is presumably willing to assume responsibility. This can mean the general contractor is of less significance in his traditional role, and that the User must go beyond that person to find expert guidance and responsibility.

Telecommunications System Vendors

Since the breakup of the American Telephone and Telegraph Co., the telecommunications industry has seen ten years of staggering growth, including its irretrievable insinuation into the business of building buildings. In 1984, the *Wall Street Journal* reported that the evolution of building developers as telecommunications brokers, installing and integrating systems in their properties for shared tenant use, was an event ranking with the introduction of air conditioning. Commercial construction began its long and continuing decline about the same time, but the importance of the telecommunications system for virtually every User/Tenant has grown exponentially. It has challenged the ability of the building industry to cope with it.

Some commercial buildings will provide a central switching and call distribution system. For the smaller or less discriminating User/Tenant, this can provide some performance as well as cost advantages over a wholly-owned system. But, of late, the telecommunications system has become more and more like a suit of clothes—even for the average buyer who does not need everything tailor-made, but still wants a fit that satisfies critical communications needs.

In virtually every Tenant operation there exists a real or planned need for good telephone service, a Limited Area Network (LAN) for internal information distribution, and one or more on-line systems connecting with major data resources. With the integration of voice and data capabilities on the service-provider side, there is so much system fine-tuning needed, and available, that the central, shared system is hard put to compete. Thus, where it is available, it should be asked to compete— service-to-service and dollar-to-dollar—on the basis of a detailed statement of User need. At this point, you might consider using a telecommunications consultant, providing you can locate an individual with the kind of experience that will benefit your project.

A Statement of User Requirements

Introduce and predicate your conversations with a telecommunication system or equipment vendor on a written statement of User requirements, couched in User terms and language. Reject any attempt to sell services and equipment based on the presumed superiority of a provider's hardware or systems, unless it is based on a full understanding of User needs. These might cover items like:

- Numbers of personnel or organization members using the system
- Their function and their physical relationship
- Their planned growth or expansion

    (All of the above is spelled out in your facilities Program, which should be distributed to telecom system vendors.)

- Current and planned local and long-distance telephone traffic, and costs—Daily, weekly, monthly and seasonal variations
- Purpose, nature and principal characteristics of long-distance traffic
- Preferred incoming call monitoring and distribution system: operator monitored; direct line and voice-mail, etc.
- Call monitoring, recording, accounting, etc. capability required
- Type of instrument and features preferred, number of single-line and multiple line instruments required, instrument mobility and flexibility, etc.
- Nature and location of internal and external data sources—Central Processing Units or computer center, work stations and/or PCs, on-line services used, dedicated lines required, etc.
- Extent of periodic system change required—how frequently do operator functions move and how rapidly are they multiplying—and cabling system preferred; overhead raceways, underfloor ducts, etc.

Present this and other information related to the unique requirements of your organization to prospective suppliers in as detailed a manner as your experience and understanding of the evolution of the telecommunications industry allows. Because the industry is constantly evolving, no one individual or organization can be reasonably expected to be on top of it, or to be able to describe the perfect system for your needs. This is why you should avoid trying to become an expert in what is going on in the field. Instead, focus on expressing the telecommunications want list of your organization as best you can, in your terms.

In preparing your request for proposal for providers, include the proviso that the item being proposed has been successfully installed in a similar configuration for another customer—not connected with the provider—for at least X months prior to its proposed installation in your premises. The X should correspond to a period of time adequate to demonstrate to all concerned that the installation is capable of performing as specified.

Training in equipment setup and use should be provided, as well as warranties. On-going post-installation training on a scheduled basis should be included with any purchase of a system or substantial piece of equipment. Compatibility with future or later or additional equipment versions should be guaranteed and unalterable capacity limitations—as in switch capacity, for example—should be avoided or provided for in contract language.

Anarchy and Chaos Prevail

A vibrant level of anarchy seems to prevail among the systems developers, equipment producers, technicians and support services of the telecommunications industry. This makes predictions and guidance, especially regarding pricing, very difficult. On the up-side of this sort of ordered chaos, technology and competition work unceasingly in behalf of the User. Software is getting better, hardware is getting smaller and cheaper to produce and to run, and every other techno-whiz to graduate from State Poly is getting into the telecommunications game. The downside of this industry environment is a near-total lack of credibility or, to put a kindlier face on it, a lack of the longevity and proven experience that contribute to credibility.

Question the basic service provider closely

This is not an atmosphere that is kind to the timid or comforting to the average User shopping for new or replacement telecommunications equipment or systems. On the contrary, it is one where you must ask for proof of performance capability at every step along the way. Be aggressive in your enquiry; start it at the bottom, with the basic telephone service provider, and cover these two major areas of concern about service providers:

(1) **Underlying System Capacity**

If you are like most organizations and dependent for service on the Ma Bell spin-off in your area, learn all you can about their switches, their trunk line capacity (number of twisted pair, fiber optics, planned or existing, etc.) and their service to the area where you plan to move. How is the area zoned for service? How is it zoned for rates, etc.? What are the plans for expanding capacity, upgrading switches, etc.?

(2) **Compatibility and Flexibility**

If you are currently under a heavy mortgage for a telephone switch that is outdated and cannot be adapted, you know the boxed-in feeling that some telecommunication equipment can give you. Ideally, all of that equipment should allow for growth, be fully programmable, and be compatible with a reasonable number of support software programs. Try to find the ideal, and if you have to give up part of it, have the satisfaction of knowing why. And look at your financing agreement. Does it obligate you to the provider, not only for the purchase of service and parts, but for replacement and expansion equipment as well? Is that kind of agreement in your interest?

A variety of Players are involved in any telecommunication equipment installation. Bringing them together in behalf of your project can be a major task in and of itself. Each utility representative, equipment manufacturer, system installer, cabling technician, rate wholesaler, long distance provider, etc., operates out of a corporate cocoon devised to protect the territory of each. It is up to the User and the User telecommunications representative to bring them into contact with one another, and to keep them collaborating with one another in behalf of a successful installation.

Furniture & Equipment Vendors

Much of what has been said above about the telecommunications industry applies to what the User encounters with vendors of furniture and equipment of virtually any kind. Useful conversations with representatives of producers in these industries must be predicated on a clear statement of the User's needs. Precede purchase orders with requests from the User for product-qualifying information, or specifications, which should be examined in detail once the overall suitability of the item has been determined.

Since we are concerned with equipment that has facility implications—that is, can occupy a substantial amount of floor space and/or require supports or utilities that are integrated with the building—we are concerned with need descriptions that, among others, clearly identify these characteristics:

- Size, for floor space
- Size, for clearance
- Clear space for access and repair
- Fully loaded weight
- Plumbing, gas and/or water
- Electrical power
- Exhaust and/or waste disposal
- Covering structure or shield(s)
- Hazardous nature
- Noise and vibration generation
- Supplies and Parts storage
- Fastening, bracing, tie-downs

These are some of the characteristics that will determine the ability of your equipment and your building to work together. However, they do not tell us much about how good the machine is at what it does, whether it is acceptable to operators and to public agencies, whether it is cost effective in operation and maintenance or how long it will last, etc. We want to be able to describe our need with respect to all of these characteristics, to establish corresponding criteria for performance, and to measure each product that comes to our attention against these criteria.

There is always a tendency to turn blindly to the traditional manufacturers of equipment to satisfy our needs—and, as a result, to suffer the price mark-ups that often go with that tradition. With much equipment used in commercial installations, particularly in retail, warehouse, shop and assembly operations, and laboratories, there are opportunities for the aware User to turn to used equipment marketers or to local custom fabricators to meet very exacting needs at less cost.

Systems Furniture

Contemporary furniture systems equate with equipment in many respects. They involve a similar level of cost and require the same attention to technical detail and performance, etc.

> Furniture systems are work surfaces, storage and lighting units that depend for their support on a system of interlocking partitions or panels. The partitions are pre-fabricated structures of wood, metal and/or a honeycomb material, often covered with fabric, and equipped with a data, power and telephone interface.

Since they are oriented almost totally to the workplace operator, the criteria for comparing products in the marketplace must be heavily skewed toward User compatibility. In fact, a detailed description of an operator's daily activity will provide the best description of workstation design and configuration.

Users that need more than a few such workstations, especially those requiring operators to be in place for more than four or five hours a day, should refer to the ANSI standard for Human Factors Engineering as it impacts workstation design and VDT (video display terminal) usage. (See the American National Standards Institute standard ANSI / HFS 100-1988 on file at your local City Hall, Library or technical bookstore).

There are many manufacturers of systems furniture. Most will have inundated the local design community with product literature of all kinds. Many will be represented at your local office furniture dealer. Manufacturer   dealer relationships vary as does the opportunity to deal on a direct basis in purchasing this equipment. As with many other office products, the size of the prospective purchase means a great deal to the manufacturer of systems furniture. As the User/Buyer, you are interested in arranging a fair transaction; this starts with the manufacturer's costs, and adds clearly detailed and acceptable costs for packing, transportation and insurance, local delivery, installation, parts and service, warranties, etc—a fair transaction does not begin with an artificially elevated retail price that is subsequently discounted.

If you are planning on saving by substituting User personnel for the manufacturer's or manufacturer's rep to install and assemble systems furniture, be aware of the tools and the special skills that are necessary to do the job. Having provided that admonition, we can always recommend User involvement in the installation of Equipment and Furniture.

We are always strong advocates of good appearance design for equipment as well as for furniture and furniture systems. Much office equipment has had a satisfactory level of attention given it by manufacturers over the years—we can always safely buy a Xerox or an IBM product with the knowledge that it will look well in our office. Not so with the cans and crates that serve, generally very expensively, as shop, warehouse or laboratory equipment and which seem to make every effort to offend one's visual sensibility. In these environments, though we do not expect every nuance of color, shape, and line; we can look for an appearance of order and consistency in these articles, along with some good human engineering. To the extent to which you, the User, can impact the look of this equipment, bring your design professional into the shop to make recommendations.

The Mover

Much as your lawyer, your design professional and your broker get to know the inner workings of your organization as your project progresses, so does the professional mover. Care, speed, efficiency, accuracy and a great eye for detail are characteristics which qualify the group that will put your furniture and equipment into place and will establish your organization in its new quarters. For this reason, interview and qualify this contractor early in the progress of your project. He should have the opportunity to become thoroughly acquainted with your operations, and the nature and location of everything you own.

The chances are excellent that there are a number of professional moving companies in your area who advertise through your local Chamber of Commerce and business telephone directory. Because of the transmigrating nature of American businesses as well as populations, most of these companies will have transcontinental experience; many will have commercial, as well as residential, moving experience.

Though this is likely to be the case, it is still important to look for commercial relocation capability in planning your organization's move. The commercial mover, in addition to valuable experience, will have unique equipment, capable of safely transporting items like mainframe computer equipment, sorting and collating copiers, and other large, delicate and expensive pieces. The commercial mover will also routinely offer the level of liability and property damage insurance you seek. Characteristics of the competent mover would include:

- Experience in moving commercial organizations
- Large, clean, up-to-date rolling stock in sufficient quantities to move you with minimum down-time
- Support equipment (cranes, transporters, rubber-tired carts, etc.,) adequate for quick, risk-free movement of your largest and most delicate equipment
- Adequate safety devices and materials for protecting your goods and the property of others in the path of the transfer process
- Personnel experienced in the disassembly and assembly of workstation or panel systems of the type you are relocating
- Storage warehouse capacity adequate for temporary storage of new furniture, branch office furniture and equipment, etc.
- A competent and experienced move coordinator

- A clear and efficient tagging and labeling system
- Sound knowledge of and experience with local codes, law enforcement practices, streets and roadways, etc.
- Appropriate state and/or local licensing and liability and property damage insurance coverage in satisfactory amounts.

The most effective way to verify these characteristics is through the Request for Proposal process, followed by an evaluation of the kind you practiced in the selection of other key team members. This process should include:

- One or more interviews with the proposed move coordinator
- A visit to the movers' operating base for an inspection of equipment
- A visit to the site of a move in progress
- Two or more calls to references given by the proposing mover

Movers' estimates and rates are based on calculations of hourly rates, or hourly rates plus mileage charges. For local moves, the latter will obviously not be a major consideration. The 1980 federal deregulation of trucking means little to the cost of local, in-city moves; however local codes and statutes can, by requiring so many workers to man a truck, for example. Man-hour rates in the industry are also quite similar, reflecting the nature of a cross-country enterprise rather than one influenced by local labor variables. Nevertheless, the User will find that the Request for Proposal can draw surprisingly varied dollar estimates of the moving cost; swings of 50 percent or more are not unusual.

Competition, desire, hunger, financial crisis, seasonal lulls, etc., can contribute to this condition, which, for the most part, is a happy one for the User who is shopping price. We heartily recommend such shopping provided you examine the heavily discounted service very carefully. The industry is prone to the use of off-the-street labor, for example, and other wage cost reduction techniques that can result in a deterioration of your service.

No amount of insurance will make up for the losses you will incur, in downtime as well as property loss and damage, from a sloppily executed move.

THE LAWYER

Because the process of relocating the workplace is replete with contracts, many involving substantial amounts of money and long-term obligations, some believe that the lawyer should be considered a natural part of that process. Others reject this notion. While comfortable spending thousands of dollars on planners, designers, architects, contractors and other consultants, they greatly resist the introduction of the attorney to the process. The User group, comprised as it is of entrepreneurs, organization managers and decision-makers, is not one which has, historically, been comfortable in the company of attorneys. The latter is trained in the language of the law—the natural adversary of the entrepreneur—and is seen by many to represent the law and its unwanted authority.

Do you want a teacher?

This is a perception which comes very naturally. Lawyers are pedagogic by nature, and none of us—not the most urbane or authoritarian among us—finds him or herself able to look upon our teacher as a peer. We feel subdued and humble in the presence of the pedagogue, the repository and dispenser of a superior knowledge which, we have been convinced from the days of our earliest childhood, extends far beyond the bounds of the subject at hand. And we also know from these early experiences, that in this superior knowledge, embodied in *teacher*, lies the ultimate authority—intellectual authority, the confidence of command grounded in logic. These are the associations we make. The attitude shifts that follow, of respect and deference and extra-ordinary attention, manifest in our behavior as we convene with our attorney.

If this is the underlying nature of the client/attorney relationship, it is a small wonder that the hard-driving, task-oriented manager or entrepreneur shuns it. Why embark on a learning experience, when there are decisions to be made and work to be done? Why bring someone else onto the scene to repeat that question that never ceases to be asked: "Have you thought about this...?"

Terms of contract are critical

The attorney of your choice should be introduced to your relocation project team at the appropriate time for a number of reasons. The principal reason, of course, is that terms-of-contract are the specialty of that profession. In the business of the lease contract, these terms, which fall into two broad groups, have great economic significance. One of these groups relates directly to the business terms of the contract and the other to all those terms which are designed to control the outcome of events which may, or may not, occur.

The role of the User attorney, with respect to the first group of terms, has traditionally been in the nature of a ratification. These terms, which include such things as amounts and time of payment of rent, operating costs, taxes and insurance, costs of improvements, etc., have been established, usually through negotiations over a period of time, by the principals to the transaction—for example, a User/Tenant on the one hand and a Landlord on the other. The contract language employed to effect that transaction must do what each of the principals had in mind in arranging it; the User/tenant attorney is important to the construction of this language. When your attorney is a particularly skilled negotiator—many are—he or she can also be valuable in arranging terms, especially when another lawyer is sitting on the landlord's side of the table.

The second group of terms encompasses a wider range of subject matter that, perhaps because of its abstract nature, seems to have a lesser claim on the attention of the principals. In this group are important considerations such as events of default and their remedies, Acts of God, subordination, insurance against liabilities of every imaginable kind, as well as protection of the interests of the parties in the event of the destruction of property or its taking by the community in exercise of its rights of eminent domain, etc. Because they are important, you will notice that the proposing party has had an attorney prepare contracts which deal with these matters.

Say again?

The attorney for the proposing party has drawn up the contract you will execute. Before your input is available, that attorney wants to do her best to create a document for her fee-paying client that will provide the latter with all of the advantages legally available. In the business of commercial leasing, such a document is referred to as a *landlord lease*. These contracts sometimes appear in a pre-printed form under the logo of a commercial printer, an industry group, a brokerage house or development company, etc. They may be represented to the prospective User as "standard" contracts, imputing a level of fairness to them that is not warranted. Establishing an appropriate level of fairness in any contract requires an attorney— one who is hired and paid by you, the User. When you are ready to make this choice, there are some common-sense guidelines to follow.

Remember that lawyers are good at contracts and usually will not pretend to be experts at a number of skills you need that logically involve other kinds of people— programmers, engineers, accountants, real estate and financial advisers, etc. But because they are often well informed in one or more of these areas, attorneys may seem to be a good resource for these other skills. Some will even encourage you to think of them as such.

Ask experts to do what they're expert at

Proceed with caution if you seek expert advice in connection with your relocation, and your concerns do not relate to contract specifics but rather to matters that could become a part of those specifics—like real estate markets and economics, buildings, construction, human resources, etc. Even though an attorney of your acquaintance may have indicated some knowledge and interest in these areas, his ability to be of real help may be severely limited. To get assistance in these matters, you must first be specific and detailed about the kind of help you need. Then seek out the individual or organization that has the most legitimate claim to that expertise.

When you call on an attorney to review one or more contracts, again proceed with caution; not all lawyers are equally good at performing this function in the arena of real estate and construction. The task requires considerable acquaintance with the arcane language, procedures and practices of the building industry, how its various facets work together and, quite literally, how buildings are built. There are lawyers and there are real estate lawyers. There are real estate lawyers experienced in the acquisition and sale of real property, who have never worked through a commercial lease agreement. For a User who is about to become a commercial tenant, an attorney with these kinds of credentials will be as useful as a divorce lawyer.

Some hiring and use practices to keep in mind.

An examination of an attorney's background and experience is thoroughly justified and highly recommended. Just as the practice of hiring a large firm of contractors or architects on the basis of the firm's size and/or presumed prestige can be a costly error, a similar mistake made in selecting an attorney can be more so. Much has been made of the outrageous level of legal fees in recent years. Here are some practices in hiring and using attorneys that concern economic sense as well as good common sense.

- Hiring a law firm without knowing, in detail, the background of the lawyer to be assigned to your project is poor practice. In addition to asking the kinds of obvious questions concerning training, experience, previous clients, rates, etc., look into your lawyer's operating style. If this is greatly at odds with your own or that of key staff, no amount of that person's brilliance will help you regain lost ground

- Hiring a law firm on the basis of the pitch made by a senior partner that the latter will "closely monitor" (or words to that effect) the activities of the junior working on your project can cost you twice as much as hiring a competent attorney in the first place.

130

- Legal fees are not sacred and should not be treated as such. They should relate sensibly to things like gross revenues, personal incomes, the cost of products or services, the risks involved in your relocation in terms of the size of your purchase or lease and the sensitivity to moving of expensive staff, equipment, inventory, etc.

- Negotiate. Lawyers can be good business-people. Many understand that a few dollars lost to a lower rate can be more than made up by the greater frequency of calls from their client.

- Be cautious with retainer arrangements; they can be an invitation to both parties to a relaxation of cost-vigilance.

- Establish guidelines for the use of expensive legal services by your staff.

- Once your attorney is on board, expect that person to know what to do for you without specific guidance from you.

- If review of a contract is in order, establish the method of accomplishing that, and the probable time required, along with the format in which legal comments are to be expected.

- Do not unnecessarily encourage lawyer-to-principal or even lawyer-to-lawyer conferencing. You want all negotiations of critical points to remain in your hands; on the other hand, unrestrained lawyers in an adversarial setting can enjoy endless hours of argument over arcane issues whose value to either principal is a fraction of the legal fees incurred in discussing them.

- Identify and look for the product that reflects your attorneys' effort and their substantial fees. Written reports are often impractical and unnecessary, but explanatory letters, memos, written instructions, annotated contracts, etc., are not. Nobody ever said all attorneys have to know how to write, but yours should do it well.

- If you are assigned an attorney by your corporate headquarters—whether "in-house", or "out-of-house"—do not relax. There could be trouble ahead. While maintaining your excellent corporate relationships, guide and monitor that person's work carefully. Negative fallout from badly wrought contracts, which may be months or years in coming, will ultimately land in your lap, not in that of the corporate attorney called in to assist you.

- Avoid the compulsion to throw every contract draft you receive into your attorney's hands. That person is trained to scrutinize everything with great care. He will do so, whether there are ten more drafts to follow or not.

Keep an Attorney on your side.

You may look at attorneys as you do dentists, hoping that you never have to see one again. But you might reflect on this simple fact. Through the various contracts that have been placed in front of them, or that they will have to wrestle with in the relocation process, User/tenants are already surrounded by lawyers. Having one on your side just makes good sense. But there is more to this business than getting somebody on your side to help you beat the other guy. The future of your organization, your staff and your employees are at stake in the complex process of relocation. Professional guidance to help you get through it includes hiring an attorney at the appropriate time.

PUBLIC OFFICIALS

As we noted earlier, of all the distinguishing characteristics that describe commercial buildings, the effects of the law on their design and development are—today and for the foreseeable future—the most critical. Building codes have an increasing impact on the design and construction process. Recent years have also seen an exponential growth of laws affecting our environment, both inside and outside the workplace. These laws intrude on our personal and organizational lives in unprecedented ways, although the captains of industry, at the turn of the century, might have thought otherwise.

In 1915, in the bowels of the borough of Manhattan, the new Equitable Life Assurance Building was unveiled. Architecturally, it was a huge, powerful neo-classic structure in the manner most admired by the captains of industry. The shear walls of this massive block fell 39 stories, without relief or setback, to meet the sidewalk on four streets precisely at the property line. It was bigger than anything ever built, anywhere, and its shadows were long and deep. The Equitable cast such a great shadow that in 1916 the City of New York, at the prodding of nearby merchants and property owners, created the city's—and the nation's—first zoning law. The Captains were greatly troubled by this unprecedented intrusion on their heretofore undisputed turf.

The new law was designed to limit the bulk of new building, and to protect the public enjoyment of sky and sunlight at street level. Buildings would be allowed to rise beyond a certain specified height only if the additional construction were set in and back a certain distance. The taller the building, the more often the setback would have to occur, creating a stepped or Ziggurat effect. Before long, this became the look of urban buildings everywhere—a look which palled on New Yorkers and the architectural community and, since New York is the bellwether in such matters, prompted a re-do of the city's zoning laws, and a rethinking of them everywhere else. Later, zoning laws and the community's efforts to restrain the commercial building developer became more Byzantine than could ever have been imagined in 1916. Writing in July, 1980, Ada Louise Huxtable said, "New York has created a monster—call it Frankenstein zoning".

Parallel to the efforts of the urban community to make sense of its built environment—enclosures of streets and walkways formed by surrounding buildings— have been efforts to police building construction. In **PART I—Chapter I, Little Bit**

of History, we noted that the development of commercial building was not the development of people space. It was the creation of economic value through the improvement of real property. Those improvements, consisting of buildings like the Equitable, brought the tax dollars that paid for the fire-fighters, streets and water mains. Thus, the evolution of our Building Codes has been the growth of measures to protect property improvements from damage and destruction with a fortunate by-product being the protection of human life.

The Uniform Building Code

The primary document for the regulation and control of the building industry is the Uniform Building Code (UBC), which "covers the fire, life, and structural safety aspects of all buildings and related structures". (*Uniform Building Code*, 1988 Edition.) The Code was first published by the International Conference of Building Officials (ICBO) in 1927, and has been updated and republished in roughly three year increments since that time. It is used in conjunction with a *Uniform Plumbing Code*, and a *Uniform Mechanical Code*, both published by the ICBO, and a *National Electrical Code*, and a *National Fire Code* published by the National Fire Protection Association, (NFPA). The latter two codes are also published in three year intervals.

The ICBO and the NFPA bear some similarity to other industry-wide organizations that research and establish standards for their constituents which may become referenced in local law. Thus, the Uniform Building Code serves as the foundation for local ordinances and statutes governing building construction in communities across the country. Depending on the inclination of the local jurisdiction, this is done by referencing the code or by wholesale adoption of it.

The Code is familiar to everyone in the industry

Since the UBC deals only with standards for construction, the enforcement of those standards—including fees, fines and penalties and/or allowed variances, etc.—become matters of choice for the community. Other local choices relate to local concerns with building characteristics that may need broader or more detailed emphasis. Thus San Francisco and Los Angeles building codes reference the UBC with a liberal peppering of seismic concerns. Building Department officials everywhere reference the UBC in some form or fashion. Virtually every developer, building constructor, architect and engineer who is plying the trade, will have a dog-eared copy on hand. It is available through most libraries, general interest bookstores and college bookstores, and through the:

International Conference of Building Officials
5360 South Workman Mill Road
Whittier, CA 90601

National Fire Protection Association
P.O. Box 9101
One Batterymarch Park
Quincy, MA 02269-9101

How does the Code affect your project ?

If the avowed purpose of the Building Codes is to protect property and lives, the greatest threat perceived by them is that of fire. Questions put to you about your project, the observations made about your space plan, and the critique of your construction will all center on this preoccupation. Corridor widths, lengths and frequency; room sizes; numbers and placement of doors; wall and ceiling construction; door and glass construction; electrical system components; etc., are elements of commercial interior construction that are subject to inspection and agency approval. In short, they must conform to code.

How is Code compliance accomplished?

Since the Uniform Building Code is a part of the law governing the construction or modification of commercial buildings in your community, there is, as you might imagine, a routine that has been established for insuring that you comply with it. Code compliance is usually accomplished through:

- User notice of intent to construct
- Submittal of plans and drawings
- Application for permits to begin work
- Issuance of permits to start work
- Periodic inspection of the work
- Interim approvals to continue the work
- Approval of the finished work

This process applies to building activities in categories like general construction, electrical work, plumbing work, and mechanical systems. Unlike the other areas, that are quite specific and focused, matters of concern with general construction can vary from project to project, with variances in plan and design. Interior stairs will warrant a thorough application of the Code, as will interior glass, penetrations or interruptions of exterior walls or interior shear walls, or drilling of columns, or installations weighing more than the prescribed live load limit, etc.

There is a casual aspect to this process which can be misleading. Users will find that no one is quite clear about when or in what manner the Building Department is to be notified of your intentions. Submittals of drawings and application for permits are, in certain respects, matters left to the discretion of the User and her Contractor. Department personnel may not appear at your site the day you start work. They may not show up during the first week, or ever, if it appears that your work does not require their attention. And you may or may not be informed of any of the above. But woe to the incautious User who fails to learn and implement the code compliance process.

Code interpretation and enforcement

Interpretation of the Code in different jurisdictions remains surprisingly consistent. Variations have more to do with community size and density than with politics or economics, though the ability of a community to devote its limited resources to building inspections weighs heavily on the performance of the building department. Consistency in interpretation has much to do with the nature of the contemporary building business, where everybody in it serves markets anywhere in the country. Interpretation of the Code may appear to be arbitrary at times, but this will not be due to local unfamiliarity with products or techniques. Your building inspector can be expected to deal on a regular basis with techniques and product types that are widely known and used.

Since the community objective is normally the encouragement of building—Bay Area readers may question this—enforcement of the Building Code is not intended to be solely punitive in nature. Rather, it seeks—in its peculiar way—to remedy faulty construction by interrupting or stopping it until the deficiencies noted by an inspecting official are corrected. A failure to correct can bring site closure and/or fines, if the violation is life-threatening. It may result in a rejection of the city approvals necessary for critical services—power, gas, water, etc.—or simply the implied threat of project delay. The threat of delay in the progress of a construction project is probably the most meaningful of the deterrents the public official has for the typical User and contractor.

How do you face the Threat?

We don't encounter the Building Code in an abstract or impersonal way. We meet up with it in the same way we meet the law when we take our drivers license exam or plead a traffic ticket or a lawsuit. That is, we come face-to-face, in an often unfriendly if not unfamiliar environment, with another human being—called a building inspector—who represents our traffic cop, our prosecutor and our judge. We are persuaded that no good can come from this meeting. Our adversary is prepared to disassemble, demolish and send us packing. A simple notation of that ominously official pen can bring our wonderfully wrought construction down around our ears like a house of cards.

We know these things from contractors and other unimpeachable sources who have described the agonies of dealing with the Building Department. With their guidance, we are prepared to use all of our wiles, even threatening language, to rid ourselves of this unwanted deterrent to the progress of our project. If reason doesn't prevail, we are prepared to offer money, or a holiday in St. Croix. If all else fails, we will simply go over their head, to the Chief, to the Commissioner or the Mayor, if necessary. Our righteousness is boundless.

What does the Other Side look like ?

The other side, that of the local agency charged with the enforcement of local building, or health and safety regulations, is not without fault in its client relationships. Its procedures are uneven, its response is weak, and its people are sometimes unavailable, brief or seemingly rude. But it fills its role in the building business with far fewer resources than any competent developer or builder would attempt to work with.

The local agency is notoriously short in community support and money. Feelings for the Building Department do not run high on Main Street. Few citizens are inclined to want to think about it, much less understand it, and their passivity extends to the agency's funding. Since it must attempt to draw its personnel from the ranks of professionals, it has to offer some kind of tenure as well as its traditional low wage. This is not easy for an agency that must count on fees from an industry as volatile as the construction industry. And those who must share in the community's General Fund are not much more secure. Many communities have simply shut down their building departments at various times for lack of funding.

Approving agency personnel are real people

The agency personnel who work, by choice, in this environment, are not unaware of their handicaps in these respects. Because wages are uniformly low, the work does not bring applicants of the type who win positions with the aggressive and highly visible architectural, engineering and construction firms. But they may have background that would qualify them for these firms, and the accumulated knowledge in the group that makes up the average building department could be awesome, were it not for a lack of ego. This failing, juxtaposed with the egotism facing it every day in the form of self-important architects, builders, landlords, etc., severely affects communication between the two groups.

Before he/she unrolls their drawings in the office of the approving agency, the architect is convinced that no one present for the other side will be competent to understand his designs. This mind-set has a very predictable effect on the architect's presentation as well as its reception. On the other side, the person(s) representing the approving agency are equally convinced that, short of explaining what it is they are designing or building, the architect, contractor, landlord, etc will use every cunning device known to modern man to get an agency approval.

Good communication means listening

Communication: it is not a new concept in the contemporary world of commerce and industry. But, in the world of building buildings—like so many rutting dogs and strutting peacocks—we substitute posturing and confrontation for communication. Forever on the defensive and poorly armed, the approving agency has one weapon, but it is an impressive one: disapproval. To gain the prize—approval—the other side must be willing to subdue the ego and get on with the business of communicating, and with that most unpleasant of all activities for the professional builder, architect and developer: listening.

Secrets for success in dealing with approving agencies

Hundreds of very successful architects, builders and landlords across the country make an excellent living while dealing with approving agencies on a frequent basis. Following are a few of their secrets:

- Understand the law, in the sense of its intent, and how it operates
- Understand who is affected by the law and what the enforcement process is
- Make a crude estimate of the cost of non-compliance. This is not a recommended alternative, but the question may be raised in your Boardroom
- Get to know the where and who of the enforcing agency
- Go to the enforcing agency and meet with the people there. Make an appointment sufficiently in advance of any construction work so that there is no pressure on you or your host to do something other than establish rapport and learn about one another.
- Call your new-found friends at the approving agency with questions as they arise. Their answers may or may not help, but you will have advanced the cause of your project immeasurably.
- Document each of these contacts and calls as you go along.

Arrange to meet informally with the inspector who may eventually visit your construction site. Such a meeting can prove invaluable in understanding the kinds of detail that person looks for on the job. Here again, understanding and being sympathetic to people motivation can be extremely important. Everyone carries some psychological baggage; for the building inspector, it may be as simple or as complex as a certain prejudice about how a convenience outlet is wired. The inspector's quirk may cost nothing to install and four or five dollars to correct, if it is not done his way. If your site has five hundred convenience outlets, it is apparent that the inspector's quirk is cheaper to follow in the installation than in the correction.

The Law in the Workplace

Compliance with the decades old Building Code isn't the end of our readers' concerns with the Law as it affects the workplace. It now reaches into many areas other than construction. Here are a few notes from our *Law-in-the-Workplace* bulletin-board:

- The San Francisco Board of Supervisors enacted the nation's first VDT Ordinance, regulating the use of the video display terminal in the workplace. The ordinance was subsequently thrown out on a narrow court ruling, but similar bills await passage in Sacramento and other state capitals as well. San Francisco vows to keep trying.

- Effective July 1991, California's SB 198 requires employers to develop a written injury and illness prevention program and to implement this program through safety committees, safety training, and abatement programs. SB 198 is classified by employers as another bureaucratic nuisance. It is largely a paperwork-generating bill, but it comes with teeth in the form of penalties including jail time.

- Along with legislation with similar intent from OSHA (the Occupational Safety and Health Administration of the Department of Welfare), the Environmental Protection Agency (EPA), the Toxic Substances Control Act, (TOSCA), The Asbestos Hazard Emergency Response Act (AHERRA), the Comprehensive Environmental Response Compensation & Liability Act, (CERCLA) - also called *Superfund* - California's SB 198 cannot be shrugged off.

- The U.S. Post Office was cited again by OSHA for its failure to modify mail sorting machines held to be responsible for cumulative trauma disorders among postal workers and, (by Post Office records), for $29.6 million worth of medical bills. The unusual pursuit by OSHA of a quasi-federal agency over workplace practices that have seldom come under scrutiny is indicative of a national mood and the willingness of these agencies to go wherever they smell a viable issue.

- In July of 1992, the Americans with Disabilities Act of 1990 (ADA) became law for businesses with more than 25 employees. The bill is designed to end discrimination in employment against the handicapped.

- The Comprehensive Occupational Safety and Health Reform Act currently before Congress will require OSHA to develop indoor workplace air quality standards by the end of '93. (A smokers' advisory)

The Americans with Disabilities Act (ADA)

The ADA has a narrowly defined and indisputable civil rights goal. The approach it takes to enforcement, however, is scary, if not completely novel. The Congress, the Justice Department and the Equal Employment Opportunity Commission (EEOC)— the most visible of four federal agencies charged with administering the ADA— seemed, collectively, to recognize the imprecision of some of the regulations being proposed and the improbability that any local jurisdiction had the expertise much less the manpower, to enforce them. Since a complaint originating in the workplace is virtually the only way the ADA might be triggered, the language of enforcement was left to hinge on litigation at the local, and very personal, level.

To determine the validity of a complaint or a company's response to it, an interpretation of such phrases in the ADA as *undue hardship* and *reasonable accommodation* is necessary. The nature of this task would seem to be beyond the capacity of most responsible agencies, leaving little choice for the complainant but to sue. As one critic put it, the definition of reasonable accommodation "is a lawsuit waiting to be created", because "reasonable people will disagree about what is reasonable".

Video Display Terminal Legislation

What we have seen of VDT legislation creates a similar sense of unease, for rather different reasons. The admirable goal of the proposed legislation is the prevention of workplace injuries. This time the potential culprit is repetitive strain injury (RSI), said by the Labor Department to account for 48% of all occupational illnesses. It is an insidious, amorphous and painful affliction. In the office, RSI is associated with keyboard operation, which is intertwined with a variety of subtle everyday workplace activities like sitting, swiveling, tilting, turning, looking, reading, etc. These seemingly simple activities, performed in an inhospitable workstation environment, can generate numbing fatigue and terminate a workday.

Before World War II, a tiny but hardy band of industrial engineers and industrial designers began to focus their talents on what they called human engineering, designing user-friendly toasters, mixmasters, cars and bomber cockpits. They gave us bucket seats in our first sports cars and tailored the Mercury capsule around the first astronauts. They measured the human body and researched its physical capacity for doing, reaching and responding to a variety of physical stimuli in different circumstances. They created a discipline called Human Factors Engineering, and a professional group called the Human Factors Society and gave us *ergonomics* and *ergonometrics*.

Worker fatigue and human factors engineering

In 1988, the Human Factors Society reached a milestone of sorts. After roughly a half-century of seeking recognition from the larger engineering community, their measurements and standards were accepted by the American National Standards Institute and were published as part of the ANSI bible of industry standards. ANSI/HFS 100-1988 became the logical industry-wide reference for any legislation dealing with human factors in the workplace. Indeed, it became the foundation for the ultimately failed San Francisco VDT legislation, an event that raised interesting questions concerning the use of such standards.

In its statement of purpose, ANSI/HFS 100-1988 says: "Human factors engineering principles and practices are highly application dependent", and "the nature of good human factors engineering is *to tailor the specifications for the unique work situation* of interest." (Emphasis ours.) These qualifications are necessary in this less than precise science; the stimuli they are attempting to measure (light, sound, color, etc.) are irrevocably entwined with our highly variable physiological responses to them. But "tailoring" to "unique work situations" means custom design and manufacture. Legislation written to require those conditions in the workplace must be careful when placing responsibility for their costs. The costs in dollars spent for products of doubtful value, or for the courtroom time needed to interpret weak legislation, could be enormous.

Legislation in a new suit of clothes

There is a big difference between the neo-legislation represented by the ADA, SB 198, VDT ordinances, etc., and the old fashioned Zoning regulations and Building Codes. The latter may have dealt with simplistic issues, but they proposed a problem, a solution and an effective—though at times obnoxious—agent of correction. The costs of compliance and non-compliance were identifiable. The players were known. Time spent getting something fixed could be managed.

Today, the neo-regulations pose the problem, ask for a solution and provide a framework for it that looks a lot like a courtroom. Dealing with this new breed of regulation will require imaginative and resourceful Users who can anticipate trouble. They will take many of the steps recommended above for dealing with the Building Department, including understanding the law and getting acquainted with the personnel from the enforcing agency. They will go further by informing their staff and employees of the steps they are taking to anticipate and remedy workplace problems. They will cultivate and refine the idea of understanding the motivation of people in their own organization. They will provide workable, short-term solutions to workplace problems when long-term answers are out of reach.

Co-opting the professional buzzards

Resourceful Users will co-opt the unions and the professional buzzards—the attorneys, consultants and experts—who have already sprung up in large numbers to mine the rich fields of the ADA and other legislation. They will put this crew out of business by representing the employees interests better, and for reasons that make more sense to employer and employee. And they will establish systems for documenting their efforts and those of their employees that will make the enforcing agencies cry uncle.

Information regarding the Americans with Disabilities Act of 1990 may be obtained from the following:

- The EEOC will send one free copy of a comprehensive technical assistance manual on the ADA to anyone who calls. It includes a 214 page directory of resources, both government and non-government organizations. Call 1-800-669-EEOC.

- The Job Accommodation Network, a service of the President's Committee on Employment of People with Disabilities, provides advice on ADA issues. Call: 1-800-526-7234.

A brand new book by Mary B. Dickson, *Supervising Employees with Disabilities*, Crisp Publications, Inc., puts a positive twist on the A.D.A. by showing Users how to take advantage of and nourish the extraordinary skills of the handicapped.

Chapter 4

THE TOOLS

Implements of the mind

In their studies of early Man, paleontologists have been able to tell us a great deal about ourselves through their examination of ancient tools unearthed in various parts of the world. As interesting as the nature and use of these early implements can be, however, the endurance and continued application of many of them is equally, if not more, surprising. The working end of the shovel and the axe today look much as their ancestors did millenia ago. The adze, chisel, rope, cup and bowl, are among hundreds of similar artifacts of the life and industry of man that demonstrate how very little our bodies and many of its needs have changed.

But in the fraction of human history represented by a fragment of the Twentiethe century, we have left the tools of the paleontologists' world and discovered the implements of the mind. With an international language of numbers, signs and symbols, we have organized and systematized information to allow us to construct new environments and build over old ones. Without abandoning the ancient tools, we have, in these latest micro-seconds of planet life, found ways to harness the power of millions of hammers, shovels and levers.

This chapter on the tools of relocation talks exclusively about information—what and where it is, how and in what form you can organize it, and what you need to do to make it work for your organization. These are tools that organize your ideas and the information you need to develop them; that give your planning concepts concrete and executable form; and that facilitate your evaluation of alternatives.

We will discuss the principal tools of relocation and how to apply them. You will invent others to fit your own needs and methodology. The latter is important because the worth of the tool lies in its ability to save you time and effort and money. We have focused our effort on content rather than format since most of our readers will want to study this material and apply it to their own procedures and systems.

COSTS AND BUDGETS

This segment will identify the costs of relocating the User organization, and discuss methods to evaluate them and to budget for them. We will look at fixed costs and variable expenses, some recurring for short terms and others for longer ones; some escalating at fixed rates and some adjusted periodically according to negotiated formulas; some billed as lump sums and others amortized into other expense figures, etc. Some of these figures play a part in virtually every real estate transaction and are well accepted. Others have been exhaustively examined and are still poorly understood. Still others are unique to the principals involved in a particular transaction and defy any general application or study.

Understanding renting helps you understand buying

Certain important distinctions exist between the rental transaction and the purchase agreement. This book emphasizes the commercial lease agreement and the financial and other obligations this contract places on the User as a tenant. One of the reasons for this emphasis is that the terms of the sale/purchase agreement, no matter how complex, are devised to effect the closing of the sale transaction. At this point, except as the terms of a new mortgage may affect the User organization, the transaction is complete. The other principal has either disappeared, or become a passive party to a loan agreement, and the User has become master of his/her real estate future. This is decidedly not the case with the tenant lease agreement, which has ongoing cost and legal implications for the User.

In our earlier discussion of Lease/Own options, we distinguished between the User as investor and the User whose concern is the use to which real property can be put to aid User productivity. It is this latter motivation that, we feel, consistently binds our readership together. There is an inherent conflict between the interests of the renter and those of the real estate investor—in the same company or in the same individual. To avoid confusion, this presentation approaches costs from a User/tenant point of view.

Finally, your concern is with the costs of facility *relocation*. Though certainly inclusive of, and largely dominated by, new rental costs, relocation must also recognize significant User expense that is not related to real property.

Relocation costs and the Cost of Occupancy

The costs to the User of renting and relocating into commercial space fall into two categories, Rental Costs and Relocation Costs. Together these equal the Cost of Occupancy. The latter represents the sum of all costs connected with getting into and living in your new quarters, for the period of time represented by the lease term. It also represents a useful figure for comparing candidate locations. The table below identifies the principal components of each group of costs.

Rental Costs

BASE RENT The cost to the developer or landlord of land and building; the cost of money; and the cost of landlord overhead and profit

OPERATING EXPENSE Taxes and insurance; the costs of operation and maintenance of buildings and grounds, utilities, and increases in any of these costs

TENANT IMPROVEMENTS Planning, design, construction and finishing of the premises for tenant occupancy

Relocation Costs

PERSONNEL Costs of personnel transfer; costs of new hire, temporary housing, housing cost differentials, wage and salary differentials, identifiable losses due to production down-time

F F & E The cost of furniture, fixtures and equipment, and systems required as a direct result of the relocation—omitting discretionary purchases

MOVING The cost of specialists and consultants not related to any of the above, graphic design, advertising and notices, voided warranties and other penalties associated with the relocation; costs of packing, shipping and moving furniture and equipment; equipment rentals, staff overtime, room and board; vehicle expense connected with the move; etc.

TOTAL **COST OF OCCUPANCY**

Let us suppose

To put some flesh and bones on the outline above, let us suppose that

A national engineering company plans to move one of its regional offices from Peoria to Schaumberg, Illinois. The office has a staff of 40 persons; Thirty are professional/technical and the balance are financial and administrative. They will lease 8,000 square feet of office space for a three year term in a contemporary two story *flex* building in Schaumberg. Their estimate of occupancy costs looks like this:

BASE RENT	at **$ 8** /sq ft /yr	**$ 192,000** for 3 years
OPERATING EXPENSES	at **$ 7** /sq ft /yr	**$ 168,000** for 3 years
TENANT IMPROVEMENTS	at **$ 5** /sq ft /yr	**$ 120,000** for 3 years
PERSONNEL	at **$ 4** /sq ft /yr	**$ 96,000** for 3 years
F F & E	at **$ 1** /sq ft /yr	**$ 24,000** for 3 years
MOVING	at **$ 0.5** /sq ft /yr	**$ 12,000** for 3 years
Total Cost of Occupancy		**$ 612,000** for 3 years

The Regional V.P. tells the national Financial V.P. the total amount of the financial obligation the company can expect to incur in moving the Peoria office. The number seems to be all inclusive and should not leave the Regional V.P. with embarrassing oversights she would have to explain later.

But the national office wants to know how the rent compares to market rates; if operating costs include utilities or if power is being metered separately; whether those costs provide for escalation and services such as parking; if tenant improvement costs are amortized in the rent; if there is an allowance from the landlord for some portion of these; and whether interest is being charged and if so at what rate? And what is the impact of a five-year term on these costs? Also, the national office does not want the FF&E costs included in the move budget—these are depreciable items and will be provided for in the corporate capital budget.

The local Vice President promises to dig up the asked for detail, but is miffed at the comment on the furniture. Her small FF&E budget provides for four badly needed work-stations; she knows how capital budget items have a way of getting lost or being deferred. Would the local landlord swap a portion of the tenant improvement allowance dollars for workstation dollars? Would the corporate office be willing to explore a different accounting treatment for these items? A lot of questions remain to be answered.

Rent and Operating Costs

Departing from this scenario for a moment, look at some of the questions raised by it and the graphs above.

The rent figure used above is isolated from the two following items which are often quoted with rent. This figure is referred to as *base rent* because it is inclusive only of "pure" landlord considerations. Many landlords are reluctant to provide the User with this figure even though it can be determined simply by deducting the other known components of rent, discussed below, from the larger quoted rent number.

Rent is most often quoted as a figure inclusive of operating expenses plus an allowance the landlord is willing to contribute toward tenant improvements. Thus, rent for our hypothetical project was probably quoted to the prospective tenant as $20 per square foot of rentable area. That is, $8 in base rent plus $7 in operating costs plus $5 for tenant improvements.

The catch-all, Operating Costs, often includes costs not legitimately a part of running the property we are leasing. Most responsible landlords will furnish a list of such costs to a tenant or a "serious" prospect.

A base rent transaction can, with mutual landlord-tenant agreement, transfer responsibility for direct payment of operating costs to the tenant.

Operating expense limits, or caps

A tenant/landlord agreement in a multi-tenant facility often includes provisions for an *expense stop* or *base-year* or other similar treatment of operating expense reimbursement to the landlord who has assumed responsibility for payment of them. The expense-stop identifies a specific dollar amount that represents the upper limit of expenses to be paid by the landlord, who looks to his/her tenants for reimbursement of all expense amounts in excess of the expense-stop. The expense-stop is negotiable and it is advantageous to the Tenant if this number can be established at a high level.

The base year establishes a similar value on a slightly different basis. It uses as a reference point *actual* expenses being incurred over some present or future period. If, as and when expenses accrue in excess of this base-year amount, the tenant is liable to pay its proportionate share of that excess. Like the expense stop, the base year is negotiable. Since it is assumed that these expenses are always rising, it is advantageous to the tenant that the most current or even a future period is selected as a base-year.

Landlords not using the expense-stop or the base year method of recovering expenses may make their rent or operating costs subject to escalation, using a conventional index, like the Consumer Price Index (CPI), for example, to advance or escalate the rent periodically—usually on an annual basis. Rental escalation using one of these formulas simplifies tracking expense amounts for both landlord and tenant, but it can result in an elevation of rent beyond that required to simply recover increases in expenses.

Using our hypothetical tenant with the $20 rent, look at the differences between the rental advances of the three methods of escalation. All increases are calculated at the rate of 6 percent per annum.

rent advance in:	Yr.1	Yr.2	Yr.3	Total
CPI	$ 0	1.20	2.72	3.92
EXPENSE STOP	$.42	.45	.46	1.33
BASE YEAR	$ 0	.42	.46	.88

The CPI Landlord has applied a 6% rise in the Consumer Price Index to the entire amount of the second and third year rent. The expense stop landlord has experienced a 6% rise over the $7 expense stop and has applied that to each year of the three year term. The base year landlord has experienced a 6% rise in first year expenses which he seeks to recover starting in year 2. (note that the *way* in which the expense increase is applied in each case is very important.)

Things—like rent—are seldom what they seem to be

The situation illustrated above demonstrates that there are quantifiable differences among different treatments of building operating expenses. These differences can take dollars away from or add them back into, the User budget. The User must do the simple math involved with each escalation plan put forward by interested landlords and carry it out to its lease term conclusion to determine its budget impact. Quoted rent does not provide an accurate picture of real rental costs.

Utility costs and rent

In the routine leasing of commercial property, water, heating fuel and electricity are most often purchased by the landlord, who resells them to the tenant in return for rent.

The modern speculative developer, building in an urban area or in an industrial park, will arrange with local utility providers for the delivery of reasonable amounts of gas, water and electricity for heating and cooling and the use of the development's tenants, and for the disposition of their uncontaminated waste water. In all likelihood the developer has had conventionally-sized distribution systems for each commodity installed in the building(s) in question to accommodate tenant needs for heating and cooling and personal hygiene. The extent, or reach, of the system within the building varies from one to another, although it is customary for water and electricity, at least, to be brought to a single point on every level of a commercial building.

The expectation is that the so-called average tenant will have an average demand for electricity and very little for fossil fuel in excess of amounts needed for heating purposes or for amounts of water that much exceed that required for personal use and/or reasonable (e.g., dental office) laboratory use. There will be some users of larger amounts of these commodities who need guidance with respect to filling their organization's special needs in their community. All Users are well advised to verify the availability of utilities directly with the providers in the area of their interest. Then, with the prospective landlord, they can check the capacity of the distribution system in the building, and the preferred manner of payment for the utility usage.

Electrical power usage and costs

For the average commercial tenant, electricity can be as much as 25 percent to 30 percent of the total operating expense cost. It is very often the single most contentious issue in initial landlord-tenant discussions of the operating expense matter. In certain sub-leases, older leases and in smaller commercial building market areas where there has been a tradition of cheap electricity, the language of electrical usage provides for an amount in the rent sufficient for heating, cooling and lighting and to run a reasonable number of customary small office machines, or those of *low electrical consumption.*

More sophisticated—complicated—leases attempt to establish an allowable kilowatt, or kilowatt-hour-per-square-foot level of consumption that might be applicable to all tenants, or to limit the rated consumption of any given piece of equipment.

Always lurking behind the discussion of landlord charges for electrical usage is the not unusual situation in which the building owner and operator also functions as a profit-margin-earning distributor of electrical power. Owners of large commercial complexes or major office buildings, for example, trade routinely in zillions of kilowatt-hours of energy consumption annually. As a result, they reap the benefit of wholesale rates from the local utility company. Even with their mark-up, these rates may be low enough to more than offset the perceived advantage to the Tenant/User of having a meter installed, for direct billing by the power company.

Do not overlook this option. It is also one preferred increasingly by those landlords who are not interested in being in the power regulation business. When the User is a major or single tenant, a dedicated electrical meter is an option recommended by all concerned, especially the small tenant who shares building operating expenses with an energy-guzzling neighbor. If your organization fits the small-tenant description, keep an eye out for the guzzler. You may be paying a part of his bill.

Estimating electrical costs

An unfortunate aspect of the power consumption/cost negotiation can be User ignorance of power need and the resulting tendency of the renter to negotiate unnecessarily for some unreal upper limit of the electricity to be made available.

As a part of the routine User equipment inventory, notations should be made of the rated power of each unit in the organization. This is easily read from the little tag or plate, usually found in some hard-to-get-to spot on the machine. It may also be found in equipment manuals. Record all notations displaying V (volts), W (watts), and Hz (hertz or frequency); these will help determine the number and type of electrical outlets needed, as well as your total power consumption.

Motor-driven equipment may not show a wattage figure but instead indicate amperage and voltage figures from which power consumption can be determined. In this case, the volt and amp figures should be noted. In addition, some indication should be made of the approximate usage the machine gets: in number of hours per day, for example. Show this compiled information to a representative of the local power utility company who can determine your organization's power usage, and give you a breakdown of rates corresponding to that usage.

The costs of tenant improvements

These costs can be viewed as the costs of the professionals involved in the planning and design of your new digs, plus the costs of the labor and materials that go into their construction—the former usually being a fraction of the cost of the latter.

Currently, the costs of the design professionals' work can range from less than $0.50 per square foot of leased space to $3.00 and more for demanding high-finish retail or office space. Construction costs can range from $4 or $5 per square foot for cleaning a space, patching walls and painting a few, to over $100 per foot for work that goes into the high-finish space. The variables in the tenant improvements cost equation lie less in who, how big and where you are, geographically, than they do in what your plans are—how many changes must be made to a space—how much detail is required.

Proposing a formula

Where does your project fall in these wide-swinging ranges; how do you begin to estimate some of these costs? In your earliest planning stages, you want to limit enquiries that can cause information leaks. So, in the privacy of your office, try the following formula:

> **Determine the probable average asking rental for the space you want. Multiply this number by 1.5 (150%) to find the probable average cost of tenant improvements for the space.**

Increase this number, for estimating purposes, if you feel that your improvements are going to be better, or more costly than the average; lower it if you intend to hold these costs below the average.

Now return to the engineering company in Peoria to see how this formula works.

First, the Peoria V.P. uses the smarts that got her the job in the first place and gets that asking rental number from Schaumberg. She is not telling how—it might have been through a client or a colleague already leasing in the area, or from the classified pages of the Chicago Tribune, which, like most urban newspapers, carries broker ads for commercial space. She develops a wide range of rental figures for the area:

Source 1: **$16** per square foot per year

Source 2: **$26** per square foot per year

Source 3: **$17.50** per square foot per year

Source 4: **$21** per square foot per year

Selecting $20 as an average figure and using the magic 1.5 multiple, she determines that it could cost as much as $30 (1.5 x $20) per square foot to improve the still unidentified space, or $240,000 for the 8,000 square feet of space the company needs to lease. Amortized over the needed square footage and the desired three year lease term, the improvements will cost $10 per square foot, per annum.

As we saw earlier, at least one landlord is willing to pay $15 ($5 per square foot per annum) for the needed improvements, leaving a balance for the tenant of $15 in so called above standard improvements to pay for. In this case, both the V.P. and her corporate headquarters decide they will spend no more on improvements than the landlord is willing to amortize in rent.

With respect to the estimated cost of professional services, our formula is not so precise that an amount for this purpose can not be considered a part of the construction cost estimate. Our Peoria engineering company opts to follow a somewhat Spartan route in outfitting new quarters and has, as a result, budgeted less than the average ($1.50 per square foot) for the services of a design professional.

The Allowance for Tenant Improvements

As we mentioned in the Tenant Improvements discussion earlier, most commercial developers and landlords structure their project financing to allow for some degree of alteration and finishing of spaces to be leased, at some level of expense. They incur this expense by making required improvements themselves or by furnishing the tenant with an allowance paid from landlord funds upon completion of the work. Almost universally, the allowance is held to the minimum dollar amount that the landlord feels may be necessary to induce a tenant to lease, and to bring the space in question to a minimum standard of occupancy.

Estimating the likely cost of your tenant improvements is difficult. But estimating a likely landlord allowance is still more challenging. It means guessing at an unknown financial transaction—that between landlord and lender—and the vagaries of landlord market judgments. Here are a couple of clues to performing this guesswork. Our model engineering company found that:

- Their **$20** rent was composed of:

  25% ($5) in **Allowance** for improvements,
  35% ($7) in **Operating Costs**
  40% ($8) in **Base Rent**

- The probable average cost of improving tenant space was $30, making the offered allowance 50 percent of estimated improvement costs.

The first set of figures suggests that the typical tenant improvement allowance is 25 percent of annual rent or $15 ($5 x 3 years). The second set of figures suggests that the allowance is 50 percent of the estimated improvement costs or $15 (50 percent x $30).

In the guesswork of estimating improvement costs, these two guidelines may give the User a point of departure for the cost estimating needed in **Preliminary Planning.**

Advanced cost estimates for tenant improvements

Once you have progressed midway through the Planning Step in your relocation process, (see **Further Planning** in **PART II—DOING IT**), and have a program in preliminary form and a conceptual space plan, you are ready to prepare a preliminary construction budget. This service is offered at substantial cost by a variety of consulting organizations, including developers, architects, construction and project managers, and other design professionals. Primary data is not readily available to these consultants, and they place a high value on brokering and presenting it. But you, the User, with a very valuable and tangible project in your pocket, do not need an information broker and do not need to pay high fees, or any fees, for construction budget preparation.

Where good budget information comes from

There are a number of sources of good budget information in the construction industry and some of them may be closer and more readily available than you think. Keith Collins, in his book *Estimating Construction Costs* suggests that the best—if not the only—source of construction cost data comes from the contractor's experience. That is, if you want to know how much it costs to build a wall or lay a floor, ask the contractor who did one on your block yesterday or last week. The next best source is the experience of others, which is where most contractors go for much of their information.

The latter may come from any one of a variety of trade sources, like **R.S. Means**, **Richardson** or **F.W.Dodge**, which publish a compendium of frequently revised and updated construction cost data. They also provide a variety of software packages designed to fit one or more of the many building types—hospitals, factories, stores, office buildings, etc.—that comprise the big and varied building construction industry. Active construction contractors in most urban areas are usually on-line with one or more of these services. Current construction cost data from these sources is also available in hard copy at your local Library. Contractors and their staff estimators may also rely on the Construction Specifications Institute to help keep them organized. In recent years, CSI has developed a Masterformat system of product classification and numbering which is said to be used widely in the industry.

Contractors readily admit that their fortunes rise and fall on the reliability of their data base and the careers of their highly prized estimators. The latter surfaces when it is time to bid on a job or estimate one—an opportunity that does not come often in the currently depressed commercial construction market. Of even greater interest to the contractor than bidding on a job, is the opportunity to talk directly with a User, without an information broker, about a negotiated contract. Most often, the contractor relishes that opportunity enough to offer to help the User by providing budget information and, with very little prompting, to do so at no cost to the User.

An excellent resource

The local contractor makes an excellent resource for the User seeking construction information. This information can be asked to be offered at no charge to the User, since the contractor who provides it can be given a legitimate opportunity to bid on the work involved. Similarly, no compromise with objectivity is implied, since the estimates being prepared are to be used only for budgeting purposes. The cooperating contractor must be careful, for obvious reasons, not to under or overestimate what a typical bid for your work would be—another advantage to the User. For your part, understand that the budget information you receive from the contractor comes from data that is readily available and does not involve a lot of detective work. This freebie will not include precise estimates of the costs of exotic finishes or equipment, etc.; it will give you useful budget figures for those items, and very accurate figures for the rest.

As to finding that cooperative contractor, a little investigation in the community where the work will be done will turn up a good candidate. Local landlords who use their services can be a good resource as can the local Chamber of Commerce, your commercial real estate broker—if you have already established relations with one— the purchasing agent with a large local employer or utility company, other tenants in the building you plan to occupy or the neighborhood you plan to move into, etc. In conversations about a negotiated contract, be honest and firm in the matter. If you can show your Board—make one up if you don't have one—that there are tangible advantages to such a contract, the contractor in question will have the best shot at it. If not, he/she will certainly have a "leg up" when competing for the job. In any case, you should feel no obligation nor succumb to any pressure to enter into such a contract prematurely.

Obviously, accuracy is the primary quality of any budget estimate—after that, perhaps, come matters of degree of detail, consistency, and readability. Without too many gyrations, you should be able to extrapolate the figures the estimating contractor gives you into useful per-square-foot budget numbers, and also be able to manipulate those numbers as the inevitable design changes come along. To do this, you need item costs for things that can vary in quantity or manufacture, like a sheetrock wall with a paint or fabric finish, or light fixtures with different kinds of lenses, doors that are of hollow or solid core construction, or increases or decreases in these things, etc. It is also important that you know the contractor overhead and profit factors used in calculating your budget, and your estimating contractor should cooperate in providing this information.

Global estimates for the cost of construction of a typical office or workspace, with large numbers of similar components thrown together under a single dollar figure, are of little help. Most contractors and their estimators understand this and will work with you to provide at least the quality of budget information represented by the generally available references noted above. When you get that estimate, go to your local library and check it against the data in the appropriate schedule published by one of the companies mentioned above.

Square footage is another rent variable

Just as rent is not what it seems, the unit designated to measure the commodity called space, or the square foot, is not either. The reason for the variable quality of the square foot in commercial building is not some variation in its geometry - it remains 12 inches square - but rather its identity, in the aggregate, in the eyes of different kinds of people.

The developer and the landlord seek buildings that will optimize their return from rentable area. The building contractor and the architect are interested in the largest gross building area assignments they can get. The interior designer is asked to draw plans for the tenant's useable area, or the actual space the tenant can occupy and work in, while the latter pays rent on the larger rentable area.

The difference between rentable and useable area, or rentable and useable square feet, is called an add-on factor, a load factor, an efficiency factor, etc. It may be expressed as a percentage—or its inverse—of some other larger number. This factor is made up of spaces in a building, other than the premises occupied by tenants, that the owner, with more or less legitimacy, will claim serves all tenants, equally. They are spaces like

- Janitor closets,
- Mechanical rooms,
- Building lobbies,
- Mail rooms,
- Restrooms and Core spaces, etc.

Core spaces include building elevator shafts, stairs, air conditioning ducts and other vertical penetrations in an office building, for example, that run from floor to floor. Sometimes all of these spaces are lumped together whether they are vertical penetrations or just rooms or spaces somewhere. These are still referred to as core spaces.

The space you lease in a multi-tenant building or project is called your premises. Premises is a part of the space you pay rent on; it is all of the space you occupy and that you may think of as exclusively yours for the term of your lease—your home, your sanctuary. Measurement of your premises results in the useable square footage you occupy.

Thus, all the premises or useable area in the building, plus all the core space in the building *should* equal the gross area of the building. Core space becomes a percentage of gross area. The resulting number becomes the building add-on or load factor:

Gross Area   = Useable Area + Core Space

Core Space = X % of Gross Area

X % of Gross Area = Load Factor

In the case of our friends moving to Schaumberg, let us say that their prospective landlord proposes the lease of 8,000 square feet of rentable area in a building with a load factor of 15 percent. In determining the usable area they would be entitled to occupy, they would divide their rentable area by the inverse of the load factor, or 1.15. (This is a quick way to find the number which, if we add 15 percent to it, becomes 8,000):

Rentable Area   = 8,000 sq.ft.

Load Factor   = 15%

Useable Area = 8,000 / 1.15 = 6,956.5 sq.ft.

Had they gone to their landlord with drawings indicating a measured useable area of approximately 7,000 square feet, the landlord would have made the following simple calculation of rentable area:

Useable Area = 7,000 sq.ft.
Load Factor = 15%
Rentable Area = 7,000 + 15% = 8,050 sq.ft.

As you can see, these last two calculations do not yield precisely the same results. Watch out for this when your space and your rent are being tallied up. Since you have no way of knowing a building add-on factor, approach the marketplace with Useable Area as the square footage number that most closely represents your organization's requirements. Multi-tenant, multi-purpose commercial buildings— young or old, almost anywhere—will have add-on/load factors ranging from a low of 8 - 10 percent to a high of 22 - 25 percent.

For a widely accepted definition of rentable and useable area in a commercial building, used by landlords, developers, and those in the architectural and brokerage communities, refer to the BOMA (Building Owners and Managers Association) definition, available through their office in your area.

Relocation Costs

To this point, we have focused almost entirely on costs over which you, the User, have little discretion and less control—the costs of renting. To a somewhat greater extent, the costs of relocation, the other not insignificant costs of occupancy, are within your power to restrain, or to fashion after your own policies and customs. These are costs which concern your organization's personnel, your movable equipment and furniture, and the minute detail that does not loom large in your budget, but is critical to the success of your operation.

Prior to 1988, the doctrine of employment at will prevailed in the American workplace—as it still does—and the responsibility of the employer to the employee in the event of a facility relocation was, presumably, entirely a moral one. In 1988, Congress passed the Worker Adjustment and Retraining Notification Act (WARN). This law places some modest requirements on employers of over 100 persons, in connection with a company closing or relocating. The financial impact of the Act seems negligible if the employer complies with certain notification requirements. Nevertheless, you should review this important legislation.

Human Resources/Personnel

The figures in our hypothetical calculation of personnel costs for the mythical Schaumberg engineering company consist of payments of:

$40,000	**for moving households**
$20,000	**for temporary renter housing**
$20,000	**for severance pay**
$ 5,000	**for site search travel & lodging**
$ 5,000	**for costs of hiring**
$ 6,000	**for down-time & miscellaneous**
$96,000	**TOTAL PERSONNEL COSTS**

These figures suggest that a small core professional staff is moving (some homebuyers and some renters) that there are limited company obligations to employees left behind, that the hiring of replacement personnel will not be costly, and that virtually no relocation-caused downtime is expected.

For a more extensive look at the personnel aspects of organization relocation, we suggest a review of the *Company Relocation Handbook* by Sharon Kaye Ward and William Gary Ward, and *Your Rights in the Workplace* by Dan Lacey and the Editors of Nolo Press in Berkeley, among others.

Furniture, Fixtures & Equipment (FF&E)

Estimated costs of FF&E are usually quite varied from one organization relocation to another. With the exception of the start-up organization, they are almost entirely dependent on a perception of need. As indicated in the discussions between the Peoria V.P. and her national headquarters, her relocation budget would only provide for four new workstations at the very reasonable cost of $6,000 each, or a total budget allowance of $24,000. (See our discussion of furniture vendors in **PART I—Chapter 3**.

Moving

With respect to the costs of moving, the engineering company chose to use a rule of thumb figure of $.50 per square foot of space for its calculation. This figure might be considered adequate in most situations for a local move, but not for one of over one hundred miles, as this one is. No provision has been made here for the cost of graphic design, stationery or other important peripheral costs associated with a relocation. (For a discussion of the mover, see **PART I, Chapter 3**, and for other move related activities which could incur costs, see **PART I—Chapter 2**.)

THE PROGRAM

The principal implement of planning the relocation is the **Program**. The word has its origins in the practice of architecture, which may have borrowed it from the performing arts. As a way of explaining the workmanlike habit of compiling lists of everything requested by the client, the architect offers the analogy of the list of performances and players provided to patrons of the music halls and theaters. The "program" is the performing company's way of verbalizing the content of an audio-visual experience.

American industry applies the word to any set of interrelated and ongoing activities that produce something, usually of a complex nature. In *Systems Management Techniques*, Paul Gill mentions the need in World War II for fresh management approaches to the development of America's complex weapons systems programs and the subsequent design of Program Evaluation and Review Technique, or PERT. Not coincidentally, PERT is an offspring of the heavy construction industry and Critical Path Method (CPM) of tracking complex residential and commercial building projects.

The Program: its purpose and its intended users

To the User facing a relocation of facilities, the program represents an orderly summation, in written and graphic form, of all the information about the User organization needed to plan, design and construct a new facility or rehabilitate an existing one. The goal of the program is to make this information as complete as possible and to put it into a form that others, who may be totally unfamiliar with the User organization, can use to assist in acquiring, building, and outfitting the User facility. Thus, the program will become an important tool for the real estate broker, the developer or prospective landlord, the architect, the mover, and other vendors and suppliers.

Program information: where does it come from ?

The information used in the program can only come from within your organization and, if you have one, your existing facility. It is on your desk, in your files and in your head. It may also be a reminder in the form of the things around you: doors and windows, light and sound, etc., or the habits of your work day: steps to the washroom, trips to the parking lot, etc. It is information within easy reach and not difficult to record. Part of it concerns what you would like to have, or want. Preparing the want list is discussed later in this Chapter.

You can record the information yourself; it can be prepared by anyone familiar with the organization who can organize and present information well. The latter includes design professionals experienced with this kind of assignment. Whoever the preparer is, remember that completeness of the information is of greatest importance. No amount of expensive consultation will insure that equipment or functions or spaces needed will be provided for, if the need is not expressed in some way by the User.

What kind of information must be recorded?

Information to be collected will relate to a variety of characteristics that are either a part of the workplace facility or directly affect the User's choice of one. These fall into three categories:

- **Site Information**, or data relating to things you need that are normally outside your workplace, but are important to it. Proximate site information includes features that are a part of the facility buildings and grounds: parking, loading docks, rail-sidings, driveways, landscaping, etc. Area site information includes features that make a site more desirable for your operation, like proximity to banks, freeways, clients, suppliers, etc.

- **Workplace Information**, or data relating to space and service needs in the workplace premises. People-space information includes assigned spaces like private offices and employee work stations; Support space information includes conference, file storage, etc., rooms, and other spaces not assigned to an employee(s) and Services information includes electricity, air conditioning, water, sinks, counters and cabinets, etc.

- **FF&E Information**, or data relating to loose (unattached) items like desks, chairs, shelving, display cases, copying and computer equipment, etc. Existing FF&E consists of items presently on hand that are intended for reuse; new FF&E consists of new acquisitions.

Information Sources

The best information source is the User organization individual or group working most closely with an item or in a space, or most directly involved in making decisions about it. Care should be taken in making information gathering assignments in order to avoid unwanted repercussions of either a practical or a psychological nature. A certain amount of probing into individual need and/or intent is necessary; this kind of enquiry needs to be handled with some delicacy. There is a natural tendency to empire-building by those who look upon a relocation as an opportunity to expand their sphere of influence, as well as to improve their own working conditions. There is a contradictory urge on the part of others to minimize their need and to overlook that of persons or functions for which they are responsible. And there is a prevalence at every level to remain ignorant of, or inattentive to, intangible human need; to such things as light, air, sound, privacy, comfort, etc.

Information gathering

Gathering program information within the organization can be handled in many ways. One extreme is that it be developed by one individual for the entire organization, such as an executive or someone designated by an executive committee or board; the other is that it be solicited from every individual within the organization. There are legitimate reasons for taking each approach, as well as virtually any in-between.

A very young organization, necessarily small and manageable, with an entrepreneurial owner or chief executive, with well-formed ideas about all of its needs can certainly define those needs for the purposes of the facility program. The risks to be run in doing this are minimal and the gains may lie in greater flexibility and more security with privileged information.

A more established organization may wish to reach into its ranks, at every level, for the wealth of new ideas, as well as data, that lie there. The gains of this approach, in addition to the often-times valuable ideas generated, lie in several areas: greater certainty that all information needed is, in fact, being obtained; a balance of emphasis between internal groups and functions is being maintained; a strengthening of internal ties, greater individual involvement and productivity, etc., are becoming possible.

The risks of widespread involvement in the program process are largely confined to time-loss and the effect this may have on time-sensitive operations, the availability of properties to move to, or funds, or key Players, etc. A certain amount of confusion can result from any dilution of the programming process, along with difficulties in decision-making. The organization should be prepared to handle these aspects of the democratization of it.

Programming space standards

Certain simple standards or conventions are applicable to the program; if used, these standards can greatly aid the communication of the information in it. Some of these standards derive from repeated use in the building industry, or the experience of others—users, architects, etc. None, except those involving the basic rules of arithmetic and geometry, etc., are to be considered so cast in stone that they can't be adjusted or manipulated.

The intent of the workspace standard is to provide for the greatest flexibility in the use of space, and the greatest economy in designing and constructing it. Here are some guidelines to understanding standards:

- Room sizes are understood in square feet, meaning the product of the length and width of a space, expressed in linear feet.

- Dividing a larger space into smaller spaces of equal size creates standard spaces.

- A set of standards that is based on the architecture of a known facility, e.g., on its column or window spacing, sizes, etc., can be applied to workspace.

- Workspace standards can be created from the sizes of rooms you have worked in or have had some experience with. To keep from alienating your architect, these room sizes should have dimensions that can be factored—multiplied or divided—easily.

- Workspace standards can be made from multiples of the dimensions of typical workstation furniture—desks, tables, counters, work-benches, etc.

- A cirulation standard is used to account for the area around work-spaces that is needed for the movement of people and equipment. It is usually expressed as a percentage, with a range of roughly 20 percent to 40 percent, of the workspace it serves.

- To keep from alienating your contractor and your staff, and further frustrating your architect, try to avoid mixing standards.

Empty space is a big ticket item

The circulation standard is worth discussing a little further; it represents such a significant portion of the total amount of space you may buy or rent. Traditional architectural practice correctly observes that the amount of space required for circulation can not be determined until a space plan is drawn. Since the program is designed to provide estimates well in advance of space planning time, and experience shows that there is a certain consistency to this kind of space, the percentage estimate is in common use. Experience also shows, however, that different workspace —office, laboratory, warehouse, etc.—can require significantly different amounts of circulation. It is common for this to occur within a single User's space. Thus, a single circulation factor applied to all User space can generate a significant estimating error.

Estimating special use areas

How does the User estimate the size of a lunch room, an auditorium, a classroom, a Boardroom, a warehouse, etc.? The size of these spaces may be based on more than numbers of people and furniture. The company lunch-room may or may not need to incorporate an area for informal client "mixing". Warehouse or store-room space may halve or double, depending on materials handling equipment and the aisle space it requires. Classroom space is a function of teaching methodology and equipment, and the kind of participation expected of students. Similar special-use areas will have space needs that must be based on your detailed appraisal of how they are to be used. Such an appraisal is a prerequisite to their design or layout. This, in turn, will constitute the best estimate of the space required by each. The layout of the room in question may be done by the design professional who will ultimately be responsible for the preparation of construction documents. Or it may be a simple sketch dimensioned by User personnel.

Job descriptions, functions and space

The appraisal mentioned above is an extension of a management tool, already in existence in most organizations, variously referred to as a personnel, function or job description. This management tool can be invaluable to those responsible for program preparation. If your personnel department has not already done so, job descriptions may be prepared to include brief descriptions of the nature of the space, equipment and furniture recommended for each position. The nature of the space described would preferably be specific as to its use characteristics but not its size or dimensions. The latter may seem to be a frivolous constraint—it is easier to say that a function requires a 10 by 10 foot space than it is to describe what goes on in the space—but it is an important one. Functions and the furniture, equipment and space needed to serve them can change rapidly. If it is logistically impossible for management to adapt to these changes at the moment they occur, it can at least take advantage of the opportunity to do so, presented by plans for a relocation of the workplace.

Working relationships and adjacencies

An important objective of the program is to describe, in workplace terms, how different User functions relate to one another. This information resolves itself on the space plan in terms of the placement of functions and in the business of programming and space planning. These preferred placements are called adjacencies —the Accounting Department prefers to be located next (adjacent) to Personnel; the President prefers to be near (adjacent to) the Chief Financial Officer and the Vice President of Administration, etc. As the organization grows larger, the matter of the interrelationship of individuals and groups becomes complex, and priorities of functional adjacency must be established. Even with priorities, satisfying these location needs can become a significant problem for the space planner trying to fit them into unforgiving structures.

THE REQUEST FOR PROPOSAL

Every organization reaches a time in its corporate life when it tires of reaching for a phone or a keyboard to recreate the same information it has provided for seemingly thousands of purveyors of goods and services to invite still another to feast at its board. The first such moment results in the invention of the organization purchase order. The relief this brings to the entire staff is palpable. No longer is it necessary to repeat the company name, billing address, shipping address, type of business, SIC Code, invoice number, terms of payment, etc., and that last bit of critical data that invariably escapes memory and causes our provider to chastise us. For a long time, that purchase order form is our salvation in hurried moments; if we have designed it well, it can be used to order everything from printer paper to company trucks.

The Request for Proposal (RFP) is a kind of purchase order form. It is an organization's invitation to providers of services, from the owners of big buildings to moving companies and architects, to offer those services and to put a price on them. You can use the form of your existing purchase order to solicit these quotations and proposals, provided you give your request the kind of accuracy, authority and thoughtfulness that will elicit the best and most complete response from your prospective provider.

To accomplish these goals, you will want to come forth with the kind of information about your own purpose in relocating that corporations a few years ago used to shy away from. Anticipate the questions you or your CFO or your Office Manager may get in some unguarded moment; calculate and prepare your answers to them now. How long have you been in business? How is your business doing? How many people have you hired in the past year? Do you want a five-year lease? How much rent do you want to pay? How much do you want to spend on improvements? Where do you want to move to? Why do you want to go there?. What does your balance sheet look like? How is your credit? These and a thousand other questions about your planned relocation will form on the lips of providers, each with a different spin or bias. Each may be deflected to some extent at least by a well executed Request For Proposal.

Five major parts

A good RFP will contain five major parts:

- A covering letter
- A statement of relocation purpose and goals
- A statement of facility requirements
- Information requested from the respondent
- User company support data including a capsule company history and a brief financial statement

This format and much of the material in it can be used effectively over and over again for a wide variety of prospective providers in the relocation process. The brief **covering letter**, which introduces the subject of the correspondence and lists its enclosures, need be altered only with respect to the type of services being sought. You should be able to run this again and again for requests going to a wide variety of providers and vendors involved in the relocation process.

The statement of relocation purpose and goals

This is prepared to satisfy anyone about the reasons for your impending move. The statement is couched in terms that point up your major concerns and emphases—for quality service, speed, economy, etc., and stresses the expected benefits to your staff of your new home—downtown, suburbs, industrial park, new city, etc.—and your new quarters. It is also an opportunity to be honest about your reasons for moving in a way that does not raise questions about your motives.

If you are down-sizing, if your industry is in a slump, if the local newspapers have just reported your loss of a major contract, etc., you are, for no good reason, placed in a high risk category by prospective providers. When you choose to relocate in these circumstances your stock, metaphorically speaking, goes down still further. Without a well thought out effort at correcting misguided perceptions, you can lose valuable negotiating leverage with developers, landlords and some contractors. In short, a poorly structured RFP can cost you money.

The statement of facility requirements

The statement of facility requirements may be taken almost verbatim from the program you have prepared, or are in the process of preparing. This may be included in its entirety with your RFP, since it gives services providers an excellent picture of the scope and nature of your move. Its very bulk also lends an authenticity and seriousness to your request for proposal which can only be guessed at otherwise. And it succeeds in answering a wide variety of questions on the part of others which can only become a continuing nuisance as time goes on. (You may wish to review the document before photocopying it to remove any proprietary or confidential information.)

Information requested from the respondent

The information you seek from your respondents will necessarily vary from one type of service to another. Your questions should, in themselves, express an understanding of how the service generally operates. The Appendix contains some prototypical request formats for each of several types of service provider. Where appropriate, prepare the RFP with blank spaces that respondents may use for their replies. You can expect that each prospective provider will respond, regardless of your thoughtfulness, with answers in their own format. The latter will be particularly true of building developers and landlords, who will not only answer your request in their format, but will reformulate your questions for you, or ignore them entirely. There is little to be done about this landlord/developer penchant for contradicting good busines sense. Since lucid answers will not be forthcoming from this group of providers on the first request, keep your first approach simple. If you establish a format for financial analysis as a part of your RFP process, insist on getting answers that will fit that format. A judicious call to a reluctant provider with a reminder of their desire to be treated fairly in your analysis may do the trick. It may be your only recourse, short of eliminating the recalcitrant provider from your review.

User company support data

This portion of the RFP can be handled quite simply. At the same time, it can establish the desired impression of User organization financial stability, seriousness of purpose, successful achievement, competitiveness, etc., and longevity. Establishing the latter in the eyes of the prospective landlord is very important for the obvious reasons that that entity survives largely on the promise of income projected over long periods of time. An extensive User history is advantageous; User ability to project an environment of future success can be just as meaningful, if not more so.

The most straightforward way to submit background data is to enclose a copy of the organization's standard brochure with the RFP. Before doing this, however, the brochure should be reviewed with an eye to how it will be seen at the other end. If it is primarily a product sales tool, laden with glossy photos of imposing looking metal housings and electronic controls, embraced by vacuous male or female models, and accompanied by an incomprehensible technical text, question its value in the context of the RFP. If, on the other hand, the standard mailer briefly, but tastefully, describes the User organization, its principals and capable staff, its broad markets and the extent of User reach into them, its assets in the form of securities, facilities and equipment, copyrights and patents, etc.,or simply a strong client list, expect it to be well received.

If your organization publishes an annual report or an abbreviated financial statement is already a part of your standard brochure, and the information in either of these is reasonably current, either should satisfy the respondent's initial need to know concerning your financial condition. Here again, is a place where a review of the quantity and quality of this already published information is recommended. Assume that the unidentified reader of your information, in the office of a leasing agent or a contractor, has an MBA in Finance and is intimate with the credit-data needs of his/her employer. Thus, that person will quickly look for clues to User organizational structure, operating incomes, debt and equity histories, typical User financing instruments, asset liquidity, etc.

Organizational structure is exceptionally important to landlords and other service providers. In recent years, most have experienced the great resourcefulness of the American entrepreneur in escaping legal liability for contract payments. The User should be aware that the corporate veil has become a rather tattered shield for the corporate executive about to sign a lease; personal guarantees are frequently sought from those with the most prestigious corporations.

For the very young organization, perhaps embarking on its first effort at finding a workplace, the kinds of materials we have discussed above will be as significant in their appearance and manner of presentation as they are in their content. For such organizations, projections of future success in their marketplace and the availability of resources to carry the enterprise through a period of limited returns are of paramount importance. In this connection, clear-eyed, straightforward and un-embellished statements are welcome. If they are submitted in an easy-to-read format, on quality paper with a well-designed letterhead and logotype, and placed in an enclosure (binder, folder, envelope, etc.) that adds to an overall sense of thoughtfulness and attention to detail, the User organization can be assured of positive provider response.

EVALUATIONS, ANALYSES & CHECKLISTS

The process of relocating the workplace would be less complicated than it is if we did not seek to make changes and improvements in the workplace, but this is largely what the relocation is all about. Growing up or growing down, moving to this part of the country or that, we want to improve our organization with our next move. In doing so we have to make comparisons, to evaluate how we have been living, to see our workplace as others see or experience it, and to stack it up against that of our best competition and our own idealized vision.

Three important checklist/evaluations

This is why this book includes a process called **Evaluation,** (see **PART II—Step E**) one of the four steps requisite to **EPDEX** and a successful relocation. Even though that step asks you to examine the place you are working in now—your existing workplace—it also gives you a framework to develop a new and improved workplace. We encourage you to study the items included in this step, particularly with an eye to evaluating those facility features that are critical to your own operation, or have failed you miserably in the past. Change factors, discussed in **Evaluation,** should also be incorporated by the User in three important checklist-evaluations:

- The Want List
- Site Selection Criteria
- Site Evaluation

A summary we refer to as a **Quicklist** follows this section. It lists each of these factors by the descriptive name used in **Evaluation.** Each is developed with a paragraph or two in **Evaluation.**

The statements of our criteria for satisfactory functioning of a building component which appear in **Evaluation, PART II,** are necessarily brief. They are explored in greater detail in a number of excellent technical guidebooks. For concerns about the inner workings of buildings, for example, refer to *Mechanical And Electrical Equipment for Buildings* by Stein, Reynolds and McGuiness, published by John Wiley & Sons. The book is suitable for engineers and architects, but is eminently readable for the User with a technical bent. The AIA publishes a quarterly review of architectural technology. **Facility Management Journal** is a bi-monthly magazine, published by IFMA, that deals with a wide range of current issues in building maintenance.

Preparing the Want List

The first and principal characteristic of the want list is that it is comprised of what the User wants in the workplace. If this means that it should look like an elephant or a pelican, then that requirement should head up the list—and the site search needs to begin very quickly. If it means the equivalent of three parking spaces for every employee, 100 foot bays, and 75 foot ceilings, then this information suggests a move away from downtown and places constraints on our thoughts about certain other facility wants as well.

The Quicklist

Start your list by jotting down any and all facility—workplace—thoughts that come into your head, as they arrive. Use the Quicklist at the end of this section to help track these ideas; they will come in spasms and spurts and take some time to develop—days, weeks, months. Let the list grow naturally; do not cull or prune. Do not leave something off your list because you think it might cost too much. Often, the very characteristic you thought most outrageous in the wanting of it already exists in a building just around the corner, at a bargain price.

When you feel you have temporarily exhausted your new-workplace ideas and have explored the pertinence of items on the Quicklist, establish some priorities among them. Among the more obvious reasons for doing this, you and your staff want to avoid over-emphasizing, or trading on a particular want-list item to the detriment of another that may be more important. Using our five-point grading system explained in **PART II—Step E, Evaluation** can help in this exercise. Finally, make sure that the prioritized want list accompanies any organization statement of facility or workplace need, such as the Program or the statements of goals and purposes that accompany your requests for proposal.

Site Selection Criteria

The method used to pick the location of your next workplace, along with the building and suite that it is in and the rent that you pay, etc., will employ some judgements and standards and comparisons that we group together and call selection criteria. These should, by rights, evolve from the want list you labored over, above, minus some of those considerations of internal and external factors that do not bear directly on real estate and structures. Here again, we offer the Quicklist on the following pages, and the **Part II Evaluation** material on which it is based as primary resources for this purpose.

While the want list affects these criteria, and may be the origin of them, selection criteria go beyond the broader statements of the want list and specify certain characteristics as being those that will determine a preferred site. You may, for example, be convinced that a responsive, high-performance HVAC installation is in the best interests of your organization and place this item high on your want list. Subsequent investigations into the characteristics of this equipment, plus your new-found knowledge of what is available in the marketplace, help you define certain performance criteria, which can now become site selection criteria. From this example, you can also see that where the want list contains items, features or characteristics that may or may not be available in the real world, the selection criteria work with the realities of what, in fact, can be delivered.

Site Evaluation

We noted above that selection criteria is an essential element in the method used to pick the best site for our organization. The method itself comprises a series of evaluations which combine to give us a site, or a project evaluation. Our Quicklist, at the end of this section, separates these evaluations into four groups:

■ **Cost Factors**

> Elements making up the cost of relocation are listed here and analyzed in Costs & Budget Estimates, earlier in this chapter.

■ **Internal Factors**

> Internal Factors result from the nature of your organization, its characteristics, its methods of operation, its people, goals and needs, etc. They are largely within your control. These are briefly discussed in **PART II—Step E**, Evaluation.

■ **External Factors**

> These have their origins in institutions, forces, events, and organizations, etc., that are outside your own group, and beyond your direct control. They are discussed briefly in **PART II—Step E**, Evaluation.

■ **Deterioration Factors**

> These are an integral part of your facility and are subject to change or deterioration with the passage of time, or as a result of normal wear and tear, neglect, damage, etc. They are briefly discussed in **PART II— Step E**, Evaluation.

Cost factors relative to rent and the construction of tenant improvements are discussed in some detail in **Costs & Budgets** in this Chapter. Used to compare sites, or projects, an analysis of costs is relatively uncomplicated and straightforward and can lead the reader to a reasonably well defined result. The mathematics of commercial renting are not complicated. They fall well within the capabilities of the average entrepreneur or manager. The tools for analysis, in the form of computer software spreadsheets, (Lotus, Quattro-Pro, SuperCalc, Excel, etc.) are also in the hands of most of our readers. The biggest problem our reader will encounter in this area is that of wringing the needed numbers from prospective landlords. A second problem may be that of making sense of the formulas and analyses provided by landlord agents and over-zealous real estate brokers.

An evaluation of internal and external factors necessarily involves your view of the content and significance of each. In those circumstances where they apply, the corporate directive looms very large (internal factors), as does the local State office of OSHA (external factors) for the paint manufacturer or clinical laboratory. There are instances when an analysis in one of these areas requires the input of a professional and our step-by-step **DOING IT** outline recognizes this possibility in **Further Planning.** The special areas mentioned are representative of the many that may be encountered in planning for the new location.

The focus of your relocation effort will be on the facility and the workplace it houses, and we lump together all of the characteristics of these places and refer to them as **Deterioration Factors**—our way of recognizing the truisms about change. From the day we start to work in a new workplace, we are changing; the facility we are in, new or old, wood, or brick, or steel and glass, starts to become less adequate to our need. Still, rather than throw up our hands and throw out all of our analytical tools, we tell ourselves that the more we demand from the workplace facility, the better we adapt it to our current—and projected—needs, the more we will get from its deteriorating condition.

Using the **Quicklist**, and its parent in the pages of **Evaluation**, review, refine and expand on these criteria for evaluation, and compare this information with that concerning the workplace proposed by prospective landlords. When performance measurements or other information provided by the landlord fails to be persuasive, pay another visit to the proposed premises, with key members of your staff in tow. Be sure to include anyone in this group who is a regular, full-time user of the space or facility in question.

Q U I C K L I S T

For the formulation of want lists, site selection criteria, building, site, and project evaluations, etc. See **PART II, Step E, Evaluation**, for a brief development of each heading, and a method of measurement.

COST FACTORS

1.   Base Rent
2.   Operating Expenses
3.   Taxes
4.   Insurance
5.   Utilities
6.   Maintenance
7.   Escalation
8.   Tenant Improvements
9.   Design Professional
10.   Construction
11. Personnel
12. Furniture
13. Equipment
14. Moving

INTERNAL FACTORS

15. Income
16. Systems
17. Personnel
18. Corporate Directives
19. New Products
20. Growth
21. Consolidation
22. Incremental Change
23. Quantum Change
24. Goals
25. Business Plan

EXTERNAL FACTORS

26. Industry Change
27. Markets
28. Competition
29. Government Regulation
30. Local Planning
31. Community Development
32. Taxes and Insurance
33. Suppliers
34. Amenities

DETERIORATION FACTORS / SITE

35. Approach and Access
36. Landscaping
37. Parking
38. Lighting
39. Drainage
40. Identification
41. Amenities
42. Outbuildings

DETERIORATION / EXTERIOR

43. Apparent Type
44. Building Entries
45. Architectural Design
46. Signage
47. Facing Materials
48. Roof

DETERIORATION / INTERIOR

49. Public Areas
50. Core
51. Planning Module
52. Walls
53. Doors

54.   Ceilings

55.   Floors

56.   Millwork

57.   Elevators

58.   H V A C

59.   Electricity

60.   Lighting

61.   Water and Waste

62.   Life Safety

DETERIORATION / MANAGEMENT

63.   Personnel

64.   Maintenance

65.   Security

66.   Billing

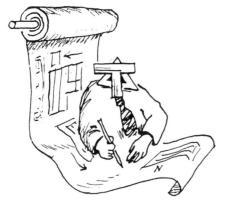

PLANS AND DRAWINGS

Preparing the commercial facility for relocation is communicated primarily, and at times exclusively, in visual terms. This does not mean that your world suddenly becomes void of comfortably familiar words and phrases in your native tongue; it is just that buildings, architecture and the objects that go into them and adorn them often resist verbal description.

The ancient discipline of architecture has, over many years, established a varied, wide ranging, and often confusing convention of signs and symbols to convey information to those responsible for constructing the designs of its practitioners. As commercial building has grown more complex, so has the complexity of this system of communication; with it, the opportunities not only for misunderstandings and faulty execution, but also for life-threatening mistakes as well.

Until recent times, the User was usually a reluctant buyer of work ridden with errors whose cause was never to be known; responsibility was endlessly shunted between architect, Client/User, contractor and tradesman. Rising costs of labor and materials, and occasional litigation, made an industry out of correcting the mistakes of new construction; the User almost invariably payed the bill.

Since the User was never a part of the traditional communication system—a system closed to Users and the unwashed for centuries—there has been little opportunity for the User to respond to communication breakdown in any way other than the occasional scream of pain at the misplaced wall or door, and the unexpected bill. This deficiency will certainly be corrected in the coming decades. But for the User hoping to muddle through plans and drawings now, following is an introduction to their preparation and usage with the admonition that you ask for translations of their arcane gibberish whenever the intent of the builder or the design professional is not absolutely clear.

The paper napkin work and the start of the grand plan

It all begins—literally or figuratively—on the paper napkin. It might be the back of an envelope or an old memorandum or piece of junk mail; it might be yours, or hers, or theirs. It does not make any difference: it is the start of the Grand Plan, the layout and design of the new work space that is going to bring a rush of success to your organization.

You might think it has the embarrassing appearance of a child's scrawl, without scale or perspective, and with words—almost unintelligibly written—across everything. It might even be accompanied with verbal apologies for its lack of finish and professional qualities, and—god forbid—being nothing more than a concept. If it is all of these things, it is traveling in exalted company, because the work of Corbu and Louis Kahn and other masters of the art of architecture has begun with sketches that perfectly fit this description.

If you happen to be with a very aware design professional when the paper napkin work is done, chances are that scrap of scrawled upon waste will be carefully folded away for future reference. Perhaps it will even be resurrected at the end of the project as the final test of the success of the original concept.

Space plans: a medium between User and design professional

Arguably, the most important single drawing to emanate from the planning and design process is the space plan. The space plan comes in two versions, a series of single line drawings in the early stages of planning, followed by a hard line drawing which fixes the planning decisions in a way that, along with certain other instructions, can be used to start construction.

The single line terminology comes from the liberty taken with the way that walls are traditionally represented (by two parallel lines in a hard line drawing), drawing these as a single line, and also with their execution in a free-hand form. The single line drawing is a medium between User and design professional, the hard line drawing works between the latter and the contractor, although the User must be able to understand both.

A lot of other drawings are done in the process of getting construction information into a useable form. The base line drawing, done in hard form, on a reproducible surface like vellum, puts down information which isn't supposed to change—exterior walls, stairs, elevators, mechanical rooms, etc.,—so the planner can draw over it as many times as he/she wishes. Block plans, also referred to as concept plans, are made to show relationships between blocks of User space of identical or similar usage. Detail drawings are like close-up pictures of how things go together. Many times, the paper napkin work will be accompanied by a detail drawing or two to suggest how the concept can actually work.

Elevations: looking straight on at things

Then there are drawings such as site plans, which are very important in explaining what goes on outside the building you may buy or lease, and elevations which are drawings that will tell you what you need to know about how the surface of an interior wall will look with shelves or other millwork, where the doors and windows are, what the building silhouette (roof line) is, how different floor levels and ceiling heights intersect, etc.

Elevations do not seem to be a favorite thing for design professionals to draw. The reason for this, alluded to above, is that drawings are done for architects, contractors and tradespeople, and not for Users. But the latter may be interested in how furniture and equipment may work with windows, entries and exits, etc. A warehouse or shop foreman, or a laboratory director may want to look at door openings and clear heights and the profiles of duct work, pipe and conduit. An office manager or corporate executive may want a side-lite glass for an office or a series of offices and, with no visual information to assist him/her, will be asked to pick its size and location. Doing without an elevation drawing, which might allow the User to adjust the location of a feature, often seems preferable to letting the design professional put it in the wrong place.

Scale: enlarging or shrinking objects

Architectural drawings are done to scale, meaning spaces and objects have been reduced in size, proportionally. The most commonly used scale in architectural drawing is 1/8th of an inch to a foot. This is an anachronistic scale, considering that the computerized design professional and contractor convert it to a decimal equivalent, but it makes it easy for the lay person to follow. With any school-house ruler, one can measure using inches and parts of inches, and multiply by eight to come up with a number of feet.

> **For example**: a room, 3 1/2 inches by 2 1/4 inches, on your daughter's wooden ruler, would be 3.5 x 8 (28) times 2.25 x 8 (18). The room would be 28 feet x 18 feet, and 504 square feet in area.

Details may be done to a larger scale, so that the object is more easily readable on the paper; elevations and site plans may be done to a smaller scale because the architect must put a much larger building or land area onto the same size sheet that other drawings appear on.

Basic information for the architectural drawing

Because the space plan—referred to subsequently as a partition plan—is such an important document from the beginning to the end of the plan-design-construct cycle, it is wise for the User to be thoroughly familiar with it. Insist that it contain necessary and useful information presented in the clearest way possible.

The partition plan becomes a base line drawing for the preparation of other drawings. That is, lighting, plumbing, electrical, telecom, etc., data are—or should be —drawn as overlays on the space or partition plan. A block of information normally appears in the lower right-hand corner of the drawing which carries the name of the design professional in large letters. This is also a good place to find other necessary information like:

- The subject of the drawing
- The scale of the drawing
- The date the sheet was drawn
- A North-South directional arrow
- A legend of signs and symbols used

The walls and columns describing the building's exterior and its interior columns and core spaces should be quickly recognizable and defined with a heavy or filled line. All spaces on the drawing should be numbered in order to communicate the multitude of information that will be generated about each space. Certain spaces of otherwise unidentifiable character, large open office areas, workshop or assembly areas, storage and lunch rooms, etc., should be labeled. A plan of the layout of critical furniture and equipment in each of this latter group of spaces should be prepared, reviewed and approved prior to approval of a final space plan.

Two and three dimensional visualizations

In the best of all circumstances, communication about your project would take place in the presence of three-dimensional models, lighted and colored to effect the desired character and mood of your workspace. Architectural projects that are of sufficient scope will merit such a model, but only if their cost is substantial—that is, well into seven-digits or more, and the design-work is thought to be unusual or distinctive. But, primarily because of costs in money and the time it takes to prepare them, they are rare in connection with the typical relocation project.

The two-dimensional visualizations most often used to convey the feel, or overall appearance quality of some aspect of a design project are called renderings. Design professionals may produce these or, more accurately, have them drawn by a contract graphics service, as perspectives or as axiometrics (axonometrics if you prefer the Greek). The latter lends itself to mechanical drafting techniques, suitable to virtually any design professional with architectural training and is more widely used, though less User-friendly, than the perspective. The perspective is liable to render interior views in a manner more compatible with the lay viewer's experience, since it can look at objects at or near eye level, with a scale and image more nearly approaching that of the nice pictures in the shelter magazines. It also lends itself to a more accurate rendition of the patterns and textures of furniture and fabrics. Perspective and axiometric views of plans developed by CADD equipment can also be generated by computer giving the viewer the much ballyhooed "virtual reality".

The Mock-up

As its name implies, the mock-up is an elaborate stage set that uses every available architectural feature, finish and piece of furniture and equipment to be specified in a typical portion of the subject interior. It is used these days by the design professional, with greater frequency and success than the traditional two-dimensional means of conveying the elusive sense of an interior design concept. Costs are kept within reason by constructing the mock-up, with the landlord's blessing, in an empty portion of the building to be leased, and by using contractors and vendors who stand to reap the reward of an eventual purchase order.

This technique offers many rewards to the User that cannot be equalled by any other interior planning and design methodology. Virtual reality becomes, simply, reality. User personnel may be invited to walk through the mock-up and touch and feel and fully experience the space being designed for them. Problems become immediately and irrefutably apparent. Design solutions do not require endless discussion and speculation. The long-term benefit of the mock-up is that everyone— from the design professional to the User organization clerk—can feel that each made a contribution to a workable solution.

CADD

Ten years ago CADD was the wave of the future in architecture and is now solidly emplaced as the engine of the present in engineering and architectural practice. As attractive as it is, the installation, setup and operation of Computer Assisted Drafting And Design equipment is still economically out of reach for many design shops and for most architectural interior installations. You may see it in your project, particularly if your bidding or construction documents are long and detailed, and you may not. Its presence or absence in a design professional's shop should not greatly affect your selection of one.

CONSTRUCTION AND BIDDING DOCUMENTS

All of the previously described plans and drawings lead up to the construction and completion of your project. However, before they appear on the construction site, they will go through a final review, receive the signatures and official stamps of the Owner organization, its architects and engineers, and become construction or bidding documents. (With respect to these contracts, you as the User, Tenant and Client, are referred to as the Owner.)

This collection of technical diagrams, details, plans, drawings, and instructions written in the best pseudo-courtroom manner describe, as well as they can, the look and content of what is to be built. When complete, they are gathered together in a bid package which is then placed in the hands of the bidder. The contents of each bid package is identical; it is intended to provide any interested builder with an opportunity to win the contract being offered.

Although not all construction work is bid, the documents that control their work remain essentially the same as if they were. Different components of the bidding documents are discussed below; let's first take a look at the why of bidding. Is it necessary? Advisable? Is it a lot of work for a small private project? To begin to answer these questions, it is a good idea to remember why we have the process in the first place.

Bidding: racehorses and art?

Construction bidding is not unlike auctioning race horses or fine art or the property of large estates. In these cases, buyers who are willing to compete with others, or bid, are persuaded to appear for an opportunity to obtain what is thought to be an exceptional value at a bargain price. This attractive possibility or risk of gain induces the prospective buyer to bid. Similarly, the tenant or landlord who wants something built offers money in the form of a contract, to any builder who will provide the requisite materials and services. Cash is flowing in a different direction in this comparison, but the concept of risk and gain involved in the bidding transaction is the same. The contractor-bidder seeks to maximize an opportunity for profit from the sale of materials and services; you, the User, hope to buy the latter at a bargain price. This opportunity to seek out the lowest price for the work you need done is a compelling reason for the sometimes tedious process of bidding.

In a weak market for commercial construction work—and we are experiencing such a market in most parts of the country as we write—there will be much interest in your construction project and many contractors interested in bidding for your construction dollars. This environment is a healthy one for construction bidding and makes the process advisable for many of you who are about to embark on a construction project. Is it not, then, advisable for all Users in this market? And what other method of hiring a contractor is there?

Where bidding is less meaningful

In any given construction market there is always a particular set of circumstances at work that can throw our generally accepted platitudes about market conditions right out the window. You may be relocating to an area where, in contradiction to the national trend, there is a healthy market for commercial construction, and where your bid package would be less likely to receive the attention you would prefer. Also, if the nature of the work you wish to accomplish, and the kinds of skills and materials required to get it done fall outside of the capabilities of a significant part of the local contractor community, the bidding process becomes less meaningful. If your project calls for designer finishes or the kind of care required for the exacting specifications of certain Federal agencies, the bidding process—a broadcast call for the best price—is only as effective as your ability to screen or qualify your bidders. There are other circumstances that tend to dilute the effectiveness of bidding in certain locales.

Builders vary in the kinds and quantities of the resources they will bring to a project. Contemporary contractors are no longer capital intensive enterprises to be evaluated by the quantities of trucks and backhoes in their yards or the numbers of carpenters and plumbers on their payroll. Nevertheless, most will have some unique resource, or special access to one, which may be particularly significant to your project. Many will own or have an equity interest in a cabinet shop, builder's supplier, lumberyard, or an electrical or plumbing contractor, etc. Others may act as local representative for one or more manufactured building components—doors, windows, floor covering, etc., or elevators and other mechanical equipment. These connections can provide the contractor with extra leverage when it comes to bidding on certain work. Why, then, don't you get the advantage of that extra leverage in the bidding process? You may, but you may not get the dramatically lower bid you might think should be forthcoming.

Negotiated Contracts

Making the additional profit available through the kinds of involvements noted above is one of the less apparent ways the contractor has of remaining competitive and staying in a difficult business. To the extent necessary to win the bid award, the savvy contractor will share his/her cost advantage with you, the Owner, but only by giving up the narrowest possible difference in price between himself and the nearest competitor. It sometimes happens that the bidder with the greatest margin to work with makes a bad guess and becomes a runner-up, making losers out of both you and the contractor. One of the ways to avoid the possibility of this outcome, and to gain more of the available margin, is to interview several contractors, and to negotiate a contract with one of them.

The negotiated contract is a frequently used option for many in the business of letting construction contracts. As its name implies, the agreement involves discussions between two parties, leading to an agreement to perform work. The quality of this negotiation lies in the ability of the contractor to understand the level of work required, and the belief on the part of the Owner that a contractor has been selected who can satisfactorily perform the work at the lowest cost. The latter determination is brought about through the Owner's due diligence; much of this can be accomplished through conversations with local contractors, and others outside of, and apart from, the bidding process. During any such conversations, it is not unwise to let it be known that the Owner is open to any reasonable negotiation.

Document preparation and the Owner/Contractor agreement

These documents will be prepared by an architect in the office of your design professional. They will be signed and stamped by an architect licensed to practice in your jurisdiction. It is not necessary that these two be the same person, but the stamping and signing professional is the one who is accepting complete responsibility for the documents, which will probably consist of:

- An Owner/Contractor Agreement
- Plans and Drawings
- Conditions of the Contract
- Technical Specifications
- Bidding Requirements

A sample of the Owner/Contractor Agreement, developed and copyrighted by the American Institute of Architects, may be obtained, for a very nominal charge, at your local office of the AIA. This form is in common use in the design and construction industries. Like all such contracts, it should be reviewed carefully and, as noted on the face of the AIA blank agreement, consultation with an attorney is encouraged with respect to its use. The agreement form assumes a certain amount of preparatory discussion between principals, including a determination of the preferred method of payment by the Owner, such as cost of the work plus a fee or stipulated sum. There are no blanket observations to be made about these two methods of payment, since each has its appropriate place in a given set of circumstances; each can be modified to fit specific circumstances. For more information concerning these contract agreements and general procedures for construction bidding, a pamphlet entitled *Recommended Guide for Competitive Bidding Procedures and Contract Awards for Building Construction* is also available from the AIA, 1735 New York Avenue, N.W., Washington, D.C. 20006.

Plans and drawings

All of the Plans and Drawings reviewed in this chapter and in our discussion of the **Design Professional** (see **PART I—Chapter 3**), will be included in finished form in the Bidding Documents package. They consist of:

- Partition plans
- Power and telephone plans
- Mechanical, electrical, and plumbing system plans
- Reflected ceiling, or lighting plans
- Plans, schedules and details for:
    - Structure—architectural detail, etc.
    - Millwork—coffee bars, cabinets, etc.
    - Finishes—wall & floor covering, etc.
    - Doors and hardware
    - Other features

Depending on the size and nature of your project, drawings may combine different kinds of information on the same sheet, for the sake of easier handling by the tradespersons. These presentations and combinations vary from one practitioner to another. As a result they require close review by the User/Owner, prior to signing. As we noted earlier, all of the information on these drawings should directly reflect your program of facility requirements.

Conditions of the contract

Conditions of the Contract are textual in nature. They serve to explain and detail the particular circumstances under which the Owner and contractor are willing to conclude their contract. The bulk of these are referred to as General Conditions and, as they appear in AIA documents, they describe a wide variety of circumstances, rights and responsibilities, acts, etc. that affect and or control this kind of work just about anywhere.

Like any other portion of the contract, these can be modified by supplementary conditions that are intended to augment the general conditions in ways reflecting your locale, your site, the unique aspects of your project and your contractual arrangements. The General Conditions, as they appear in the AIA contract documents, are claimed to be widely used in and generally accepted by the industry —they are approved by the Associated General Contractors of America. Nevertheless, we suggest that our User/Owner scrutinize this portion of the contract document as carefully as he/she might any other with strong financial, technical and legal implications. Make such changes in them as appear to be necessary to protect User interests.

Technical specifications

These may also come in the form of written text, which might be augmented by a drawing or diagram from time to time. They are included when it is necessary to detail a component of the work in a way that is not suitable for the documents described above—in the case of carpeting, for example, when the composition, fabrication, coloring, weaving, etc., of the surface fiber and its backing are of critical importance to the User.

Similarly, such a specification might describe the required characteristics of wall-covering or millwork, or a mechanical component of your installation such as a dishwasher, waste disposal unit, elevator, door closer, exhaust, etc. These specifications are often inserted in the bidding documents in the form of a tear-sheet or brochure, etc., provided by their manufacturer, a procedure which can be acceptable if the information provided is what the User needs to evaluate the installation. This procedure is preferred over that of furnishing the User with a generic description of an item which can vary substantially in manufacturing detail and quality from one maker to another.

As mentioned earlier, bidding documents (i.e.: construction documents) will be much the same whether your project is bid or not. But those items that will not be necessary for the negotiated contract will be the papers referred to as bidding *requirements*. These are necessary to the business of administering the process of bidding itself, and may consist of an advertisement, and/or an invitation to bidders, instructions to bidders, a bid form, and provisions for changes and addenda, etc. The User/Owner architect is normally considered to be the person responsible for the administration of the bid process and the preparation of these papers. The cost of this service may be minimal when the need for the bid process is identified early and it is included in the original menu of services for which the User contracts the architect.

THE LEASE AGREEMENT

In our earlier discussion of **Costs and Budgets**, we apologized to those readers who, in realizing the relocation of their organization, would enter into a contract to buy or build a piece of commercial property. We did so because we spend a lot of time talking about tenants and leasing, and not a whole lot about buying. We pointed out the nature of the difference between the two transactions and how the sale-purchase agreement is the terminal point of your due diligence, as a buyer. As we have pointed out on a couple of occasions, the thrust of your concerns as a buyer/owner takes on a substantially different orientation from that of the tenant once the sale transaction is complete.

The User/tenant, on the other hand, must perform the same due diligence, and then enter into a contract that takes on a life of its own and binds its participants to considerable mutual obligations over a long period of time. It is a contract which, at its best, establishes a partnership between two parties who have much to offer each other, and who are willing to enter into an exchange with a true sense of shared responsibility.

It is a contract which, at its worst, is dogmatic and rapacious, violating, if not the letter of the law, the laws of good-will, trust, common-sense, and fairness. It is a contract that has come to us, unaltered and undiluted, from the Sheriff of Nottingham and the days of Sherwood Forest and Robin Hood. It is grounded in the ancient laws against poaching and for the landlord whose rights over his tenants were absolute and unsparing of property or life.

This contract is called a Lease. If there is any question in your mind about who puts it together, who creates its terms and its language, establishes its biases and its points of view, and determines the behavior of its signatories, it is decidedly *not* the User/Tenant.

The quality of lease language

This combination of historical characteristics, reflecting another time and another way of life, plus a viewpoint inherently protective of the rights of the property owner, work to give the lease document a flavor unlike that of any other in the lay person's experience. It is a document still redolent with the social values of entitlement, position and a language, starting with the word *landlord*, which grew out of Parliamentary law and serves to express those values very well.

"It is essential to the relationship of landlord and tenant, whether created by lease or otherwise, that the occupancy of the tenant be in subordination of the rights of the landlord" is a textbook summary of a tiny portion of the code of the state of California. It is an unequivocally clear and correct statement of the contemporary tenant/landlord relationship. It is a way of saying what every tenant knows: establishing tenant rights in a lease agreement is critical because, for starters, you do not have any; it is an uphill battle all the way to get them.

Where the purpose of language elsewhere may be to clarify or edify, the apparent purpose of the language of leases is to confuse. Actually words are the least of our problems with lease agreements. In addition to the mandatory sprinklings of hereofs and wherefores and hereinafter defineds—they seldom are—we see curious things like indemnification, subrogation, eminent domain, estoppel, metes and bounds, prorate parts and proportionate shares, and other words and phrases that are not a part of our everyday usage, but which are not beyond our grasp, all other things being equal, which they are decidedly not.

Be alert for language which, intentionally or otherwise, can have more than one meaning, or whose meaning is obscured by mountains of intervening detail or ambiguous words and phrases. No excuse is adequate to relieve a landlord from the responsibility to provide a Tenant with intelligible lease language. The innocent-sounding phrase, *time is of the essence*, is a sample of the many offenders of lease language clarity. It is a phrase that has seen widespread usage in English literature and speech, and might be said to be in the public domain. There is nothing in that usage, or in the common meaning of those words, which would indicate a criticality of day and hour, but when used anywhere in the lease document, the phrase signifies a legal requirement for absolute conformity to all date and time references in the document. This is not the creation of a single wayward landlord or attorney; it is a part of an ordained and time-honored system of legal obfuscation.

Needles, haystacks and no-punctuation pages

There is an essential characteristic to the language of all leases in which lawyers delight. It is the no-punctuation-page; most leases that have been in the hands of an attorney will have one or more of them. They probably originate in the lawyerly notion that there is only one way to—safely—write a set of assumptions and that once that is done it is best not to disturb their meaning by separating them from subordinate and related material with interruptions like commas and periods. The result is just like the windy sentence we used to describe this phenomenon: the appendages to the original set of assumptions weigh them down, scramble and bury them.

Another questionable pleasure is that of hunting for all the other places some key word or phrase may be repeated or referenced, and thereby implicated in another context. For example, searching for all of the events of default in a lease is one such pastime that has very serious overtones. If the landlord wishes to subordinate the rights of the tenant in the strictest sense of our textbook quote above, any violation of any term of the lease can become an event of default, and trigger the severe measures provided for it.

Misinterpretations hurt both sides

It is not always the intent of the landlord to create ambiguities or to cause certain outcomes as a result of an interpretation of unintended lease language. Often, it is the landlord who is also trapped by this language and who, as a result, must backtrack quickly to limit the damage done by misinterpretations. Compounding the language problem, or making it more acute, can be the great distance between principals in the initial transaction due to geography, the passage of time or multiple layers of bureaucratic responsibility.

In many cases, the lease document becomes the only record of an agreement between absent principals who, were they present and so disposed, might conceivably enlighten the interpretation of a poorly written lease. Sadly, the history of the lease tells us, time and again, that even when the principals *are* present and able to respond when a question arises, their recollection is faulty or spotty or biased. They are human, after all. And all parties concerned still have to interpret the meaning of a document written in their native language.

There are a couple of valuable lessons about lease language:

(1) It is not incumbent on you to subscribe to the landlord's lease in the form and language in which it is currently written, and

(2) It is critical to the partnership you are forming with the Lessor that you (the Lessee) feel you have the most complete understanding possible of the language of the agreement you are about to sign.

The lay view of lease structure: more alphabet soup.

Leases are fat, over-ripe concoctions of which many in the legal profession are proud. Though we felt strongly moved to call in a favorite attorney to tell us how they are put together, we did not succumb to that temptation. The lease is a tool for communication between two entrepreneurs. So, this is a business-person's view, a layman's presentation garnished with the experience of multiple encounters with this dinosaur of contemporary real estate.

The lease is referred to, formally and ponderously, as a document—a paper setting forth a number of ideas, describing an agreement, illuminating or affirming a set of concepts, etc., and fixing them in the record, so to speak, for some period of time.

The Bill of Rights is a document, as is the mortgage on your house, your credit card agreement, and your lease. Their common denominator is a kind of literary anarchy. With the exception of our first example, a paragon of clarity in comparison, these documents have no beginning, middle or end—no order and no organization. Though they employ sentences and paragraphs, read from left to right, and have first and last pages, their content is alphabet soup. They are intended to record very important information for the world but nobody in the world can find the important information needed from them in something approximating a reasonable period of time—if at all.

Whose lease? Yours or the landlord's?

The lease agreement has only recently become thought of as a classroom text might be: with simple explanations of purpose, intent and the train of thought to be followed, and a sequentiality that is something more than using every character, major and minor, in the Roman and Arabic alphabets. Because the commercial lease has grown in length, if not in meaning, in recent years, landlords, their attorneys and agents—all of whom must spend a great deal of time with this instrument of the renting process—have been clamoring for greater simplicity in it. This, coupled with the fact that the User/tenant who pays for this luxurious document in rent dollars has a right to clarity in it, gives you ample cause to demand it. And demand you must, because the tradition behind obscure lease language is powerful.

In the **Documenting** section of **PART II—DOING IT**, we include a step that suggests substitution of your organization's lease form for that of the landlord. This is a good option for the organization involved in regularly recurring renting in multiple locations, especially when sole tenancy is involved or the location selected is considerably less sophisticated about lease preparation than you are. In other circumstances, it is an approach that can cause the average User headaches and hard work.

Many readers will consider a relocation to a multiple tenant site: an office building, shopping mall, industrial park, etc., or to a site operated as one of many by a professional commercial landlord. In these cases, the landlord's lending partners will have requested a consistent lease format, to establish rents and/or shares of expenses, etc.,in an equitable manner. The tenant who wants to negotiate the best possible terms for a rental in one of these properties will meet far less resistance doing so in the context of the landlord's lease.

The look of the Lease; starting with the basics

At first glance, the look of the lease document can tell you a great deal about the quality and intent of the owner of the property being proposed to you. Whether you are leasing 500 square feet or 500,000, it should be printed in clear, legible black type on white, letter-size paper. At a minimum, it should contain the following components, in approximately this order:

- A **Cover** or **Title page**, noting the nature of the agreement, a date, the names of the principals, the Civil Code and/or statutes under which the lease is drawn, and other information that is required on this page by local law

- A **Table of Contents**, listing every article and attachment in the agreement, with its corresponding page and paragraph number

- A **Summary** of the key business terms of the lease referencing the specific language of the lease

- **Definitions** of key words and terms used in the lease

- A **Notices** page, or list of the names and addresses of key participants in the lease process

- A **Lease Body**, containing the pages, sections, articles, paragraphs, etc., comprising the lease agreement, in the order stated in the Table of Contents

- A **Signature Page**, with blanks for the signatories clearly identified by the names of their organization, authority, title and/or position and handwritten date

- **Exhibits, Appendices, Attachments and Addenda** in the order noted in the Table of Contents and clearly referencing their content and purpose

This kind of formatting of the lease is common, though certainly not universal, and represents a minimal attempt to organize complex material. If you find this outline useful but encounter objections to it on the part of local landlords or their agents, ask if those objections are legal in nature. If they are not, and you want a lease document that does not triple the man-hours you have to spend wading through the language of your agreement, ask for it in a language and form agreeable to you.

Beyond appearances: the organization of lease content

We noted in our earlier discussion of **Lawyers, PART I—Chapter 3**, that there are some general observations one can make about the lease contract. Perhaps the first is that there are no two alike and certainly no such thing as a standard lease. Even in instances where one has an opportunity to compare leases in the same building, emanating from the same landlord, there can be enough difference between any two to suggest a great danger in skipping over seemingly familiar or repetitive clauses.

We also pointed out that one can distinguish between those parts of the lease that deal with scheduled payments of money and those parts that deal with events which may or may not occur. Thus, every commercial lease will address:

- **Business Terms**, which include discussions of rent, operating costs, escalation, tenant improvement costs and allowances, etc., and the formulas and terms which work to modulate those costs in any way

- **Contingencies**, which include discussions of the distribution of the proceeds of insurance, actions and remedies in the event of default, responses to Acts of God and the exercise of eminent domain, assignments and subletting, etc.

Interwoven throughout the lease and in many respects supporting those Business Terms and Contingencies are provisions for necessary services, the establishment of responsibilities, and the administration of the agreement. Thus, every commercial lease will also include:

- **Service Components**, which describe the conditions, terms and rules of the use of the property and the premises, the various services to be provided, and the manner and conditions under which they are provided

- **Responsibility Components**, which point out who takes care of the property, how it can be altered or repaired or damaged or sued, who provides the remedies and how

- **Administrative Components**, which provide for a regulated means of communication between the principals, and between them and a large supporting cast of financial partners, employees, contractors, agents, other tenants, and the general public.

The following discussion will expand on these categories and the more frequently seen clauses in the commercial lease. A look at the *workletter* and other important elements of the Addenda to the lease follows.

Business Terms

Remember that you are reading a lease prepared by a landlord and/or given to you in behalf of a landlord. If you, the prospective tenant, find a statement, alteration, or omission that is questionable in terms of your understanding of your agreement, the likelihood is that it has been deliberately made in the interests of the landlord. If you fail to raise the question that comes to your mind, that failure or little oversight can come back to bite you.

Also remember that you are dealing exclusively with the meaning of the written word, and not with what someone has said, in conversation, to you or to someone else.

Definitions prepared by the landlord are intended to limit a concept, not define it. Look for important omissions in the lease definitions of the building, the project, the premises, the parking garage, and other facilities or parts of facilities to which you are supposed to have a right. Some definitions may be overly expansive, like those for operating expenses and taxes. These are charged back to you and should have specific limitations attached to them.

Square feet, rentable area, net rentable area, building rentable area, etc.,should be clearly defined and the relationship of one to the other should be clear to the reader. Check the math on the figures given to you; see that they correspond to architectural drawings and measurements.

The tenant's proportionate share represents the tenant's rentable area divided by the total building or project rentable area. This percentage figure is used to calculate your share of monthly operating expenses and other costs. It should be scrutinized. Be aware of who your neighbors are, what they do, and how your building is used. Determine whether you are you paying for the operation and maintenance of storage or loading dock facilities, outdoor or atrium food service and retail facilities, or public meeting room facilities, etc., which accrue, for all intents and purposes, to the exclusive benefit of others.

Business Terms; more about rent

Rent figures appear differently in landlord proposals than they do in landlord leases. Check the math. Make sure monthly and annual rental figures correspond to the rates and square-footage figures proposed to you. Look for an exact statement of the rentals due on a monthly, annual and term basis. Verify the size of the total lease obligation. Ask your attorney for a clear statement of the local statutes relating to your contract and lease obligations, in the event your organization is unable to fulfill those obligations at some future date. If you are being asked to provide a guarantee of rent, make sure its terms are not more damaging than the those of the lease or local statutes.

Additional rent is the often-used catch-all for payment of operating expenses, taxes and insurance, etc., that are billed with rent, and for the payment of extra-ordinary expenses like repairs and alterations. Unlike rent, some items of additional rent can, reasonably, fall into dispute. Since non-payment of rent constitutes an event of default, the non-payment or delay in reimbursement of an often insignificant amount can cause disproportionately serious results, unless lease language is appropriately adjusted.

Any debate over the nature and amounts of operating expense is pointless unless the landlord who controls the record of them is prepared, not only to release that record for inspection (i.e., allow an audit), but to maintain it in a business-like manner. The tenant right to audit should expressly include the right to inspect invoices for goods and services.

If you anticipate them prior to lease signing, future benefits can be provided in the form of renewal rights and the right to expand your premises. The latter is usually a consideration during the firm term of the lease, and often involves the reasonable need of the tenant for contiguous space, something the landlord will be reluctant to offer. The tenant right to renew the lease may be surprisingly easy to achieve, but it will be a toothless clause without some landlord commitment to an acceptable rental or a fair formula for determining one.

Contingencies: the unlikely events clauses

We refer to the contingency language of the lease as the unlikely events clauses because the events provided for do not occur very often, even though we spend a great deal of our time preparing for them. They are, of course, of prime interest to the insurers, actuaries and attorneys who have to wrestle with their terms.

Principal among this category of lease terms are those relating to the event that all parties are initially certain cannot happen: the default of one or another of the parties. An event of default is one in which the lessee or lessor fails to perform some act promised by the lease agreement—or performs it badly—and, as a result, actuates a remedy also provided for in the lease. The most grievous offense is considered to be the non-payment of rent, and the most painful remedy, the deprivation of tenant rights to the use of the premises.

A series of remedial steps are usually provided for between the one act and the other, to allow the parties opportunities for correction of the deficiency. The User/tenant should pay particular attention to the timing of these steps, as written in the lease. Where notice is to be given, be sure enough time is allowed for that notice to be received and a response formulated and returned. If the notice must travel to a distant headquarters office, or response involves a search of tenant or landlord records for a lost or misfiled payment, sufficient time should be provided. Even when the lease appears reasonable in the eyes of both landlord and tenant, a dispute can arise that cannot be resolved through direct negotiation. Anticipate these occurrences and see that arbitration is provided for in the lease.

The terms of the lease regarding insurance and subrogation, eminent domain, destruction or damage to the property, and Acts of God are important in determining how you and your organization fare after such an occurrence. Your contract for the lease of premises always has value for the landlord who, under certain circumstances, can realize that value in the event of catastrophe and loss of property without replacing your much needed workplace unless your lease provides for it.

Service Components

The use to which the tenant is allowed to put the premises is defined early in the lease and, as with other landlord definitions, tends to be limiting in its scope. This stems from rather ancient landlord experiences with tenant tradesmen who used to occupy a property under a certain acceptable guise, only to alter it subsequently to something nefarious, or odious to other tenants and neighbors. We suggest to both tenant and landlord that those days and circumstances have largely disappeared in modern America. If your organization is openly engaged in a set of entrepreneurial activities that could expand with growth, something of interest to all landlords, the use definition in your lease should be expanded to encompass those possibilities.

The services to be provided by the landlord should be completely spelled out and should include some reasonable standard of performance. That is, there should be some way to measure what clean is, and how often the elevator or air-conditioning will break down.

The hours and days of service should be well defined and acceptable to the tenant. The landlord may appear to be accommodating by offering to provide 24-hour service every day of the year, when the reality of that service is that on weekends, holidays and after-hours—all of landlord choosing—it is being charged to the tenant at overtime rates.

What happens if the landlord fails to provide a service, or to provide one adequately or in a timely manner? The tenant may want to withhold all or a portion of rent. This can sometimes seem like drastic action, particularly when the consequences of non-payment of rent are so onerous. (You may withhold rent for the best reasons in the world and find yourself in default). When the circumstances are such that it seems practical to do so, the tenant can hire and pay for such a service and charge that cost back to the landlord, provided the lease allows such action. The lease language dealing with this kind of provision is referred to as self-help, and its insertion in any tenant lease is recommended.

Every commercial property comes equipped with building rules, the rough equivalent of housekeeping rules or rules of deportment, a violation of which can, when the lease is interpreted closely, represent an event of default. They are referenced in the lease, but actually appear in an attachment to it, which is frequently missing and often overlooked. They should be examined closely for items that violate the nature or intent of your lease.

Attachments to and Alterations of the premises by the tenant may be permitted by the landlord with the proviso that the premises are restored to their original condition upon vacating, or that tenant built-ins become the property of the landlord. The tenant is well advised at the time the lease is being prepared to attempt to make a determination of his/her probable interest in this regard, and arrange the language of the lease accordingly.

Along with the payment of rent and landlord permission to use the premises comes the right of the tenant to the quiet enjoyment thereof, and/or the non-disturbance of the tenant therein. Perhaps surprisingly for the average tenant, these do not represent rights which automatically appear in the landlord lease. Equally surprising is that they are seldom high on the tenant list of requirements, when they should be. Without the innocent sounding language of the non-disturbance or quiet enjoyment paragraph, the landlord is free to enter into an agreement to finance, sell or otherwise obligate the future operation of the property without regard to your good standing as a rent-paying tenant. The simple insertion of this highly recommended language in your lease makes it incumbent on any new owner to observe the terms of that lease. (See the Subordination provisions of your lease.)

Service components: the right to sub-lease

One of the benefits of your lease is provided for in the paragraphs dealing with your right to sublease or assign your premises. It is also one that falls back on tradition and which the average modern landlord wishes would disappear altogether. As a result, the language providing this right is highly restrictive and designed to prevent you from going into the real estate business at the landlord's expense. Since your intent is to concern yourself with your business, you will want to assure yourself of the right to lease out a portion, or perhaps all of your premises when you have to move or expand or withdraw from the area, or provide a sister company or a subsidiary with necessary space. If you stand to make a small profit on the transaction, the landlord will want all or a big part of it. But there is no particularly good reason for him to share in this windfall. Being a sub-landlord does not come without considerable responsibility and expense. Sharing your excess rental income could very well leave you with the kind of deficit you were trying to avoid by sub-leasing in the first place.

The landlord will also want the right to withhold approval of your sub-tenant and it is the opinion of some that even when approval is not preceded by the word *reasonable*, many courts will insist that the landlord must be so. This is not the case in some jurisdictions, and unless he otherwise expresses a willingness to be reasonable in the lease agreement, the landlord can be entirely unreasonable in this matter of subleasing. In short, see that the word reasonable modifies landlord approval in your sublease language. While you are about it, see that that word is used to modify any and all landlord actions provided for in your lease.

The traditional distinction between the assignment and the sublease has become blurred with the not unexpected insistence of the contemporary landlord that the primary tenant's name remains on the lease in either case. There are places and circumstances, of course, where it is beneficial for all parties that an assignment of all the rights and obligations of the tenant's lease be made in lieu of a sublease.

The Responsibility Components of the Lease Agreement

Whether it is the lease you have been operating under for years or the one that has just fallen into your hands, the responsibility for compliance with an overwhelming number of its provisions lies with you, the tenant. You have been granted an immense privilege—your landlord would have you believe—in being provided sanctuary in a mega-million-dollar building. As a result, you must protect its owner from possible damage to it, and to their financial interest in it.

In recent years, the once lowly tenant has, with some success, taken the position of a risk-sharing partner in the obligations of the lease. Where the lease calls for limitless liability to fall on the tenant's shoulders, the tenant can suggest that the landlord bear a similar burden. Where the landlord asks for the tenant to indemnify in every conceivable set of circumstances, the landlord can be asked to respond in kind. Where the lease can ask the tenant to perform a certain task or provide a notice or pay a bill in X days, and the landlord is given X plus sixty days to perform the same task, with express reservations about whether that party needs to perform the task at all, a process of equalization of treatment can take place.

The great debate about responsibility has come about largely because the private commercial building with access limited to a privileged few has become a public building with access to all. In spite of their exotic and expensive security systems, building owners have experienced an exponential growth in trouble-makers and law-suit seekers. The assumed culprit used to be the tenant and his grubby visitors, so leases were written accordingly. Unlike the old days, this convenient formula is no longer applicable.

Administrative Components of the Lease Agreement

The balance of the paragraphs in the body of your lease document are, for the most part, administrative. They deal with seemingly minor, but very important details like the names and addresses of people and organizations to whom notices are to be sent. Since these can concern actions involving tenant dollars, it is important that their receipt is not delayed by erroneous address information.

The administrative components of the lease include minor nuisances like the Estoppel certificate that the landlord asks that every tenant complete to demonstrate to financial partners, bankers, buyers, etc., that tenants are really paying rent. It resembles a one-page summary of the lease and should not commit the tenant to anything not already detailed in the lease.

Abandonment, as it appears in the commercial lease, is a term that implies leaving with no intention of returning and can be used to give the landlord the right to take over your premises if you are seen moving furniture about. You may wish to move some furniture, or take some away, or not use the premises for a period of time, or use the premises seasonally, etc. You should be able to do any of these things if you continue to pay rent and have a reasonable definition of abandonment in your lease.

There used to be a curious code of honor among landlords with respect to breaching the sanctity, so to speak, of the tenant's premises by entering at will. It was not done, except in the most dire emergency. Today, the landlord, in the form of security guards, building engineers, maintenance and repair contractors, and housekeeping personnel, is there almost as many hours as the tenant. The landlord cannot be faulted for attending to his/her responsibilities, but these constant visits can be intrusive unless lease language concerning Entry by Lessor is designed to control them.

In an orderly lease progression, as the term winds down, the tenant may elect to vacate rather than renew. He advises the landlord of his intent, by notice, in accordance with the lease, and all parties concerned expect that the tenant will be gone, on or about the day of lease termination. Very often circumstances conspire to make a delay inevitable. The lease provides for this eventuality in its Holding Over language. This clause allows the tenant to stay on—provided adequate notice of intent is given—but usually at a substantially increased rental rate. The traditional rationale for the higher rate is the unscheduled delay in new rent starts to be suffered by the landlord, plus the notion that a long line of tenants eager to pay elevated rentals is waiting for the opportunity to lease the space to be vacated. Prior to lease signing, question whether this rationale is applicable, particularly at the Holding Over rate requested.

The Workletter: the lease guide for construction

The traditional term for that portion of the lease governing the construction of the premises, or the work, is the Workletter. The workletter gets a brief mention in the lease body, where reference is made to its location in the lease addenda, attachments or appendices. Its location in this out-of-the-way place is not due to its lack of importance—its subject matter can account for 25% or more of the value of the lease—but to its unwieldy size and nature.

Because it provides for preparation of the premises prior to occupancy by the tenant, the workletter does several important things. It:

- Describes how the premises are to be built
- Describes responsibility for payment
- Establishes a lease commencement date
- Determines when rent payment starts

How the premises are built

There are three principal approaches, or means by which the various players involved can accomplish the construction of the premises:

A.   The Landlord builds all tenant spaces;

B.   The Landlord builds all building standard work and the tenant contractor builds all above building standard work;

C.   The tenant contractor builds all tenant spaces to tenant specifications.

In **(A)** and **(B)**, the workletter will provide for what is perceived by some to be a rather cumbersome procedure of task-deadline-approval-deadline, task, etc., in its schedule for task performance. To accomplish the latter with some semblance of order and fairness, an intricate system of debits and credits for tenant delay and landlord delay is established, in conjunction with the schedule for design and construction.

In **(B)**, where there is a division of project responsibility, there is always an opportunity for conflict between the two contractors and the claims of their principals. Since the workletter is prepared by the landlord, its language in this regard is heavily protective of the latter's desire to complete the landlord portion of the work quickly and expeditiously. If left unedited, this language can leave the tenant's contractor in the untenable position of having to re-do or work over already completed work, to schedule work in costly bits and pieces and/or to charge the resulting excessive costs back to the tenant/client.

In **(C)**, the bulk of the workletter is greatly reduced, as is the confusion often generated by it, since the burden of planning, design and construction is placed entirely with the tenant. The workletter sets forth procedures allowing the landlord to approve and verify the tenant selection of contractors, including the design professional, and to check the nature and progress of the work.

Responsibility for payment

A simple statement may be made in the body of the lease under the workletter or similar heading (e.g.,preparation of the premises; construction of the premises, etc.) concerning responsibility for payment of tenant improvements. A typical statement would acknowledge landlord responsibility for improvements within the context of the building standard workletter, provided in a lease attachment. This workletter would be the briefest possible statement of the landlord's intent to install so-many walls and doors, and carpet, etc., with the materials listed in another attachment, usually called building standards.

In **(A)**, payment may have been arranged prior to lease execution, to allow for all of the landlord's improvement costs to be paid for in rent. Since there is always a possibility that the tenant can ask for some improvement not contemplated by the landlord, the workletter provides for a system of approval, voucher and payment for this excess work. Landlord work is seldom done in combination with a tenant improvement allowance.

In (**B**), the landlord's standard work, typically, will be paid for in rent, the balance for over-standard work being billed directly to the tenant to be paid for in the manner agreed to by the tenant and the tenant contractor, and/or the landlord, if the latter is in fact the contractor. The landlord may have agreed to a limited improvement allowance for over-standard work which the tenant can apply for this purpose. Obviously, a conflict of interest exists when the landlord provides an allowance from which the landlord is reimbursed as contractor. The fact that the landlord may hire a third party contractor of the landlord's choice to perform this work does little to relieve our concern about this conflict.

In (**C**), the tenant is responsible for making all contractor payments, all or some portion of which may be reimbursed by the landlord/tenant-agreed tenant improvement allowance.

Years ago, when the concept of the allowance came into practice, landlords limited its use to strictly utilitarian kinds of alterations or additions to the building in question. In the intervening years, the practice has broadened. The allowance has become a *tenant inducement*, allowing the tenant a freer rein with unique interior design treatments or a fund from which to purchase needed furniture and equipment. When the landlord provides an allowance for this use, the tenant should not be surprised to see a whopping rate of interest incorporated in it.

Lease commencement and the start of rent payments

These two dates, which may or may not coincide, are closely intertwined with the progress of the work described in the workletter. They are dealt with in the early part of the lease body, where they may appear to be set down in rather definitive fashion, but are clearly a function of when the premises are in a condition to be occupied. This, in turn, may be a function of the terms of the workletter.

In (**A**) and (**B**) above, we noted the inclusion of a more or less carefully detailed schedule of tasks to be performed by landlord and tenant to the conclusion of construction and the acceptance of the premises by the tenant. The latter is predicated on an almost, but not quite final, inspection of them by the tenant at the invitation of the landlord, since the terms of the workletter require acceptance upon substantial completion of the workletter work. This latter term signifies a level of completion which allows the tenant to take possession of the premises, and to start using them without any noticeable interference from some minor ongoing construction work.

Acceptance of the premises may or may not trigger lease commencement and the start of rent payments, or of the rental period, if the lease agreement provides for an abatement of rent. In leases that have been so formulated by the landlord—and neglected by the unknowing tenant—a lease may commence without any regard to whether the premises are ready for occupancy. This is not an infrequent occurrence when the workletter calls for a combined landlord-tenant construction effort as noted in (**B**) above. When the workletter and the lease recognize the tenant need to complete its work after completion of landlord work, acceptance can occur with an allowance for the time necessary for the tenant to complete its work before the start of rent payments. An example of the order in which this confusing array of steps may fall is shown below for the three tenant/landlord work arrangements identified above:

	(A)	(B)	(C)
1. Delivery of the Premises			●
2. Start Construction	●	●	●
3. Complete Construction	●	●	●
4. Punch-List the work	●	●	●
5. Notice of Substantial Completion	●	●	●
6. Tenant Inspection of the Work	●	●	
7. Tenant Acceptance of the Work	●	●	
8. Delivery of the Premises	●	●	
9. Start of Tenant Work	●	●	
10. Completion of Tenant Work	●	●	
11. Acceptance of the Premises	●	●	●
12. Tenant Takes Occupancy	●	●	●
13. Lease Commences	●	●	●

Notice that Delivery of the Premises occurs before anything else in situation (**C**), where the tenant must be free to work unencumbered by the landlord or landlord contractors. The tenant will want to insist in this case that, since the premises are of no use in the lease sense of the term, the lease should not commence until improvements are substantially completed. The landlord may insist, in turn and not unreasonably, that this lapse of time be restricted to that needed for completion of the equivalent of standard improvements. Before the tenant starts construction in these circumstances, an assurance should be provided by the Landlord that certain minimum base building conditions have been met.

As you can see, in the best of circumstances, the lease—or your rental abatement period—will begin, along with the companion requirement for rental payments, on or after the day on which you occupy the premises. If you are not attentive to the details of your workletter agreement, lost in the oft ignored pages of lease addenda, it could begin well before that time and cost you in unnecessary construction dollars in the bargain.

Addenda and Exhibits: the tail that sometimes wags the dog.

Perhaps surprisingly, those papers that are not considered a part of the lease body and, like a tail, are simply attached to the end of it, can have as great an impact on the transaction as anything in the lease, proper. From the User/tenant perspective, these papers might be said to fall into three groups:

- Support Documents
- Workletter Papers
- Sideletters

Exhibits that develop the official and legal aspects of the transaction or amplify and detail portions of it are part of what are referred to as support documents. These would almost invariably include a legal description of the property underlying the building(s) you are leasing, a to-scale site plan of the property showing the location and orientation of the improvements on it, and a floor plan of the floor(s) and space(s) your organization is leasing. These three documents are very important. They represent the only place in this costly agreement where you are told where you will be living in relation to the street, the railroad tracks, the setting sun, and the bathroom.

When the landlord and his/her agent make their heated pitch to win your tenancy in their building, they show you slick brochures with certain architectural, site plan and facility information that both of you think is important. You think it ought to be a part of your lease because it represents facility features you are expected to pay rent for. Most often this information does not make its way into the lease. Insist that it appears there as it did in the landlord's marketing brochure, or in the form of an acceptable substitute.

Building rules and regulations and parking facilities may be referenced in the body of the lease. They should appear in the lease addenda in detail, as should a complete specification of janitorial services. Prior to lease signing, the tenant should feel free to recommend additions or alterations to these specifications, when they appear inadequate for a reasonable level of maintenance of the User facility.

The workletter agreement and all of its supporting papers would be found in the addenda or attachments to the lease. Since there is much cross-referencing from workletter to lease body, care must be taken to see that these references are made correctly and stated accurately.

Sideletters are the kind of anomaly in the lease transaction that should make any law-abiding User/tenant uneasy. They are a way of saying that there is something important to the transaction, that it wants to be documented, and that no one can find a comfortable place for it. It may have to do with an exchange of property that is a part of the lease consideration. It may concern the assumption of some other lease, or a mortgage obligation, or a unique concession on the part of one or another party to the transaction. It generally concerns something with a short-term or one-time effect, like a rental abatement, and may be executed at the request of financial partners or banking interests.

Administratively, the sideletter and subordinate agreements like it, are often a nightmare to understand, record and manage, and have a disturbing way of getting lost—not being attached to a lease document—at inappropriate times.

Chapter 5

THE LANGUAGE

A morphological stew

The language of relocation is necessarily the language of architecture and construction, real estate and law, of engineers, vendors, haulers and mechanics. It is a complex idiom, rooted deep in the traditions of American industry and, indeed, in the history of building in Western civilization. It is a rich morphological stew, made from the ancient Greek that permeates our architecture and engineering, the Latin building blocks of our laws of property and trade, and all the modern and ancient vernacular of Europe and our own Anglo-Saxon tradition. It is millennia of invention, interpretation and layered nuance, built up stone upon stone, as the western world has been. It is still growing.

But this language of relocation is not pure romance. It is for you to use, and put to work for you, to help you grow and build, and not obstruct or delay or contribute to failure. Because it can do all of the latter by contributing to failures of communication and in this business, the clear conveying of instruction and intent is the essence of success. And what is the price of failure? It may be indicated by the numbers of managers who take on responsibility for relocation of their organization and subsequently lose their jobs. It may be in the seldom recorded stories of delays, cost overruns and things built wrongly that are too expensive or impossible to correct, which negatively contribute to worker attitude and performance.

Good communication is much more than defining words, but a good list of word definitions, such as the Glossary which follows, can help. There are problems with any glossary: each "definition" is built on the shifting sands of current usage, geography, individual interpretation, professional bias and other variables. Many of the terms are also an integral part of a complex discipline that may, itself, be undergoing a sea change. Much of this language is adapted from words and terms in our everyday usage with which we think we are thoroughly familiar, until we are, perhaps not pleasantly, surprised.

Like all glossaries, ours is intended to deal with the terms we have used in this book which need interpretation or suggest a troublesome ambiguity. We hope we have identified those that puzzle you. And we encourage you to look for clarification and to ask questions of your service providers.

A GLOSSARY OF TERMS

Abandonment: In lease terms, abandonment of tenant obligations and/or failure to pay rent, sometimes accompanied by tenant quitting of the premises without notice and with no apparent intent to return.

Abatement of rent: A delay in the payment of rent granted to the tenant by the landlord. It is often erroneously termed "free rent".

Above standard: Usually applied to improvements to tenant space which, in the aggregate, exceed a quantity of items or a dollar value established by the landlord or by tenant-landlord agreement.

Acceptance of the premises: An acknowledgment by the tenant that the leased premises are suitable for occupancy and fulfill the landlord's obligation to provide acceptable premises. The landlord usually requests a written statement to this effect from the tenant to initiate rent payments.

Acoustics: Having to do with the transmission of sound. In the workplace, the characteristics of spaces, materials, surfaces, etc., which modulate sound and/or reduce undesirable noise.

ADA: The Americans with Disabilities Act of 1990. This federal legislation became effective for most businesses in 1992, and requires conformance to a number of criteria affecting the design and construction of workplace facilities.

Add-on factor: One of the terms used to represent the difference between the amount of workspace or floor area represented by the tenant's premises and the larger area upon which rent is paid. Landlords will define this factor in different ways, but the "add-on" is calculated as a percentage of the area of the tenant's premises, or "useable" space.

Additional rent: A term used by many landlords to embrace all of the charges that might be assessable under the terms of a tenant's lease, regardless the amount, frequency of occurrence, etc.

Additional services: In contracts for professional services, those services, usually listed under this heading, that are not included under the terms of the contract and that can be provided at additional cost.

Adjacency: A phrase peculiar to design professionals, and/or those providing programming services, that refers to the proximity of one user function to another and the interrelationships of their needs for "adjacency".

Adze: A rough sturdy iron blade attached to a long handle and used for de-barking logs or other wood lumber shaving tasks.

AIA: The American Institute of Architects, an industry group serving the architectural profession whose members are largely registered architects.

Allowance for tenant improvements: An amount of money or in-kind services contributed by the landlord toward the cost of constructing improvements in tenant premises.

Ambient light: In the workplace, artificial or natural light, of a general or diffuse nature, that might originate with a row of windows, ceiling luminaires, work-station fixtures, etc. It may be designed to complement the function of "task" light.

American National Standards Institute: Or ANSI, an industry organization governed and funded by a combination of national industry and government groups, promulgating elective standards for a wide range of products incorporated in the workplace.

Americans with Disabilities Act: See "ADA".

ANSI: See "American National Standards Institute".

ANSI/HFS 100-1988: The set of ANSI standards adopted from the recommendations of the Human Factors Society, establishing safe limits or design standards for all products destined for human use in the workplace.

Approving agency: Any municipal, county, state or federal body that regulates construction of, or installations in the workplace and whose approval is required before the workplace can be legally occupied and used.

Architect: The person or firm, often registered and/or licensed, responsible by contract to a User for a variety of services related to the planning and design of the workplace.

Architectural engineer: The person or firm licensed to practice engineering in connection with workplace structures, and generally associated with or available through an architect or architectural firm.

As-built drawings: Dimensioned drawings of all or any part of an existing workplace. They may be prepared by a competent design professional immediately following workplace construction or upon selecting or moving into a workplace for which no such drawings exist.

Asking rental: The workspace rental rate, sometimes called "quoted rent", which is more or less indiscriminately advertised by a landlord or agent. The term implies that rent may be negotiated to some lesser amount.

Assignment: In lease terms, the assumption by one party of all of the rights and obligations of tenancy of another, with the approval of the landlord.

Axiometric drawing: In architectural practice, a three-dimensional representation or line drawing of a structure created by projection of orthographic views of the structure. The drawing is characterized by parallel lines rather than the converging lines of the "perspective" drawing.

Axonometric drawing: See "Axiometric drawing".

Base building: A commercial building approved for occupancy, prior to the installation of improvements for its tenants.

Base building conditions: The level of completion of the components of the base building, or that portion of one with which the User is concerned, which should be reached before construction of tenant improvements begins.

Base line drawing: In architectural practice, a hard line drawing done on a reproducible medium, carrying basic information, such as names of the principals, site or building outline, etc., common to all or most of the drawings to be done for a given project.

Base rent: Rent less its discretionary components, such as utilities, parking

fees, improvement allowances, etc. See "Quoted rent", "Market rent", "Effective rent".)

Base-year: In the commercial lease, a reference date used to calculate the portion of building operating expenses for which a tenant will be responsible. Under this formula, the tenant may be asked to pay a pro-rata share of the expenses that exceed those accrued in the base year.

Bauhaus: The German school of architecture, art and crafts of the 1920s and 1930s that emphasized the inherent logic and beauty of structure and became synonymous with modern architecture in America in the 1950s, 1960s and 1970s.

Bay: In commercial architecture, the modular unit of a plan or floor defined by structural elements, such as columns and/or walls. Since bay dimensions are consistently used throughout the typical commercial building, they represent important information for the interior planner.

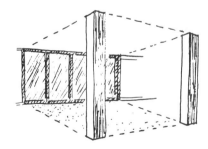

Bid: In commercial construction, the offer presented by a proposing contractor to a developer, landlord, tenant, User, client, etc., referred to as an "Owner", for construction of the work defined by the Owner.

Bidder: In commercial construction, the contractor offering a bid on a construction project, or a sub-contractor on a portion of one.

Bidding documents: The drawings, specifications, documents and instructions, etc., usually prepared by the Owner's architect, which are necessary for the preparation of an accurate bid by interested contractors.

Block plans: In architectural practice, those drawings that are intended to convey the design professional's planning concepts through arrangements of large blocks of architectural space.

Blocking: In interior construction, the material, usually rough lumber placed inside of dry wall construction, used to back up or support millwork, other construction, equipment, etc.

Blue-line Print: In architectural and engineering practice, the common print appearing on photo-sensitive white paper with a dark blue (or black or brown) line produced for working drawings, construction documents, etc. A notable characteristic is the strong ammonia smell that accompanies a freshly made print.

Blueprint: A term in common use that is intended to refer to a print of an architectural drawing. Since the blueprint is no longer made and is now a highly sought after relic, safer usage is "print", or "blue-line print". (They also come in other colors.)

BOMA: The Building Owners and Managers Association, a national industry group primarily concerned with commercial property management techniques and practices in behalf of their membership.

Broker: In commercial real estate, the individual licensed to facilitate a transaction between principals in the sale or leasing of real property.

Broker commission: In commercial real estate, the traditional compensation for the real estate broker, paid by the property owner, and often based on a percentage of the value of the transaction.

Building block: See "module". An architectural metaphor for the units of space involved in building planning and design.

Building Owners and Managers Association: See "BOMA".

Building rules: In multi-tenant commercial buildings, the guidelines established by the landlord for the use of common areas by building tenants. These rules are usually enforced through remedies provided in the typical lease.

Building site: The real property on which the commercial building is, or is planned to be, situated.

Building standard: A term used by commercial building owners to describe the limits of their budget for building components. It can refer to quantities installed (e.g., light fixtures, convenience outlets, etc.) as well as unit prices for such items, and is often indicative of a level of building "quality".

Building rentable area: The space which, in the aggregate, is available for lease in any commercial building.

Built-ins: In lease workletter terms, those items in tenant space that have been constructed by substantial attachments to building structure (e.g., wet counters, executive lavatories, etc.) with the requisite approval of the landlord, and that become the property of the landlord, or require landlord approval for their removal at the termination of the lease.

CADD: Computer Assisted Drafting and Design. In architectural practice, the computer driven equipment used in some planning and design and for the production of architectural plans and drawings.

Cap: In any discussion of recurring costs in the tenant lease (e.g., rent, expenses, parking fees, etc.) the concept of establishing a limit or ceiling to the escalation of such costs.

Ceiling cavity: In architecture and commercial construction, the space remaining between a floor slab and the ceiling hung below it, and which becomes space available for placement of conduit or ductwork, etc., or for the transmission of sound, smoke, odor, etc.

Cellular: In construction, a ceiling, floor, raised floor, etc., that is designed, for purposes of economy and structural rigidity, to be constructed in "egg-crate" fashion of a series of hollow cells.

Certificate of occupancy: C.O. In construction and code compliance, the written certification by the responsible local agency of a building, or tenant premises in a building, that they are suitable and approved for human occupancy.

Change factors: In terms of site or facility evaluation, those characteristics of an organization and its workplace that can alter the viability of any facility for the purposes of the organization.

Chase: In construction, an enclosure for or encasement of conduit, pipe, ductwork, etc., usually carrying some utility from one part of a commercial building to another part of the same building. The chase often represents a vertical "penetration", passing from floor to floor in the building.

Circulation: In interior space programming and planning, the interior space required for the movement of people and equipment. It is most commonly represented by corridors, aisles and hallways, etc.

Clerestory: In current architectural usage, the horizontal row of windows or "lights" arranged immediately below the roof line (or at any ceiling line) of a building.

Client decision time: The time required by the User, for whatever reason, to make required choices or reach decisions concerning work under contract. For construction contractors, professional service providers, vendors and ultimately the User who pays for it, this time/cost factor is second only to production cost in dollar size.

Closing: The formal conclusion of the transaction in the sale of commercial property. The term is less commonly used in leasing, where a relationship between principals continues, following lease execution.

CMU: "Concrete masonry unit". The trade term for any pre-formed brick or cement block used in construction.

Code corridors: In terms of approving public agencies and the Uniform Building Code, the allowable dimensions of interior circulation, and especially exit, corridors.

Computer Assisted Drafting And Design: See "CADD".

Concept plan: In workplace planning and design, any drawing intended to visualize, in the simplest way, the larger, more meaningful, etc., ideas affecting the function and/or appearance of the workplace and its component parts. (See also "block plan")

Conditions of the Contract: In terms of contracts for construction, professional services and vendors, the seldom-read assumptions of the service provider, often buried in the body of the written agreement, intended to define the working relationship between buyer and seller.

Conformance: Usually used with respect to the requirements of approving agencies, and/or the Uniform Building Code, indicating that certain work has or has not been completed in accordance with those requirements.

Consideration: A contract term referring to the payment of something of value, usually money, in return for a service or an agreement to provide a service. A necessary component to the construction of a legally binding contract.

Construction manager: The individual or organization charged by the User or the construction contractor with responsibility for supervising construction.

Construction Specifications Institute: See "CSI"

Consumer Price Index (CPI): See "CPI".

Core: In terms of architecture and commercial building, that portion of a building interior dedicated to general use, such as stairs and elevators, and to building operation and maintenance, etc.

Coring: In construction, drilling that results in the taking of a sample of soil from the building site, or of concrete from a poured slab, for testing purposes, or for the installation of an electrical outlet, etc.

Cost of Occupancy: The sum of all costs associated with a relocation of the workplace and the assumption of new lease or mortgage obligations.

Co-terminous: In tenant lease language, two or more leases sharing a common termination date. Such leases may or may not share the same buildings or landlords, or other lease terms.

CPI: The Consumer Price Index. An average of the costs of certain commodities and products considered by the federal government to be a measure of American consumption. Though it may not bear much relation to such costs, this index is often used to calculate the tenant share of increases in building operating expense.

CPU: In computer terms, "central processing unit": the component of your PC or any data processing system that contains its basic memory.

CSI: The Construction Specifications Institute. A national industry group representing those bearing responsibility for writing the detailed specifications required in building construction.

Cumulative trauma disorders: A quasi-medical catch-all for the variety of aches, pains and permanent injury, usually occurring with the back, neck, arms hands, eyes, etc., which are cumulative in their effect and suffered by increasing numbers of workers in a variety of workplace situations.

Curtain wall: A normally non-load bearing exterior sheathing, which may be solid, transparent or some combination thereof, associated with the design and construction of modern multi-floor building of steel construction.

Custom fabricators: Any of a variety of local shops dedicated to the production of building materials and/or furniture and furnishings made, to unique designs or specifications, and often capable of providing unusual economy and quality.

Default: In the commercial lease, the failure to perform an act or meet an obligation, as required by the lease.

Demising wall: In commercial leasing and construction, the wall built to separate demised premises, usually of double wall or heavier construction than that of other interior walls.

Detail drawing: In architectural practice, the drawing(s) of joints, connections, fastenings, component parts, and other detail necessary to instruct the building contractor. They generally appear grouped (or scrambled) together on one or more sheets of a set of construction drawings with more or less clear reference to other drawings of which the details are a critical part.

Developer: The individual or entity providing the necessary risk capital and assuming responsibility for assembling the various parts of the commercial real estate venture that will result in improvements dedicated to commercial use.

Diffuser: In construction, the visible slotted or perforated grill placed over the end of an appliance or duct at a wall or ceiling surface.

DPE: Direct Personnel Expense. In service contracts, that portion of the formula, usually a "multiple of DPE", for charging the User/client that is attributable to the components of wages or salaries paid by the vendor.

Draft curtain: In commercial building, a construction hung from the underside of a roof or floor structure as a "fire-stop", inhibiting smoke or flame-feeding drafts of air.

Drainage: In construction, the capacity for a building site, or a portion of one, to drain or eliminate standing water. The drainage "system" may be natural due to site slopes and/or soil conditions, or man-made.

Drive-by: A term common to the jargon of real estate brokers who may suggest to their client that they "do a drive-by", or make a quick visual inspection of a candidate property.

Dropped-ceiling: Any ceiling, or portion of one, which is constructed at a height lower than that established for the greater part of the space it is in. The term is also commonly used to refer to the typical commercial hung ceiling which is "dropped" below the underside of the floor above.

Due diligence: Careful scrutiny, examination or study.

Dumb terminal: A rapidly becoming archaic term for a video display terminal equipped to receive and transmit, but not to manipulate data from a central processing unit, (CPU).

Duplex: In electrical construction, the junction box containing two convenience outlets or plugs usually for common low-voltage workplace appliances.

EEOC: Equal Employment Opportunity Commission, a Federal agency.

Effective rent: In commercial real estate brokerage, a term used to identify the cost of rent after adjustments for the cost of tenant improvements, abatements, operating expenses, etc.

Efficiency factor: In architectural practice, the ratio of the useable interior space of a building to its total built area. This factor can vary substantially from one building to another, as well as in its definition by architects and building owners, and should be examined carefully by the User who attempts to derive some useful meaning from it.

Elevation: In architectural practice, a view drawn of any vertical surface of a structure, like a wall.(See also "orthographic projection".)

Eminent domain: The right of the community to take private property for the purposes of the community upon payment of just compensation.

Employment at will: The doctrine at work in most instances of employment in private industry that holds that an employer has a unilateral right to hire and fire.

Entry by Lessor: The right, usually expressed in the typical commercial lease, of the landlord to enter the tenant's premises at any time, with or without notice, for purposes deemed reasonable by the landlord.

Envelope: In architectural practice, the conceptual enclosure of a structure which may differ from the limits of the built structure itself. An uncovered atrium, an arcade or a building setback, etc., may be considered to fall within a given building "envelope".

Ergonometrics: Part of the vocabulary of human factors and product design that refers to the measurement of the human body in attitudes found in a wide variety of work-related human activity.

Ergonomics: Concocted of "ergon" (work) and "nomics" (law). An applied science, conceived in the Nineteenth century and referred to in the mid-Twentieth as "human engineering", involving the study of the human body

in relation to man-made implements to provide product design guidelines that will result in safer and more effective product use.

Errors and Omissions: The term that generally refers to the insurance developed for professional service providers to cover the risks of liability that arise from the performance of their services under contract.

Escalation: In commercial real estate leasing, the term applied to any of a variety of formulas for incrementally increasing tenant rent payments, usually assumed to be for the purpose of compensating for periodic increases in the costs of building operation.

Estoppel: In real estate, a doctrine pertaining to the legitimacy of a claim of ownership, or other fact of real property, that leads someone, like a lender or an investor, to act on that claim. Its significance to the commercial tenant comes with the landlord request for tenant execution of an "estoppel agreement", consisting of a statement of the basic facts of the tenant lease.

Event of default: In terms of the commercial lease, any failure by the principals to perform a duty or to discharge an obligation.

Exclusive: In commercial real estate brokerage, this term is shorthand for the written agreement providing the right, given by the User as a prospective tenant or buyer of real estate, to a broker to represent the former in a real estate transaction. The nature and binding character of the

213

"exclusive" agreement is variable and dependent on the intent of the two parties.

Expense stop: In the lease rental agreement, one of the devices, usually in the form of a fixed dollar amount arrived at in tenant/landlord negotiation, which is available to cap the amount of operating expense reimbursement required from the tenant.

FF&E: Furniture, Fixtures and Equipment. A term of ancient origin for those needing a category for everything in the workplace is "loose" or not an integral part of the building in which it is located.

FOB: A term of the American rail and trucking industries meant to designate the point at which responsibility for a shipment of goods terminates for the shipper and begins for the receiver. Also written fob, F.O.B or "Free on Board".

Facade: In architecture, the exterior front of a building, especially its most important face. From the Latin and Italian for "face".

Facility: In workplace terms, any improvement of real property that may be used for commercial purposes or to facilitate productive work.

Facilities Program: See "Program".

Fee developer: An individual or firm which performs the functions of a developer for a fee. The latter is usually provided by the principals in the ownership of a project. (See "developer.)

Fee maximum: In professional service and construction contracts, the fee arrangement in which a total cost for services is set that is not to be exceeded. Since the User is, theoretically, the sole beneficiary of the provider's efficiency, there are usually some risk-sharing features attached to this fee arrangement by the provider.

Fire-rated: In construction, materials and/or building components such as corridor walls, ceilings, etc.,that meet the strict minimum requirements of the Fire Code.

Fire-wall: See "fire-rated"

Firm term: See "term".

Fixed fee: In professional service contracts, a fixed or inflexible dollar amount agreed to be paid by the User/client for the services provided. The fixed fee is understood to be somewhat higher than a fee arrangement under terms in which the User elects to share some of the risks of the contract. It is closely related to, and sometimes confused with the flexible fee-maximum. (See also "Fee maximum".)

Fixturing: In construction, the process of attaching an element to finished construction, a pendant light fixture, a drinking fountain, etc.

Flex space: In commercial leasing and space planning terms, area within the User's premises that is dedicated to future expansion and that currently may be used for added circulation corridor, storage, visitor work space, etc.

Footcandle: The conventional American Standard (AS) unit of measure of light falling on a surface. One lumen of light energy (luminous flux) produces an *illuminance* of one footcandle or approximately ten "lux", the corresponding metric unit of measure.

Footlambert: An AS unit of measure of *luminance* or the intensity of light reflected from a surface. It is measured in the direction the surface is being viewed since materials such as fabric can exhibit different luminances at different angles of view.

Footprint: In architectural and real estate jargon, the perimeter outline of a building.

Fossil fuel: An energy source that is dug out of the earth, like coal or oil.

Free on Board: See "FOB"

Freehand drawing: Technically, any drawing done without the aid of tools; straightedge, compass, etc. Practically, the "freehand" architectural sketch is often drawn without mechanical aids over a hard line drawing done with them.

Friable: Easily crumbled or pulverized. The term is common now as urban society tries to rid itself of cancer causing "friable" asbestos. The latter is still commonly found in non-friable form as vinyl-asbestos tile (VAT) in many modern buildings.

Functional adjacency: In architectural and facility programming practice, a further refinement or a redundancy of the "adjacency" or proximity of worker functions to one another. (See "Adjacency".)

Furniture systems: Different pieces of furniture, designed to go together as a visual or functional ensemble. In the workplace, the term is most frequently applied to an assembly of desks, cabinets, shelves and lighting, etc., all mounted to supporting panels to make up a work station. Interchangeability of parts, variability in size and configuration, and mobility in the workplace often characterize the furniture system.

GC: See "General Contractor".

General Contractor: (GC) In construction, the person or entity hired to take responsibility for all aspects of the construction of a project. The GC is directly accountable to the User or Owner for the quality of all materials and the performance of the GC's staff, and sub-contractors the GC elects to use on the Owner's project.

General Conditions: In construction, those conditions applicable in the same way to all or most aspects of the work to be performed. They are often administrative or procedural in nature and most will have a direct or indirect implication for the cost of the project. (See also "Conditions of the contract").

Glazing: In construction, the general term for window glass.

GO,NO/GO : In project planning, the shorthand used to indicate the points in the flow of a process, determined by its logic, at which a decision may be made to halt, terminate, or proceed.

Grid: A pattern of rectangles or squares. In construction, the metal framework, forming a grid, for holding ceiling tiles in a hung ceiling system.

Gross area: In architecture, all of the built area under a building roof. The term is usually meant to be inclusive of area falling under other definitions; rentable, useable, net, core, etc., and may vary in usage from architect to building owner to real estate broker. (See "Net rentable area.)

Guarantee: In commercial leasing, the security often required of a tenant by a landlord at or prior to lease execution, usually in a form common to commercial lending practices.

Hard line drawing: In architectural practice, in contrast to a single line drawing, a dimensioned and scaled drawing or plan of a structure executed with the aid of drafting tools.

Historic building: In urban development or renewal, a building having historic value and so designated by a local, state or federal agency. Such a status may come with certain restrictions on use or the nature of allowed improvements.

Holding over: In commercial leasing, the status of a tenant in premises for which a lease has expired and who remains in the premises, with landlord permission, usually for a brief period and at an elevated rental.

Hourly rate multiple: In professional service and other contracts, the practice of charging a fee determined by multiplying the hourly rate of the provider employee by some agreed or commonly used factor. Its use is normally restricted to short term work. (See "DPE)

Human engineering: See "Ergonomics"

Human factors engineer: One who practices ergonomics, the applied science of human engineering.

Human Factors Society: An industry group dedicated to the advancement of the principals and purposes of ergonomics and human engineering.

Hung ceiling: In commercial construction, a type of dropped ceiling consisting of a metal grid, usually designed to receive a fiberboard or acoustic tile, which is characteristically hung by wires from overhead and adjacent structure. (See "Dropped ceiling".)

HVAC: Heating, Ventilating and Air Conditioning. In construction, the term used to identify systems for providing cooled and heated (conditioned) air to a commercial building.

ICBO: International Conference of Building Officials. The periodic convening of persons responsible for the promulgation of regulations affecting the design, and construction of commercial buildings.

Illuminance: In the science of illumination, source light, measured in footcandles (fc) or lux (lx).

Illuminating Engineering Society See "IES". An association of lighting industry professionals.

Improvement allowance: In commercial leasing, money set aside by the landlord to pay for the outfitting or improvement of tenant space prior to occupancy. This budget or "allowance" may or may not cover all of the costs of such improvements. Any expense in excess of the allowance is expected to be reimbursed by the tenant.

Improvements: In commercial leasing, any change or addition to the construction of a finished building for purposes specified by a building owner, including the outfitting of tenant spaces.

Indemnification: To protect against loss, to insure. In the lease agreement, the promise of either principal to protect the other against claims which

might arise in the course of their contractual relationship.

Interior design: The planning, arrangement and decoration of elements of interior workplace architecture, and furnishing, in an aesthetically pleasing and functional manner.

Interior designer: The individual trained in the practice of interior design and charged with responsibility for the design of an interior space or spaces.

Interior spaces: In terms of workplace planning, building interior spaces located away from exterior window-walls that, characteristically, do not have exterior exposure.

International Conference of Building Officials. See"ICBO"

Labor and material bond: In the construction contract, the security required of the successful contractor. It is intended to assure payment of the contractor's obligations to workers and materials vendors.

Landlord: Lessor. The person or entity who lets real property in return for rent.

Landlord delay: In the commercial lease workletter, the period of time required or taken by the landlord to respond to a notice, provide an approval, etc. It acts to extend the time required for construction of tenant improvements and could, in turn, result in a delay in tenant occupancy. (See also "Tenant delay".)

Lay-in: In construction, the term for a material that is set into or laid in place, like ceiling tiles, or light fixtures, in a commercial hung-ceiling grid.

Lease: A contract between lessor (landlord) and lessee (tenant). In commercial leasing, this contract conveys certain rights of ownership and provides for the exclusive use by the tenant of the premises described in the contract for an agreed term (time period) and rental (money), and under such other terms and conditions as the two parties agree upon.

Lease commencement: Refers to the date fixed in the lease for the start of all of its obligations and privileges. This may be a date that is dependent on such critical conditions as completion, delivery, acceptance, etc., of the premises.

Lease-term: The period of time that the lease is effective. A valid lease contract must specify a term, usually of less than 99 years.

Legal description: In commercial real estate, the means by which real property can be located on the ground by reference to approved maps, surveys, etc., and by which a legal title may be researched. This information can be found in the public record in most jurisdictions.

Lessee: A tenant; one who rents real property for money, and receives in exchange a right of temporary possession of the portion of it, defined by the lease, for an agreed term.

Lessor: (See landlord).

Leveling of floors: In construction, the process of correcting the commonly uneven surface of a poured concrete slab floor, so that items of equipment or loose furniture that may be set on it remain level.

Life safety: In code enforcement, architecture and commercial building, the category of built features, items of construction and equipment, and other considerations relating to human safety in and about the workplace.

Light: In commercial construction, a window or a part of a window.

Liquidated damages: In construction contracts, the practice of enforcing timely contractor performance through the assessment against the contractor of a sum of money fixed in agreement between the principals. Its purpose is to provide at least a partial reimbursement to the User for losses suffered as a result of delay in the use of the construction.

Load factor: In commercial real estate a term used to identify the difference between useable and rentable area. (See "Add-on" factor.)

Long-lead items: Construction materials, equipment, furniture, etc., that customarily require an unusual amount of time to process, manufacture, ship and deliver, etc., from the time they are ordered.

Lumen: In the science of illumination, the unit of measure of the light energy that radiates from a light source. It is a measure of light power as perceived by the human eye.

Luminance: In the science of illumination, reflected light, measured in footlamberts and described as "brightness" when referring to its physiological effect.

Lux: The metric equivalent of footcandle, a measure of illuminance. (See "Footcandle".)

Market rent: In commercial real estate terms, the rent considered to be at a level representative of the average (if one were taken) of rents in similar building types and in a similar area. This is an experiential figure, with limited applicability beyond preparation of the User's preliminary budget.

Masonry: Construction using brick, stone, tile, cement block, etc., to form a supporting structure, veneer, decorative element, etc.

Masonry unit: A brick, stone, tile, or cement block, CMU, etc., used in masonry construction.

Metes and bounds: Measurements and boundaries. In real estate, the term for the identifying features of a parcel of land and the measurements relating to them which may be used to describe a parcel of real property.

Millwork: In construction, a category of work consisting of furniture and fixtures traditionally made of wood (now including plastic, metal, etc.) which may be processed and finished in a factory, and assembled and fitted

or "built in" to a prepared part of the workplace. Shelves, cabinets, counters, etc., and architectural woodwork like paneling typically fit into this category.

Mock-up: In interior design practice, a full-scale, three-dimensional means of demonstrating and testing the effectiveness of a set of design ideas previously approved in two-dimensional form. It usually involves some temporary interior construction, furniture and finishes, etc., planned for use in the finished interior.

Module: In architectural practice, the linear or two-dimensional unit of measurement conceived by the architect as the appropriate "building block" to be used in planning or determining the configuration of a structure. In workplace planning, the module may reveal itself in window size and spacing, bay sizes, ceiling grid pattern, etc. The term may also refer to building products, furniture and equipment, etc., whose design involves use of a "module".

Monument: In electrical installations, the rounded metal housing for a duplex outlet characteristically mounted to and protruding upward from the surface of a floor.

219

Mullion: In architecture, the subordinate vertical member of a glazing framework which separates the lights of a window. It is also commonly used to refer to the horizontal and vertical portions of the fascia panels separating windows in commercial buildings.

Negotiated contract: In terms of construction contracts, one that has been structured through two-party discussions between a User/owner and a contractor, in contrast to a contract awarded through the bid process.

Net Rentable Area: More accurately, rentable area. In commercial leasing, the terms "net" and "gross" tend to have definitions which are unique to the landlords and others who use them and who should be asked to define them. (See "rentable area".)

Non-disturbance: In commercial leasing, the term applied to a clause that reiterates the right of the tenant to continued enjoyment of the lease in the event of a change in ownership of the property being leased. A commercial lease without such a clause can place a tenant in jeopardy as the result of such a change.

Notice: In commercial leasing, the advice required to be given by one party to another, usually in writing, concerning an event or act described in the lease. The written record of the notice can be critical to the settlement of tenant/landlord disputes.

Operating costs: In commercial leasing, the costs associated with the day-to-day operation, management and maintenance of a building that are paid by the landlord and are expected to be reimbursed by the tenant. The usually wide variety of these costs requires that they be itemized and defined in the lease, and carefully accounted for by the landlord.

Operating cost limit: In the commercial lease, any device or formula (such as a "cap") limiting the amount of an expense that may be charged to a tenant, or that restricts their definition. (See also "cap".)

Operating Expense: See "Operating costs".

Orthographic projection: In architectural practice, the traditional method of drawing views of a structure in which, to greatly simplify, an imaginary line from the viewer's eye is always perpendicular to the surface of the structure being drawn. Typical views are called "plans" and "elevations".

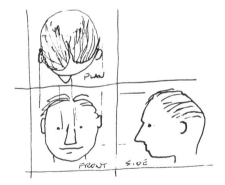

Owner: In architectural and construction contract terms, the individual or entity for whom services are to be provided and who is responsible for their payment. The "owner", in this context, may or may not hold title to property.

Parapet: In commercial building, the upper part of the exterior walls of the building that rise above and enclose the perimeter of the roof.

Partition plan: In architectural practice, the drawing showing the location of the interior walls of a commercial space. (See "space plan".)

PCB: Polychlorinated biphenyl. In construction, a chemical compound previously used as a cooling medium in electrical transformers that has been found to be toxic and has been banned from further use.

Penetration: In construction, an opening in a structure planned for the horizontal or vertical passage of people, light, air, utilities, etc. Also, an opening planned to be made in a built structure which could reduce its safe load-bearing capacity and/or for which strengthening of the structure may be required before the penetration is made.

Percentage fee: In professional service and construction contracts, a fee for services based on a percentage of the value of the cost of the work, as agreed between the principals in the contract.

Performance bond: In construction contracts, the assurance given the Owner by the contractor, in the form of a bond executed with a third party in the amount of the approximate value of the construction, that the contractor will complete the Owner's work in accordance with their contract. In the event of contractor default, the bonding entity assumes responsibility for completion of the construction contract.

Personnel: People employed by the User or User organization.

Perspective: In architectural practice, a method of rendering a view of a structure to give it a three-dimensional quality. The drawing is characterized by lines, known to be parallel in the structure, made to converge in the drawing to "vanishing points". (See "Axiometric".)

Phased occupancy: The moving into or plan to move into new quarters in stages or steps separated by more than a few hours, or a few days time.

Pier and beam: An ancient and still very current type of building structure in which supporting vertical piers carry horizontal beams.

Pipe-chase: (See "Chase")

Plan: In orthographic projection, a view, drawn from an imaginary point above it, of any horizontal section, such as a building site or a floor, etc.

Possession: In commercial lease terms, tenant enjoyment of the rights of the lease, having taken possession of the premises following completion and acceptance of improvements.

Premises: In commercial leasing, the building(s) or space(s) dedicated by a landlord to the exclusive use of a tenant, through a properly executed lease, for the rights to which the tenant pays rent.

Print: In architectural practice, a drawing reproduced by photo-chemical or mechanical means.

Program: In architectural planning, the process of collecting and cataloguing the User information necessary to plan and design a building or a workspace.

Program standards: The measurements or other guidelines established by the User, with the help of the design professional, to facilitate the process of planning, design and construction of the User workspace.

Proportionate share: In commercial leasing, the ratio of the rentable area leased by a tenant to all of the rentable area in the tenant's building which is of a similar nature and used for purposes similar to those of the tenant.

Punch list: In architecture and construction, the list of deficiencies in the work, or in any product or equipment installation, which are found upon inspection of the completed work. The request for the punch list is usually initiated by the responsible contractor or vendor and made by a design professional or other qualified third party.

Quiet enjoyment: See "Non-disturbance.

Quoted rent: In commercial space leasing, a term used to indicate a broadly announced rent figure as opposed to one which is negotiated or otherwise considered "firm". (See "asking rent".)

Raised floor: In construction and interior planning, a load-bearing floor often pre-fabricated of modular metal supports and removable tiles, installed over and supported by the building floor, creating a space between the two for the placement of necessary ducts and conduit.

Raw space: In architecture and construction, space in a completed commercial building approved for occupancy and not yet improved for tenant use. The term is also used to describe space in an existing building the improvements to which can be demolished to bring it to a state of "raw space".

Reasonable: A critical term in commercial leasing, usually intended to have the meaning of its common usage, and the absence of which can signify a right to act (usually by a landlord) in an "unreasonable" manner.

Reflected ceiling plan: In architectural practice, a plan of the workplace ceiling with its lighting and other fixtures in place, viewed (and drawn) as if it were "reflected" in the floor below it. Drawing the ceiling in this manner allows the viewer to see the ceiling in relation to the furniture and other objects below it.

Reinforced concrete: Any construction utilizing concrete reinforced with steel bars.

Remedy: In terms of the commercial lease, the means available to correct a deficiency. More specifically, the action(s) that may be taken by the landlord in the event of a tenant default.

Renewal option: In commercial leasing, that part of the lease agreement that allows the tenant, sometime prior to its termination, to request renewal of the lease. Landlord approval is usually conditioned only on the prior performance of the tenant with respect to lease obligations. In current practice, unless the renewal option has been formulated to provide for the business terms of the renewed lease, the renewal is also conditioned on the success of the negotiation of these terms.

Rent: The return or compensation for the use of property. Money promised to be paid by the tenant and accepted by the landlord in exchange for the use of landlord premises.

Rentable area: The floor area available for lease in a commercial building, or all of the floor area under the roof, less those areas and spaces dedicated to common use. The latter would include space taken by walls, chases, elevator shafts, etc., as well as building lobbies corridors, restrooms, etc. For purposes of calculating tenant rent, the landlord arrives at a "rentable area" by adding to the space occupied by the tenant an amount of space equal to a share of the common use area, the share being proportionate to the space occupied by the tenant.

Reproducible: In architectural practice, the translucent paper or film, such as "vellum", "mylar", "sepia", etc., which,

when drawn on, is capable of reprinting the drawn information on printing equipment commonly available for this purpose. (See also "Vellum".)

Request For Proposal: (RFP) A written statement, in the form of a request for services, prepared and issued by the User to a small number of pre-qualified service providers, containing the information necessary for the provider to respond with an accurate statement of work and related costs. Some forms of the Request for Proposal are designed to constitute a contract when executed by the provider.

Retainage: In construction contracts, that portion of the money scheduled to be paid for some portion of the work performed which is held by the User/Owner, in accordance with the terms of the contract, until its completion is verified. The practice of retainage is less a form of Owner assurance of satisfactory contractor performance than it is a means of reducing an otherwise immense accounting task.

RFP: See "Request for Proposal".

Right to represent agreement: In commercial leasing, the agreement between User and real estate broker providing the broker with the right to represent the User in a real estate transaction. (Also see "exclusive".)

Scale: In architectural practice, to proportionately reduce the size of a structure in drawing it. The scale of a drawing is determined by the design

223

professional executing it and is largely dependent on the size of the sheet on which it is being drawn. It is common practice for commercial buildings and their interior spaces to be drawn to a scale of 1/8th of an inch to a foot, (the metric system is still waiting in the wings) site plans to be done in a smaller scale, and details and furniture to be drawn at a larger scale.

Self-help: In the commercial lease, the tenant right to correct deficiencies or provide certain services which are the responsibility of the landlord, and which the landlord is delinquent in providing, and to look to the landlord for reimbursement of their cost. Also, the assertion by the tenant that such a right is implicit in the lease.

Sepia: See "reproducible".

Setback: In architecture, construction and code compliance, the placement of a structure or a portion of one such as an upper floor, away from a property line, in the direction of the interior of the property, as required by local zoning law.

Shear wall: In commercial building structures, interior load-bearing or structural walls placed in seemingly random locations to counteract the potential effects of twisting motions.

Shimming: To insert a shim. In carpentry, to level or plumb a framing member by the addition of a small piece of wood or metal of triangular section.

Sideletter agreement: In commercial leasing, an agreement pertaining to a

lease and executed by its principals, which is not an integral part of it and may not relate to the day-to-day operation of it.

Single line drawing: In architectural practice, a drawing, usually with the quality of a sketch, or "freehand" drawing, which represents partitions and walls with a single line instead of the customary double line. This is done in the interests of economy of effort and time.

Site plan: In architectural practice, a scaled plan drawing of improved property showing the relationship of improvements to each other, and to natural and other man-made features of the site, and indicating the relationship of site and improvements to adjacent sites.

Skin: In architecture and construction, the term often used to refer to the exterior surface of a building of curtain wall construction.

Smart-building: A trade term of less than precise usage indicating that a building has been equipped with certain information monitoring and control devices and equipment.

Space plan: In architectural practice, a scaled plan showing the arrangements of spaces in the workplace interior and the location of architectural features such as walls, doors, windows, stairs, elevators, millwork, etc., and sufficient furniture to indicate scale and other relationships. The space plan may be executed as a single line or a hard line drawing.

Stipulated sum: In construction contracts, the agreement between Owner and contractor in which the basis of payment for the work is a fixed price. (See "Fixed fee".)

Structural modification: In construction, any alteration in a building which requires a change in its structural system, or arrangement or composition of structural members. The term applied as a form of discouragement to any request for a building alteration.

Sublease: In commercial leasing, a transfer to a third party of the rights of a lease, usually by a tenant with the permission of the landlord, under terms and conditions agreeable to all parties. In contrast to an assignment, the sublessor (the original or primary tenant) remains responsible for all of the obligations of the master lease, even when the sublessee makes rent payments directly to the landlord.

Subordination: The placement of a right in an inferior position. In the commercial lease, the customary subordination of the lease itself to any mortgage or deed of trust encumbering the property of which the tenant premises are a part.

Subrogation: The assignment to a third party, such as an insurance company, of the right to sue for damages. In the commercial lease, it is customary for each party to the lease to waive the right to make such an assignment in matters covered by the insurance required by the lease.

Substantial completion: The state of completion of improvements under construction that allows them to be used without jeopardizing the work or interfering with the operation of the User in any way. In the construction contract, this is the first step in the process of completion, approval and acceptance of the work by the User/Owner, and allows for deficiencies of a minor nature to be observed, recorded and scheduled for correction following Tenant occupancy of the premises.

Support space: In terms of User space requirements and programming, those spaces required by the User organization that are not strictly defined by personnel workstation needs. Storage and warehouse spaces, reception areas, conference rooms, etc., fall into this category.

Systems furniture: See "furniture systems".

Take possession: See "Possession").

Task light: A light fixture intended to focus on and illuminate an individual's work, in contrast to "ambient" light, which is designed to provide general light in the workplace. (See "Ambient light".)

TBS (See "Tight building syndrome".)

Tenant: Lessee. In commercial leasing, one who has the right of possession of premises under an agreement, such as a lease, to pay rent.

Tenant right to audit: In the commercial lease, the right of the tenant to examine the landlord record of operating expenses for which the tenant is required to pay some share.

Tenant delay: In the commercial lease workletter, the period of time required by the tenant to respond to a notice, provide some required information or approval, etc. which, in the aggregate, could extend the time required for construction of improvements, and delay tenant occupancy. (See "Landlord delay".)

Tenant inducements: In the marketing of commercial space, any offering by the landlord designed to induce a prospective tenant to lease space. Such inducements can come in any form, but usually relate to deferred or abated rent payments, or some privileged use of the property in which the premises are located, like parking, signage, meeting room use, etc.

Tenant improvements: In commercial leasing and construction, the physical alterations and additions to leased premises which are considered necessary and/or desirable for tenant use. The nature and extent of tenant improvements is greatly variable and range from the "building standard" (which may be no improvements at all) provided by the landlord, to the most elegant outfitting that the tenant can afford. (See also "Improvements" and "Building Standards".)

Tenant improvement allowance: See "improvement allowance".

Tenant premises: See "premises".

Tenant's proportionate share: See "proportionate share".

Term: In commercial leasing, the period of time for which the premises are leased by the tenant. The term may be modified by agreements (options) with the landlord to extend, renew, terminate early, etc., leading to the phrase often used in lease analysis, "firm term", or term of the lease after consideration of all of its modifications.

Tight building syndrome: (TBS). In commercial building management and maintenance terms, the phrase adopted in an effort to explain the persistence of contaminated air circulating in many office buildings.

Tilt-wall: A type of commercial building construction, usually limited to one or two story structures, characterized by pre-cast walls tilted into place on the building site.

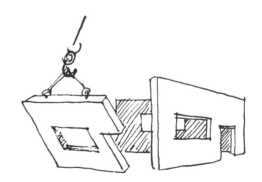

Time is of the essence: In the commercial lease, a phrase signifying that the times or dates to which the term refers are critical, and that failure to meet implied deadlines will trigger the remedies called for in the lease.

UBC: See "Uniform Building Code".

Uniform Building Code: (UBC) In commercial building construction, the set of rules and guidelines promulgated by the ICBO, and incorporated in laws and ordinances regulating the construction of buildings in most localities in the U.S. (See also "ICBO".)

UPM: User Project Manager. In terms of the User embarking on a relocation, the User staff member assigned the responsibility of overseeing all aspects of the relocation project.

Useable area: In a commercial building, the total floor area, or portion thereof, occupied or available for use as tenant premises. For purposes of determining rent, the landlord adds to the useable area an amount of space equal to a proportionate share of the building common use area.

User Project Manager: See "UPM".

User: Any individual or organization using commercial services who might otherwise be identified as a "buyer", "tenant", "client", "owner", etc.

VAT: A composition floor tile that, before the fall of asbestos, used to be understood as "vinyl asbestos tile", or "vinyl asphalt tile". Laid in place,

unbroken, VAT is not considered "friable".

VDT: See "Video display terminal". A television or computer related monitor or screen.

Vellum: In architectural practice, a durable, high quality translucent paper that may be used to make reproducible drawings.

Veneer: Any thin surface material with some distinctive visual or intrinsic value, laid over and bonded to a construction of more common support material. Hardwood "veneers" are bonded to plywood; gold leaf forms a "veneer" on wooden picture frames; marble, brick, and many other materials are "veneered" to commercial building surfaces.

Video Display Terminal: (VDT) The monitor or "screen", integrated in the home TV set, and found as an independent element in computer or word processing, etc., equipment.

Want list: A list assembled by the User at the start of relocation planning which goes beyond "user requirements" to include anything the user believes would enhance workplace activities in any way.

War room: In User terms, the space set aside, usually in existing quarters, to act as a headquarters for the planning and management of a relocation.

White sound: In the commercial interior, the overlay of sound, usually but not always by means of the User speaker system, intended to make otherwise intrusive conversations and noises of the workplace unintelligible and unobtrusive.

Wire management: In interior planning and construction, the arrangement of telecommunication cable and wire in conduits, channels, raceways, etc., to make it more accessible for system changes.

Work permit: In commercial construction, a permit required by the agencies regulating local building construction to be in evidence at the construction site prior to the start of construction. In every locality, there are certain types of usually minor interior improvements that may be made without such a permit.

Workletter: In commercial leasing, the portion of the lease dealing exclusively with matters concerning the construction of tenant improvements.

PART II

DOING IT

An Introduction to DOING IT and EPDEX

Doing It describes what you need to do to start your own organization on a path toward relocation, and a successful move. It consists of four steps, or sets of related activities—**EPDEX**, for:

- **E EVALUATION**
- **P PLANNING**
- **D DOCUMENTING**
- **X EXECUTION**

The first step is incorporated to give the relocation process a point of reference, so that you can know what has worked for you in the past and what has not. Use it to help shape your expectations and your want-list, and different project and building evaluations. **Evaluation** is separated into three parts that correspond to the different groups of Change Factors—Internal, External and Deterioration— explained on the next few pages. The Change Factor is captioned in the left-hand column, and a description of normal or acceptable characteristics of it are in the right hand column.

The next three steps follow a traditional order that allows you to apply your **Planning** skills to the design of the workplace, to **Document** the results, and to **Execute** the plans you have documented and the move you have been working toward. **Planning** is separated into three components to give you a sense of control over the process, as well as a feel for the progress you are making. A 10-question review and a scorecard to help you measure your progress follow Preliminary Planning and Further Planning. Commitment Planning represents the decision-making portion of the planning process that naturally precedes **Documenting.**

In the presentation of the three steps, a brief caption in the left-hand column identifies the step, and a highlighted sentence in the right-hand column explains the instruction. Below the highlighted sentence are brief paragraphs that further explain the instruction or note some resources (including references to material in this book). Additional observations or precautions appear in italics.

Review the outline at the start of each Step to get a sense of its content and the suggested sequence of activities. Feel free to rearrange this sequence to fit your unique circumstances and methodology.

Step E

EVALUATION

Step E **EVALUATION**

EVALUATION

Evaluation of the facility requires that we look closely at those places where our organization, people and operations interface with it, that we identify and isolate them and see how they alter with our use over time, and that we devise some means of measuring the impact of the changes we see.

Change acts on people and events and, in the workplace, on things that are a part of the buildings and facilities we use. We call these things *change factors.*

Change Factors Explained

Change factors in the workplace lessen the effectiveness with which the organization can operate. They may be tangible or intangible, and originate within our organization or others, or may be a part of the facility itself. Change factors are often positive forces in and of themselves, but their overall effect produces inadequacies in our facility which can be expected to lead to change. They fall into three groups:

Internal Change Factors

Internal change factors result from the nature of our organization, its characteristics, its methods of operation, its people, its goals and needs, etc. They are largely within our control.

External Change Factors

External change factors have their origins in institutions, forces, events, and organizations, etc., that are outside our own and beyond our direct control.

Deterioration Change Factors

Deterioration change factors are an integral part of our facility and are subject to change or deterioration with the passage of time, as a result of normal wear and tear, neglect or damage, etc. Usefulness for our purposes has diminished as a result.

The Measuring System

The measuring system quantifies Change Factors, so that we can determine a level of performance acceptability for each. Using a five grade measuring system, one grade would be given for each Change Factor. Grades would have the connotations indicated below, and could have values corresponding to the order shown. The best characteristic would receive the lowest value or, in reverse order, the best could have the highest value.

(1) Highest Rating

Excellent; best; most satisfactory; works very well; probably could not be improved; has no noticeable defects; greatest economy, etc.

(2) Next-to-Highest Rating

Very good, very satisfactory, works well, no important defects; overall effect is positive, very good economy, efficiency, etc.

(3) Medium Rating

Satisfactory, acceptable, positives balance negatives; defects can be corrected; etc.

(4) Next-to-Poorest Rating

Poor, not satisfactory; does not work well; not efficient; too costly; significant defects; in many ways unacceptable; many negative effects.

(5) Poorest Rating

Most unsatisfactory; unacceptable; works very poorly or not at all; must be improved soon; very costly and inefficient, etc.

Factor Correlation

There are few, if any, guidelines of a general nature that are meaningful to the correlation of values of the various change factors. They are apples and oranges. Each is an integral part of the workplace without a measurable relationship to another. Some priorities will need to be established, however, as the time comes for funding of facility improvements. At this time, the most recent update of the **Facility Evaluation** should be reviewed by the User organization in order to compare the returns in productivity that might be anticipated from specific improvements.

Performing the Evaluation

Evaluation can be done by one person or by several. The opinions of internal experts can be useful; lab technicians, engineers and drafts-persons, word processors, telecom systems operators, etc., can provide unique input to the facility evaluation. Direction or guidance given to those performing the evaluation should be limited to that required by administrative procedures, schedules, etc.; avoid coaching concerning factor grades, evaluation outcomes, etc. It is most helpful if the User/respondent is well acquainted with the item in question.

To start the Evaluation process in your facility, look through the following outline of change factors. Then, start your own list. Add or delete factors that are appropriate to your organization and your building. Create your list in such a way that you can include columns corresponding to the five-point measurement system described above.

Take your list of deterioration change factors with you on a practice walk-through. Make notes on how things look to you. Do they look like they can do the job? Are they performing as though they were new or freshly installed? Is their appearance, noise, smell, etc., acceptable? Use good judgment, but don't be afraid to use personal, subjective judgment.

Take your list of internal and external change factors with you to the next Planning Committee or Management Committee meeting you attend. Note the current status of some of those change factors as they come up for discussion. Give some grades. Make some ratings. Keep your grades, notes and observations on file, and review them at periodic intervals.

INTERNAL CHANGE FACTORS

Internal change factors result from the nature of our organization, its characteristics, its methods of operation, its people, its goals and needs, etc. They are largely within our control. Listed below are some internal factors commonly found to generate organizational and workplace change.

Income   **E1**   NOI, gross revenues, sales, etc. Your measure of the productivity of the organization. If this measure is available by organizational unit (division, department or section, etc.), use that of the smallest group. It will be easier to relate that productivity figure to features of the group's facility.

Systems   **E2**   Systems change can mean an addition or deletion of a work unit, its up- or down-sizing, change in working relationship with other units, or the addition or reduction of major equipment, etc. Look over your recent history of these kinds of changes. Then look at system changes that are planned.

Personnel   **E3**   People changes may or may not occur as a result of changes in income or systems. Cyclical change is less important to measure than long-term change, which could result in unused or in overcrowded facilities. Note functional changes that require workstation changes and shifts in population characteristics that impact facilities.

Corporate Directives   **E4**   If you are part of a larger organization whose headquarters or decision-making personnel are elsewhere, you may receive periodic instructions regarding new procedures, new policies, new products, etc., along with specific guidance regarding the size and use of facility space. Locally generated directives will, obviously, have the same effect.

New Products and Services   **E5**   These are introduced from time to time, and bring with them a need for people, equipment and space. Anticipating new or changed products or services can help determine the kind of changes in facilities that will become necessary.

Growth	**E6**	Many organizations use historical data to predict a growth rate for stockholders, investors, creditors, etc. If you have an idea of the composition of this rate (e.g., net worth, sales, stockholder equity, etc.) you can use it to predict facility growth.
Consolidation and Expansion	**E7**	Organization change may have involved the gradual acquisition of separate locations performing a requisite service or producing a critical part. Periodic review of the efficiency and productivity of these locations is probably being done. This information can be followed to help determine either the wisdom of consolidating these units, or of breaking them down further.
Incremental Change	**E8**	Changes occur in any organization that cannot be laid to any single cause or set of factors, but are simply the result of the nature of the organization's experience. They are relatively small and incremental and manifest themselves in the facility in growing numbers of pockets of unused space *or* in the increasing density of people space and/or support space (storage, records, equipment, etc.).
Quantum Change	**E9**	Many organizations have one or more opportunities in their lifetime for dramatic change to occur. It may be caused by the approval of a long-awaited product, a buy out, a major influx of funds, the loss of a major customer or a major supplier, a joint venture, a new partner, a merger, etc. It is different than an act of God in that its occurrence has a degree of predictability and you would like to be able to anticipate its impact on your facility.
Goals and Needs	**E10**	We state what these are with some degree of regularity, because they can change as our organization matures. We want either to validate the existing or identify new ones that respond to changed conditions in our world. Look at the facility impact of these restated or altered expressions of organization goal and need.
Costs	**E11**	Facility costs are a normal everyday concern, but their relationship to other operating and overhead expenses can alter gradually in ways that, once

perceived, suggest a facility change. Rent, operating expense, maintenance, taxes and insurance, etc., should be monitored as a percent of one or more preferred productivity measures to serve as a good indicator of the need for facility change.

Business Plan   **E12**   Your organization's plan for a coming period of time may be prepared with an emphasis on operations and financing. It also reflects your goals and effectively predicts facility change.

EXTERNAL CHANGE FACTORS

External change factors have their origins in institutions, forces, events and organizations, etc., that are outside our own and beyond our direct control. Listed below are some external factors commonly associated with organizational and workplace change.

Industry Change   **E13**   Watch your industry for short- and long-term signs of expansion or contraction, or of geographic shifts, both domestic and international. Industry publications also generate predictions based on feedback from member organizations, which can be helpful in determining the impact of these factors on your facility.

Markets   **E14**   These are in a constant state of change as market demographics shift in their population concentrations, purchasing capacity, interests, etc. As they shift from nearby locations to areas further from your facility, try to anticipate the point at which a facility change may be necessary.

Competition   **E15**   Look beyond the larger elements of your industry and industry markets. See what your local direct market competition is doing, especially in terms of their facilities. Does the latter play a part in increasing or diminishing your own stature in your market? Are you sufficiently aware of competitor plans for the near and long-term?

Government Regulation   **E16**   Measure the facility effects of two kinds of regulations: those that apply in a generic sense to commercial facilities of all kinds, and those that are specific to your industry and, perhaps, to your own unique operation. Be aware of proposed legislation and probable schedules for enactment. Plug this information into your facility plans.

Local Planning and Zoning   **E17**   Municipal and County authorities can enact changes in land usage and restrict or alter the availability of important community facilities, like roadways, water, and sewage. Be aware of proposed changes.

Calculate their timing and effect on your operation and your facility.

Community Development **E18** Regulated and unregulated changes in the fabric of the community surrounding our facility are important to us if they can restrict access, increase traffic, or limit parking availability, etc. Monitor neighboring properties for developments planned by private as well as institutional owners, and measure the probable effects of these changes, if any, on your facility.

Taxes and Insurance **E19** In our volatile climate for taxing and litigation, those responsible for measuring the need for facility change should watch these items carefully. Even as tenants, be aware of the damaging effects of the kind of abrupt tax increases that result, in some areas, from the resale of commercial property.

Suppliers **E20** The quick availability of certain products and/or services is critical to your successful operation. Be aware of prospective changes in that availability. The shifting of a warehousing function caused by a supplier change, for example, could mean either a substantial reduction or a significant increase in your need for facility space.

Amenities **E21** You would like to be as close as possible to certain amenities commonly associated with an urban environment, regardless your location. Nearby banking, grocery and clothing stores, repair shops, theaters, and food service, etc., are facilities that benefit you and are a convenience for your employees.

DETERIORATION CHANGE FACTORS

Deterioration change factors are an integral part of the facility and are subject to change or deterioration with the passage of time, as a result of normal wear and tear, or neglect or damage, etc. Workplace usefulness, for your purposes, has diminished as a result.

The items representing change factors on the following list are grouped roughly by where or what they are.

Site Deterioration Factors

These are elements of the building's real estate, the buildings and grounds immediately around it, and the larger community of which it is a part.

Exterior Deterioration Factors

These are components of the building exterior and its structure that affect your sense of its utility, security, integrity, etc., as well as its image.

Interior Deterioration Factors

These are physical characteristics of the building interior that comprise its public spaces and shape the "raw space" of your premises.

Building Systems Deterioration Factors

These are the equipment and other means by which utilities and essential sevices are made available to building occupants.

Management Deterioration Factors

These are the systems and methods, etc., used to manage your building and your premises, and the experience and approach of those using them.

In the right-hand column, the description of the characteristics of these change factors represents them at an acceptable level of performance or appearance, etc. It is intended to correspond to things that you can walk up to and see, touch, hear, smell, etc., and can make some personal judgments about.

Evaluate these change factors in terms of your anticipated length of stay, their importance to your operation, etc.

SITE DETERIORATION FACTORS

Approach and Access   **E22**   Easy to access by auto, pedestrian and handicapped. Drives and walkways are in good repair, unobstructed, adequate in width, well-curbed and clean.

Drives and walks are well-lighted as needed at all hours of the day or evening. Directional signage is clear and easy to find.

Landscaping   **E23**   Planting is attractive, well designed and well maintained. Landscape materials are sensitive to locality and climate.

The building foundation is properly protected from wet areas and sprinklers.

Standpipes are placed in the locations required by code, but are screened or are otherwise unobtrusive in appearance.

Parking   **E24**   Preferred parking area is covered and immediately adjacent to the workplace facility.

An adequate number of spaces are available for organization employees, staff and visitors. Spaces are striped, well-planned and visually unobstructed. Surface parking is well-paved, planted and curbed.

Covered and surface parking is well-lighted for early morning and evening hours; covered parking is well-lighted at all hours. Parking area entry is secured and/or monitored.

Lighting   **E25**   Lighting is adequate for visual identification and security purposes. Lighting marks driveways, walkways, signs and building entries. Light sources are veiled from driver or pedestrian eyes.

The color of light is complimentary to landscaping, building materials and signage.

Drainage   **E26**   All approaches, parking and landscaped areas are well-drained. No standing pools or large depressed areas are noted.

Walkways are raised; curbs, gutters and storm drains are appropriately placed.

There is no rotting woodwork or plant material.

Identification and Signage

E27 The building(s) is well and clearly identified by number and/or name.

Both relate to city and/or postal directory information. Street number appears at curbside or is otherwise easily visible to driver and pedestrian.

Appropriate directional signs for drivers, visitors, deliveries, pedestrians, emergencies, parking, entries and exits, etc., are well-located and clearly visible.

Identification markings on glass are duplicated on opaque, well-contrasted materials.

Amenities

E28 Image and amenity conscious organizations can note the spaciousness of landscaped areas, setbacks, pools and fountains, sculpture, outdoor furniture, etc., and the attractive placement and design of these features.

Outbuildings and Equipment

E29 Freestanding building equipment and storage facilities are located well away from building entries on sturdy foundations. They are walled or screened from view by appropriate building materials, and clearly signed to indicate their function, hazardous contents, if any, etc.

EXTERIOR DETERIORATION FACTORS

Building Type   **E30**   Mid-rise; high-rise; low-rise; single-story; masonry; curtain-wall; tilt-wall; reinforced concrete; pier-and-beam; steel-frame; wood-frame, etc.

Make a determination based on reasonably ascertainable visual information. Confirm this with an architect or engineer; it is important to your evaluation of other kinds of structures you could work in.

Building Entries   **E31**   All barrier-free code regulations are satisfied.

Entries are architecturally identified. They provide covered and ramped access to clearly marked doorways appropriate in number and size.

A sufficient number of entries allow for convenient access to the building(s) from driveways, walkways, parking areas, loading areas, etc.

Adequate vehicular turnaround is provided.

A well-lighted protected walkway runs from surface parking areas to the building, there are well-lighted and secured walkways, waiting areas and elevators or stairs from interior garages.

Architectural Design   **E32**   The building is well-situated on its site, comfortable in relation to adjacent landscape and buildings, and presents an overall pleasing appearance.

It matches your concept of the look and/or visual features most appropriate to your organization. Its architectural style and detail (or lack of same) are satisfying.

Signage   **E33**   The visibility characteristics of building signage are equal to or better than that above for site signage. It is well-placed and sized, well-lighted, and repeated if not visible from different points of view. Lettering is easily readable and identifiable, and contrasts with its background. Clear directions are provided for different entries and building functions, etc.

Facing Materials **E34** Materials on the face of the building are generally in harmony with its type, location, size, etc. They are sturdy looking, clean, well-detailed and well-joined, in the case of pre-fabricated panels or masonry, weather-proof. Patchy signs of streaking, staining, oxidizing, chipping, etc., do not show.

If tinted, vision glass is free from discoloration or peeling; tinted or clear glass is solidly framed in a durable, well-sealed casement material.

Roof drains, or scuppers, are not visible or are architecturally integrated with the materials and design of the building.

Colors and textures are in keeping with the nature of your organization, its purposes and its people.

Roof **E35** The building roof can be walked if it is of the built-up, parapet type. It is easily accessed, with owner permission, from a well-lighted interior space.

The roof surface is well-drained, consistent in color and texture, and firm underfoot. Gravel, if used, is spread about evenly.

Roof joints, at sloped or vertical surfaces, parapets, hatches, roof drains, equipment footings, etc., are well-caulked, sheathed and flashed without cracks or separations.

Rooftop equipment is securely fastened and is not visible from the ground near the building. Loose materials are not stored on the roof.

INTERIOR DETERIORATION FACTORS

Public Areas **E36** Building lobbies or foyers are central and adequately sized for peak building occupant and visitor load. Directories and directional signage are well located and clear and well lighted. Vertical transportation is quickly and easily accessed. Corridors are wide and well lighted.

Floor, wall and ceiling materials and finishes emphasize visual character, as well as utility, and are clean and well-maintained.

Lighting is adequate for the purposes of tenant and visitor traffic. It is selected for visual effect as well as utility. Built-in features and furniture are apparent.

Art, sculpture and planting are on display.

Core **E37** This area gathers together various building services and utilities in a central location on each floor.

Principal-floor core may comprise mailroom, shops, copy and data center, building office, etc., with elevator(s), stairs, janitor and mechanical spaces, lavatories, drinking fountain, mail-drop, etc. Areas and services are grouped together and not scattered. *(Stairways are separated by Code.)*

Interior materials and finishes are equivalent to other public areas.

In multi-tenant developments, electrical equipment is centrally located in a secured space, accessible on request for verification of panel board and riser capacities, etc.

Size and configuration of core area has implications for planning of User areas.

Planning Module **E38** Usually rectangular, this is the unit of the building planning grid that determines the placement of most building columns, windows, ceilings, etc. The less variety in it and the more uniform its components, the more the user gets from the interior space. *(This information is most easily verified from an architectural drawing.)*

Rectangular plan shapes are dominant, windows are the same size and evenly spaced; interior structural columns are evenly spaced and in line with window mullions and module dimensions are multiples of ceiling grid dimensions.

The variety of planning modules is kept to a minimum.

The bay size is a multiple of the module.

Walls   **E39**   Walls are vertical and lie in a single plane. Smooth or rough, their finished surface is even.

Visible horizontal joints indicate a change in material only (e.g., sheetrock to metal to glass.); vertical joints indicate a change in material or a connection between prefabricated panels. All joints are tight and sealed. Walls of similar construction and use are uniform in thickness.

A durable base material (e.g., vinyl, wood, metal, stone,) is applied to the full length of the wall where it meets the floor.

Wall-to-floor and wall-to-ceiling joints are tight and finished evenly and uniformly.

Reveals and caps are uniform.

Demising walls, core, load-bearing (shear) and sound walls are continuous from floor slab to overhead slab or beam. Fastening and sound transmitting characteristics are seldom uniform and walls or wall segments must be tested for these purposes.

Doors   **E40**   Doors to people spaces are 36" wide, and are of solid wood construction, hung with at least three hinges from a hollow metal or wood frame, securely mounted to adjacent walls.

The door closes firmly along its full height (84" or more) with little closing effort.

Openers are lever handle type; closers and locks are optional.

Finishes are clean and uniform in color and pattern, except for variances in wood grain. The door is cut at the bottom to clear the finished floor.

Ceilings   **E41**   Ceilings may be finished or unfinished.

Finished ceilings may be a uniformly surfaced material —like plastered gypsum board or acoustic tile— attached to a metal supporting grid hung from the structure above, at a height sufficient to clear ducts, pipe and wire above and doorways below.

The ceiling is hung no lower than 9' above the finished floor, and is consistent in height.

The ceiling grid is uniform and consistent with respect to building architecture, and allows for consistent and good spacing of light fixture placement.

Ceiling openings for exhaust fans, speakers, building air, etc., are functional and are appropriately covered with clean diffusers, or grills.

The ceiling surface is clean and free of spots, streaks, stains, cracks, breaks or unfinished openings. The ceiling tile design, finish and color, etc., are uniform. True acoustic tile is used where acoustic properties are specified.

Louvered or perforated grills or registers cover only the ends of the duct or pipe they serve. Their flanges fully cover cut ceiling openings, are tight to the ceiling surface, and are finished in the ceiling color. Acoustic or perforated lay-in tiles fit down tightly in their metal supporting grid.

Unfinished ceilings expose duct and pipe work, etc., and the underside of the floor above. Materials and surfaces exposed this way are free of loose, flaking or peeling, etc., particles, and are uniformly finished or painted.

Draft curtains are hung where required by fire code in large open areas—warehouses, etc.)

Floors   **E42**   The floor consists of the surface you walk on, plus the platform or deck beneath that surface. The surface varies from soft to hard; from easy to clean to less easy to clean.

It is uniform, solid, level, tight and durable, without open joints, seams, cracks or wrinkles.

Necessary changes in surface material, or interruptions in the surface for ramps, junction-box monuments, raceways, equipment hold-downs, etc., appear only in areas with little or no traffic.

Surface materials (tile, masonry, carpet, other rolled material, parquet, etc.) may be glued down or stretched. (Stretched carpet is only acceptable in low traffic areas.)

Raised floors, for which all of the above applies, leave ample clear height for personnel and equipment.

Millwork   **E43**   Millwork comprises built-ins of any kind, appearance or utility, constructed as a part of the building interior for general use at the time of original construction or, for a specified use, later. Applications include dry or wet counters, work surfaces, cabinets, shelving, moldings, soffits and other interior architectural detail, etc.

All millwork is firmly fastened to building sub-structure, and is of durable, well-finished materials.

Millwork of other than homogeneous materials like stone, glass, hardwood, etc., is composed of core materials (plywood, flake board) enclosed on all surfaces with a durable laminate (melamine plastic). Laminated surfaces are not peeling or discolored.

Doors, drawers and shelves are level, plumb and do not sag, tilt, or stand open.

Cabinet doors are equipped with automatic closets. Corners and edges of exposed counter tops and cabinets are rounded or softened. Drawers release easily, extend their full length, and re-set firmly.

Cabinet and drawer interiors are finished in stain resistant, wipeable surfaces.

Colors and finishes are uniform and/or well-coordinated with other interior finishes.

Fixed horizontal work surfaces used regularly by equipment and/or VDT operators and technicians are fully adaptable to operator function and comfort.

BUILDING SYSTEMS DETERIORATION FACTORS

Elevators   **E44**   A commercial building over one story high has one or more elevators. Building permits and inspections are required for their manufacture and installation. Documents confirming these are available for your inspection.

One or more elevators may be set aside exclusively for the moving freight. These elevators are not for passenger use and are not required to meet passenger elevator specifications.

Waiting areas for passenger elevators are ample enough for peak waiting periods, without spilling over into traffic corridors. Door openings are not less than 42" wide and permit the simultaneous passing of two or more persons.

The criteria of elevator service quality for passenger use are understood to be average waiting time, handling capacity and travel time. Acceptable waiting times are in the 15 to 26 second range; a 75 second elevator trip is considered tolerable, a 120 second trip is not considered so.

There is no noticeable elevator-generated noise or side-to-side movement in the moving elevator cab. The cab is well-ventilated and supplied with appropriately warmed and cooled building air. Passenger control panels and buttons are clearly identified and easy to reach, for wheelchair as well as standing passengers. Braille indicators and annunciators are provided.

The American National Standards Institute (ANSI), publishes the specifications which form the basis of most municipal code regulations affecting elevator design and installation. The National Elevator Industry, Inc., 600 Third Avenue, New York, NY 10016, publishes Suggested Minimum Passenger Requirements for the Handicapped.)

Heating, Ventilating and Air Conditioning

E45

The HVAC system is designed to meet the requirements of building user comfort and to meet specified building interior environmental control criteria that are based on assumptions about human comfort.

ASHRAE (the American Society of Heating, Refrigerating and Air Conditioning Engineers) publishes comfort standards that have evolved from detailed studies and calculations of physiological responses to heat and cold, psychological and cultural factors, the clothing we wear, etc.

Operative temperature is used to measure these standards by means of a globe thermometer.

Operative temperature represents an average of the air temperature of a space and the average of the various surface temperatures surrounding the space. (p. 36, Mechanical and Electrical Equipment for Buildings, 7th Edition; John Wiley & Sons.)

Winter and Summer recommendations are made by ASHRAE for mainly sedentary office workers, dressed in appropriate seasonal indoor attire as follows:

> *Winter optimal   : 71° F*
> *Summer optimal : 76° F*

The relative humidity (rh) range at these optimal operative temperatures is 30 percent to 70 percent. The sling psychrometer measures air temperature (dry bulb) and relative humidity (wet bulb).

HVAC equipment is installed in the building to provide all work areas with conditioned air to meet the above minimum standards of individual comfort at specified hours and days of the year. This equipment is supplemental to passive warming and cooling designs and devices that are directed to the same goal of individual comfort.

Points of air supply and their controls are as frequently and strategically placed as possible.

Air being supplied to the workstation is directed away from its occupant and is not of sufficient force to lift or move loose paper or other light objects on work tops.

Supply air is free of odors, fragrances, visible dust, etc., and is tested periodically for the presence of harmful bacteria. Records of this testing are available for your inspection. These and other characteristics of minimal supply air quality are uniform throughout the workplace.

Heating and cooling devices in the workplace (supply and return air ducts, exhausts, flues, radiant heat devices, switches, thermostats, etc.) are located to be compatible with normal work activities and placement of furniture, equipment and lighting.

With the exception of an acceptable level of rushing-air sound near supply air outlets, the workplace is free of HVAC equipment noise.

Electricity   **E46**   With the exception of electrical system failures or outages causes outside your building, your equipment gets the power it needs to operate at all times.

Your telephone and electrical equipment is located in a dry, secured, dust-free space exclusive to your use, in or near your premises,

There are sufficient convenience outlets in all areas of the workplace. They are sized correctly for typical office machine usage, and placed at the appropriate height on the wall, or on the floor underneath or immediately adjacent to workstation furniture.

Outlet receptacles are properly grounded and polarized where required. *Receptacles connected to different voltages, frequencies, or current type on the same premises must be polarized so that attachment plugs are not interchangeable.*

Spaces or rooms with laboratory or computer or other equipment requiring greater than normal or building standard power usage, are equipped with their own panel board and main circuit breaker.

Unless specified for your usage, all building wiring in your premises is copper. *Aluminum wiring creates a heavy oxide at joints which, unless carefully maintained, creates a resistant build-up with high-heat and incendiary possibilities.*

The wiring system in your building (and on your floor and at your premises) meets current code. Documentation of this fact is available for your inspection. *Code compliance provides assurance of minimally acceptable levels of power delivery and safety.*

Wiring work for workstation changes or equipment relocation can be accomplished quickly and relatively inexpensively. All walkways and work areas are free of exposed cable and raceways. No cable is exposed at ceiling tiles or wall-ceiling intersections.

The wiring system (cellular floor, underfloor duct, power pole, ceiling and cavity wall, raised floor, etc.) provides the flexibility you need for planning your operations.

Transformers are located outside your building or your premises or are properly installed in a sound treated interior vault or closet. They are of the dry type or are liquid cooled with other than PCB coolant. *(Polychlorinated biphenyl has been banned for this usage.)*

The electrical demand control system in use by your building or your local utility is in keeping with your organization's power requirements and the peak demands of your operation.

Your building provides both emergency and stand-by backup electrical systems. (The emergency system is required by code for fire safety reasons. The backup system may or may not be required by code but may be essential to your uninterrupted operation.)

Your local utility and/or your building owner provides adequate spare capacity in power available to your premises for future growth.

Lighting **E47** Daylight in the workplace interior can be modulated, and is well-integrated with interior artificial light.

Primary light sources are obscured from view, and general area and circulation area ceiling light fixtures minimize ceiling surface reflectance.

Movable task lighting is provided at workstations involving repetitive or continuous operator functions. There is a good balance between task light and ambient or area light.

Task and ambient light sources are selected and arranged in ways to minimize or eliminate veiling reflections (glare) on the work surface and to reduce excessive brightness, shadows, contrast, etc.

Furniture and work surfaces may be oriented to daylight exposure in such a way as to keep the daylight source at the operator's back or side, but not so that VDT (video display terminal) screens will reflect the light from such a source.

When work area light measurements are made, measures of luminance (light reflected from work or other surfaces, in footlamberts) as well as illuminance (source light, in lumens and footcandles or lux), are made.

In the absence of a specific lighting design, Illuminating Engineering Society (IES) guidelines are followed regarding the establishment of a non-uniform lighting system.

Lighting fixtures, whether task or ambient (ceiling) fixtures, are so located that they cannot reflect in an operator's monitor screen.

Task lighting can be manually positioned at the workstation. *This is, strictly speaking, a furniture consideration, not a facility matter.*

The spectral (color) composition of light being used is capable of rendering colored objects in the workplace (graphics, machine coding, lettering, signage, artwork, etc.) as closely as possible to their intended color and intensity.

Switching of building light fixtures is arranged in a sensible and energy-saving way by work area and traffic pattern so that areas temporarily not in use may be switched off, and corridor and walkway lighting may be independently switched. *The DOE recommends switching off spaces not in use for ten minutes or longer*

Multi-lamp fixtures can be dimmed in areas (e.g., storage, reception and conference rooms, kitchen) where general lighting requirements are lower than those for detailed-task areas.

Lighting fixtures located in areas where useful daylight is available can be controlled (switched or dimmed) separately. An area of any length times an interior depth from the window wall of twice the window height is recommended for separate switching.

Placement of ceiling fixtures is coordinated with furniture arrangements in work areas where the latter are stable. Interior finishes, walls, floors, ceilings, millwork, etc., are light in color, but work tops are not white or given a reflective surface.

In open ceiling or high-ceiling spaces, fixtures are hung low enough to provide effective ambient light.

There is no perceptible ballast noise or flicker from fluorescent fixtures. Fixtures installed are not dirt and dust collectors, and do not require heavy maintenance for dusting, cleaning, lamp-change, etc.

The required emergency lighting system is in place, in accordance with your local code, to restore lighting in the event of a general power failure, a building system failure or a fixture failure.

**Water
and Waste**

E48

A system of water supply and waste water disposal is in place that is adequate at all times for your personnel and operating needs.

Water is available in the locations and amounts and at the temperatures required for your use. It is provided free of turbidity (suspended matter such as silt), color, taste and odor.

Supply water is tested periodically and regularly for toxics (lead, barium, arsenic, etc.) cyanides, nitrates and fluoride in excess of the amounts programmed for dental care purposes, chlorides, pesticides, and disease producing organisms, bacteria, protozoa, etc. This testing is documented and records are available for your inspection.

Water temperatures for cleaning purposes are available at 140 F. degrees, for washing and 180 F. degrees, for sanitizing. Instant water heaters are installed for quick availability of heated water for brief, occasional use.

The water supply system is not noisy; pipes and fixtures are well-supported and do not sag or vibrate with use and are not used to carry the weight of lavatories or other hardware.

Cold water pipes are wrapped to prevent leaking from condensation.

Sinks, lavatories, drinking fountains, etc., are free from any odor of pipe gas.

Washrooms are conveniently located and readily accessible to concentrations of organization personnel.

Washrooms are designed to meet, at least, the minimum requirements of the Uniform Building Code, whether the code is applicable in your community or not.

Provisions are made for handicapped person accessibility that is; washrooms and toilets are barrier-free.

Washroom entries are designed so that persons at or using lavatories or toilet fixtures cannot be seen from the entry or outside it.

Troughs are not used as urinals.

Washroom floor and wall surfaces are finished with non-absorbent materials at least to the extent required by the Uniform Building Code.

Washrooms are ventilated mechanically, independently of the building supply-air system. Their ambient air pressure is maintained below that of the balance of the floor or building.

Separate washrooms are provided for men and women where code and/or common sense require. In the case of unisex facilities, fixtures needed by each (urinals, sanitary napkin dispensers, etc.) are provided. Permanent partitions separate all waterclosets and urinals, and both of these from lavatories.

Drinking fountains are provided in numbers and locations to meet, at least, minimum code requirements of one per 75 persons. Water is cooled to an acceptable range. Fountains are not located in washrooms.

Washrooms and their interior enclosures are well lighted, at least to the level of the general work area. (See "Lighting", above.)

Where employee rest areas are provided, they are adjacent to, but not inside or integrated with, lavatory facilities.

Eye-wash and shower equipment is installed according to code in areas where hazardous or toxic materials are in use.

Adequate space and facilities are made available for disposal of the organization's solid waste material at a location within or immediately adjacent to the building or the premises.

If the user organization is required to carry solid wastes away from the building, an adequate and easily accessible loading dock or off-street off-loading facility is available.

Life Safety   **E49**   The design of your building and its fire detection, alarm, suppression and evacuation systems are adequate to protect your organization and its people, and to meet all current requirements of the National Fire Protection Association Life Safety Code. Documentation of regular Fire Department inspections and approvals is available for your inspection.

You have been made aware, through clearly written notices and well-designed strategically placed maps and diagrams, of building features affecting life safety. Periodically, you have an opportunity to practice approved building evacuation procedures.

Building public areas, corridors, walkways, passenger and freight elevators and staging areas, loading docks, etc., and other entries and exits are kept free of obstacles, debris and flammable materials.

The building is protected, to the extent possible, against fire from adjacent properties (e.g., open fields, brush, debris, flammable storage, etc.)

Building fire detection and alarm systems are well-designed, located and maintained, and are provided with emergency power back-up and a communication system that can relay fire location data to a live monitor.

Fire exit doors and stairs are properly located, sized (44"W), identified with well illuminated signs, easily accessed, unobstructed and useable from the floor interior at all times.

Individuals on the upper floors of high-rise buildings (above seven stories, or the reach of typical Fire Department ladder equipment) have a designated fire and smoke protected refuge area available to them in the event of a fire emergency.

Fire-rated doors, walls, draft curtains (fire stops), fire hoses, etc., are properly located, installed and maintained and are operational.

Sprinklers, with flow control devices for automatic shut-off, are installed in all parts of your premises or building, regardless the local status of this code requirement. A back-up water supply system, independent of that provided for general building or Fire Department usage, is dedicated exclusively to sprinkler system operation.

Users in natural hazards areas of the country (those susceptible from time to time to earthquake, cyclones, tornadoes, and hurricanes, etc.) are provided with specific action guidelines for steps to take in the event of an occurrence.

Protective measures are apparent in the building design, construction or retrofitting, and maintenance and operation that are equal to or exceed those required by the Uniform Building Code.

MANAGEMENT DETERIORATION FACTORS

Personnel **E50** One or more landlord representatives are located in the building at all times during normal building operating hours and an office space is set aside for their use.

A landlord representative is available to receive telephone calls at all times during the day.

Landlord representatives are thoroughly familiar with, and have the means to contact, available emergency services such as hospital, fire, police, etc.

On-site landlord representatives are courteous and responsive, and are reasonably knowledgeable about their building, its various spaces, functions and operating equipment. They are familiar with services provided both by the landlord and those available through the community, like mail and package delivery, etc.

Maintenance and Housekeeping **E51** All landlord maintenance and housekeeping services provided for in the lease are performed, as scheduled, in a complete and workmanlike manner.

Public areas inside and outside the building(s) are clean and kept free of trash. Walkways are swept regularly (although water conservation will prevent hosing in many areas), landscaped areas are cut, trimmed, weeded, etc., as necessary to preserve healthy looking plantings.

Garage, parkway, surface parking area, and walkway lighting is functioning, and lamp lenses are kept clean. Lamps are replaced as needed, immediately.

Building entries, glass, hardware, floors, walls, any public area furniture and/or fixtures, elevators and lavatories, etc., are kept clean and fresh smelling.

Broken, cracked, worn, peeling, rusting or oxidizing, etc., materials and surfaces are resurfaced, repaired and replaced as necessary.

Tenant-floor public areas are cleaned and maintained in a similar manner, in accordance with your lease, but in any event so that wall and floor coverings are kept in good condition, stairs and railings are in good repair, and are safe and clean, and public area lighting is adequate and well maintained.

Your premises are cleaned, daily, in accordance with your lease and/or your housecleaning contract. In either case you should have an opportunity to examine that contract and the services to be provided in detail to see that the level of housekeeping, and security, you require is being provided for the fees you are paying.

Security **E52** The site, entries, drives, walkways, parking areas and garages are well lighted at night and periodically patrolled during the day, if open to the public.

Building areas, entries and spaces that practically can be, are walled or fenced and gated, or doored off with security devices controlled by the landlord and/or the tenant.

Billing **E53** Landlord billing is done on a regular basis, in a consistent and easy-to-interpret manner.

Commercial leases generally require monthly payment of rents, without notice, on the date specified in the lease. Most landlords provide a monthly bill, however, to charge for variable operating costs and repairs, etc., as well as rent. Repairs made at tenant expense should have prior tenant approval.

Extraneous or variable cost charges, such as rent escalations and operating expense shares, etc. are well detailed and conform to the formulas provided in the tenant lease.

Billing for repairs and/or alterations made in the tenant's behalf is accompanied by copies of the service providers' bills and/or a statement of the hours and billing rate of landlord personnel.

Step P

PLANNING

PLANNING

Understanding the Step

This is the beginning of the first step in the relocation process that is pointed at the goal of relocation.

Planning begins with the less than organized, often subconscious, process of testing ideas about something—in this case, about the idea of a workplace and all the qualities it might have. Preliminary Planning puts words and form to this process. The Review and Scorecard which follows can be used to check your progress.

Further Planning carries the process into the consciously purposeful act of organizing for relocation. In this part of planning, information gathering and thinking about budgets and schedules is going on in earnest, and you probably need to get others in the organization involved with you. Another Review and Scorecard are provided as a part of your ongoing re-evaluation process.

Farther along in the planning process you have the opportunity to make some decisions regarding outside resources, consultants, vendors, and a variety of advisors who can help you achieve your goals. You are starting to make some commitments to the idea of a new location which involve more than yourself and your close associates. This part of the process is called Commitment Planning.

The logical sequence to all the steps described will be unique and distinctly different for each reader. Read through Planning; then go back to the outline of Planning on the previous page and place these steps in an order that fits your circumstances.

PRELIMINARY PLANNING

NEED
DESCRIPTION

P1 **Put together a want list of your workplace needs.**

If your organization is getting ready to operate in its first workplace, get together with your associates and make a list of the things you would need to work with.

Specifically, describe those things that have to do with place, with the kind of town, neighborhood and building you would want to be in.

List the features of the desired building itself. See our discussion of the Want List and Quicklist in **PART I, Chapter 4**. Review, add and delete items, etc., as necessary to fit your organization or business plan.

> *Focus on things that are liable to take space, like people, equipment, furniture, etc., and/or that require utilities like power, water, telephone, etc., and/or support facilities like loading docks, warehouse or storage space, etc.*

> *Try to ignore probable cost. This is a want list.*

> *Do not project your facility wants beyond one or two years; the likelihood of more facility change in that time is too great.*

Review Your Facility Evaluation

If your organization is already at work and you have been evaluating your facility on a regular basis, update and review that evaluation now.

Use this evaluation to prepare your want list for a new location.

If you have not evaluated your existing facility, use the material in the preceding section to do that now.

Prepare a preliminary Program of space and facility needs.

Use your want list and your existing facility evaluation, if you have one, to help you.

See the discussion of the Program in **PART I, Chapter 4**, for guidance.

> *Remember the preliminary program is based on educated guesswork that will be refined and altered later, as necessary. When making estimates, guess up.*

> *Information control is important in this stage. Do not reach out too far—preferably not beyond the confines of your own office—for data.*

IN DEPTH
STUDY AREAS

P2 **Identify activities that substantially affect your day-to-day operations, the impact of which needs study before any relocation decision can be made.**

Look closely at the impact of any dislocation or interruption to telecommunications services, power availability, toxics management, human resource availability, etc., and similar activities and needs that are unique to your organization.

> *At this time, consider only the kind and extent of the information you might need, and the outside resources that might be necessary to generate it—engineers, technicians, personnel consultants, etc.*

Discreetly collect information on resource availability and cost.

EXTERNAL
CONSTRAINTS

P3 **Identify activities or outside factors beyond the control of you or your organization, which could impact your facility decision.**

See the section on Evaluation and the list of External Change Factors.

Add to this list as you see fit, with Change Factors which are appropriate to your unique situation. Discreetly collect information about them that will be helpful in your facility planning.

INTERNAL CONSTRAINTS

P4 **Identify activities or internal factors that are largely or completely within your and your organization's control, and that could impact your facility decision.**

See the section in **PART II** preceding this one; see Evaluation and the list of Internal Change Factors.

Consider the timing of your facility needs. Note the circumstance that would make it necessary or desirable to move very quickly, and those that would lengthen the necessary lead time.

Consider the numbers and experience and demographics of key personnel, the desirability of their relocation beyond certain limits and the probability they would move outside a certain area.

Consider information at hand concerning ongoing personnel assignments, budget changes, production and marketing schedules and other internal constraints that could affect the accomplishment of a move.

For relocation planning purposes, be expansive in your estimates of market and personnel growth, new products and services, etc. There will be ample opportunity to scale back to a better defined reality.

OWNING VERSUS LEASING

P5 **Consider the advantages and disadvantages of owning your facility versus leasing one.**

See the discussion of *Owning Vs. Leasing* in **PART I, Chapter 2**, for the pros and cons of being an operator of real estate and being a rent-payer.

The discussion of *Owning Vs. Leasing* does not discuss the financing of a purchase of real estate. Review your and your organization's resources for accomplishing this.

COSTS AND
BUDGETS

P6

Consider your organization's financial resources and the probable limits to your expense for facility needs.

See the discussion of *Costs and Budgets* in **PART I, Chapter 4** for guidelines to estimate the cost of relocation.

Establish an internal budget cap on facility expense, based on percentage of overhead, gross revenues, product price, or willingness to pay, etc. Write this figure down and keep it for future reference.

Check the newspapers in the area of your probable interest for local commercial real estate advertising and published rental and property sales offerings.

EXISTING
LEASE
REVIEW

P7

Review the terms of all documents comprising your lease(s) on all of the spaces you now occupy that could be affected by your decision to relocate.

Look for and examine all lease language that might affect your ability to accomplish a relocation such as:

- **Lease termination dates**. If you have more than one lease, are the various leases co-terminous? (Do they end on the same date?) Is your lease termination at least one year away? You will need that much time or more to get ready for and make a move.

- **Holding over penalties.** Should you pay the additional rent for extending your stay in current quarters, if necessary, or should you try now for a short-term extension at your current rate?

- **Renewal options**. Do you have such an option? Does it establish a new rent rate that you can use to compare facilities costs at other locations? Can you set new terms now and still keep your relocation option open?

- **Terms of default**. Can you estimate the cost of leaving your lease with a substantial remainder? Would that remainder have market value?

■ **Sideletter Agreements**. Are there any third-party agreements that would substantially alter the above terms.?

See our review of the Lease document in **PART I, Chapter 4**.

The information you seek is available in your own files. Be certain you review an original lease, correctly dated, and signed by your landlord.

If you have serious doubts about some important interpretation of your lease, contact your attorney for help. Remember that this review is preliminary in nature.

PRELIMINARY PLANNING REVIEW

Take a break now and review your preliminary planning.

Circle one answer for each question below that comes closest to matching your observation after your preliminary planning. Add the values of the numbers preceding your selections and compare your total with the scorecard guidelines that follow the questionnaire.

How urgent is the need to relocate?
(1) We must move.
(2) We ought to move.
(3) It won't make much difference.
(4) We're somewhat better off here.
(5) We're much better off here.

Are relocation costs affordable ?
(1) They're surprisingly low.
(2) They're costly but affordable.
(3) They're just manageable.
(4) They will be a problem for us.
(5) They will be extremely difficult for us.

Are rents affordable?
(1) They are less than we are now paying.
(2) They may be less or about the same.
(3) They're a little higher but OK.
(4) They're higher and barely affordable.
(5) They're a lot more than we're paying now.

Can you get what you want somewhere else?
(1) We can get everything we want elsewhere.
(2) We can get most of what we want.
(3) We can make a little improvement.
(4) We probably can't do better.
(5) We definitely can't improve.

What is the impact on Operations?
(1) Very positive, we'll function much better.
(2) Positive, we'll function better.
(3) OK. we'll function about the same.
(4) We may not operate quite as well.
(5) We may have problems elsewhere.

What is the likely impact on personnel?
(1) High approval likely. No losses.
(2) Approval likely, few losses.
(3) Some will like it; some won't.
(4) We may lose some key people.
(5) We risk major losses.

Are there places to move to?
(1) There are lots of choices available.
(2) Good selection of locations.
(3) There are some choices.
(4) There are few choices.
(5) Alarmingly little available.

How soon can you move?

(1) Within the next six months.
(2) Within six to 12 months.
(3) Within one to two years.
(4) Within two to three years.
(5) More than three years away.

Will the existing lease penalize you ?

(1) No penalties of any kind.
(2) Minor holding-over penalty.
(3) Some extra rent, but manageable.
(4) A big portion of the lease will remain.
(5) We'll need a big lease buyout.

Can you deal with Internal and External factors?

(1) No problems.
(2) Some very manageable problems.
(3) No problems we can't solve.
(4) There are some difficult problems.
(5) There are extremely difficult problems.

TOTAL ( ) TOTAL

SCORECARD

If the total of the answers you have checked is in the range of:

40 to 50 You don't have to move. There is little to gain, and the move would be costly in many ways. Think about terminating the planning process now.

30 to 40 Gains may not equal losses if you relocate, but you may want to continue the planning process until you get better direction.

20 to 30 The probable gains seem to outweigh the negatives. You are on the right track and should continue the planning process.

10 to 20 The signs seem to be clear that a relocation is a good idea and continuing the planning process is very much in order.

FURTHER PLANNING

PROJECT
STAFF

P8

Invite, assemble, delegate and/or appoint one or more of your assistants or associates to help you move the relocation project along.

Prepare an informal job description for the help you will need.

See **PART I, Chapter 3** for a description of the User Project Manager (UPM) and the support that person usually requires.

Determine where you can locate—in what office or workspace—the person(s) who will manage the project.

Determine to what extent you wish to advise others in the organization of your plans to relocate your facility, and the part they might play, if any.

PROJECT
PROCEDURES

P9

Meet with members of your staff whom you wish to have informed about, or participate in, the management of the relocation project, and discuss ways to efficiently advance the project.

Identify your designated UPM and that person's assistants, if any.

Establish overview responsibilities for broad areas of concern such as Finance, Operations, Compliance, etc.

Establish procedures for information collection and distribution, approvals and decision making, etc.

Determine the need for confidentiality, if any, of information with respect to other staff and employees, clients and customers, trade associations, and soliciting real estate brokers and developers., etc.

The nature of the facility relocation project is such that activities and participants must often cut across traditional lines of organization

273

practice and protocol. Discuss ways that your organization will handle these circumstances.

Review your organization's guidelines for procedures applicable to major project management, or develop informal guidelines compatible with organization philosophy and practice. Establish a protocol that recognizes the unusual temporary conditions which project personnel will have to operate under.

PROJECT
GOALS

P10 **Identify some desirable and achievable goals and discuss these with concerned staff.**

Look at:

- Relocation cost parameters
- Target locations
- Best site, building and space
- Personnel changes
- Operations changes
- Facility changes
- Move in date
- Image, etc.

Use information gathered in your Preliminary Planning to plug into the goals list, above.

> *It is important that project team personnel have targets, no matter how flexible or liable to change. Target dates, budget ceilings, etc., should be flexible and conservative and capable of adjustment with new data.*

If real estate information you have assembled appears inadequate and you require more detailed availability and rental rate information, consider retaining a broker for that limited service.

(See *The Broker* in **PART I, Chapter 3.**)

LONG LEAD
TIME ITEMS

P11 **Note major items whose delivery involves substantial delay or whose installation in a new**

location must occur on a pre-determined and specified date.

Check your Want List and your Preliminary Program for items like the following:

- Production or laboratory equipment
- Data processing equipment
- Warehouse racks
- Motorized library or file racks
- Telecommunications systems
- Above standard floor covering
- Executive furniture
- Workstation or panel systems

Initiate a process of detailed specification of long lead-time items.

Research distributors, dealers, manufacturers, etc. in the local area. Identify the best and alternative resources for each item.

Collect information on:

- Product construction
- Price, discounts, mark-ons, etc.
- Delivery lead-time
- Warranties, buyer protection
- Contracts,deposits, cancellation rights
- Toxic or hazardous materials
- Installers and installation procedures
- Public agency approvals required
- Product chain of distribution
- Probable shipper(s)
- Off-site warehousing and costs
- Product discontinuations, new items
- User training

RESOURCE NEEDS

P12   **Identify relocation-related services and resources that will be needed and are not available in-house.**

Identify the information needed and the type of expertise required.

Real estate data may need to be refined and may require a broker. Specification of telecommunication equipment may require a specialist in that area. An architect may be needed to make refinements to the architectural program and/or delineate planning and design ideas.

Be detailed and specific in your descriptions of need. Outside help has a way of creating dependencies and still greater expense. Identify the correct specialty needed: lawyers for contracts, designers for color, engineers for structures, etc.

IN DEPTH
STUDY :

P13

PROGRAMMING

Update, refine and expand your preliminary Program of facility needs.

Review the discussion of the in-house *programming* process in **PART I, Chapter 4**

Discuss and prepare space standards for offices and work-stations. Define the optimal adjacency relationships (who needs to be near whom) among the various functions in your organization.

Prepare procedures for collecting needed information, delegate data gathering and processing responsibilities.

Prepare forms and questionnaires.

Schedule interviews and walk throughs of your existing workspace.

Consider the use of a design professional with programming experience to assist you. Describe the way that professional would best fit into your process. Limit services at this time to Programming plus a conceptual space plan or block plan.

Guide, instruct and collaborate with the design professional, if one has been retained for the programming task.

IN DEPTH
STUDY:

TELECOM

P14 **Develop a telecommunications plan that anticipates the organization's long term voice-and-data equipment needs.**

See the discussion of telecommunications and management information systems in **PART I, Chapter 3,** *Vendors*.

Prepare a want list similar to the one you did for the facility as a whole. Focus on your need for the best possible intra-office and inter-organizational communication. If you have not had a chance to think of your telephone service as a MIS, or Management Information System, now is an excellent opportunity to do this.

Consider your needs for frequency and volume of all, including the most incidental, telephone traffic, from point to point within the organization, and between various points within and outside of the organization.

Consider your needs for data storage, data retrieval and processing, and the speed with which retrieval and processing should be accomplished.

Collect detailed information on local telephone dial tone company services, capabilities and limitations, and on private systems and equipment manufacturers and installers.

Try to collect cost information from these organizations that will allow you to determine per call costs of all telephone usage, regardless its origin, purpose, destination or frequency.

IN-DEPTH STUDY:

POWER AND UTILITIES

P15 **Develop an equipment plan that anticipates the organization's needs for power and other utilities normally provided through community infrastructure, (power, water, waste disposal, gas, etc.)**

> *The purpose of this plan is to determine the extent and cost of your dependency on local utilities, the resulting impact on your operating flexibility, and the changes in equipment and utility needs that may be suggested.*

If, in your experience, your power and other utility needs substantially exceed normal or standard requirements for a commercial facility, detail these needs now.

Inventory existing equipment, noting power and utility requirements for each piece, as well as size and weight for space planning and structural planning purposes.

Contact local utility companies for service and rate information, and managers of major users in the area in which you are interested in relocating for indications of service failures or problems.

IN DEPTH STUDY:

HUMAN RESOURCES

P16 **Develop and/or review your staffing plan with a view to the impact on it of a facility relocation.**

Review information concerning needed skills and skill levels.

Review information at hand, or solicit such information from public and professional agencies in the community of your interest, concerning:

- Local skills and human resources
- Housing availability and costs
- School availability and quality
- Public transportation
- Automobile commutes
- Local and state taxes
- Public facilities and amenities

For demographic studies, see the local Chamber of Commerce; city, state departments of finance, trade, commerce, health, etc., the Rand McNally Commercial Atlas, the U.S. Bureau of Labor Statistics, local economic development associations, local universities and colleges, local newspapers, trade associations, transportation authorities, etc.

Review Federal, State and local statutes and union agreements regarding employee rights in the event of a relocation of the employer. Establish internal guidelines with respect to wage differentials and housing cost differentials.

Determine the timing and manner of your announcement of the relocation to organization personnel, and estimate the probable impact of that announcement on key personnel.

IN DEPTH STUDY:

SPECIAL AREAS

P17 **Examine areas, other than those discussed above, that are critical to your operation and the planning, design and construction of which have an impact on, or are affected by, your facility.**

Consider the following:

- Collection and temporary storage facilities for toxic wastes,
- Storage bins, sheds, vaults, enclosures, etc., for hazardous material storage,
- Truck access, circulation and loading dock facilities,
- Ramps and special entry doors for materials handling equipment, over-sized loads, etc.,
- Raised floors for data-processing areas,
- Surface and/or overhead raceway systems for cabling and wiring
- Overhead cranes, overhead observation or control booths, ceiling structure mounted exhaust system ducting and stacks, etc.

279

■ Over-standard clear spans requiring structural reinforcement, etc.

Your new location, wherever it is, will routinely and customarily provide a limited number of generic features or accommodations designed for your type of operation. These will not fill the type of need noted above, but will provide the necessary underlying structure.

Structures, attachments, millwork, etc., left behind by a previous tenant are often available, but will seldom meet technical specifications, nor be suitable for more than temporary use.

PUBLIC
AGENCY
REQUIREMENTS

P18

Investigate the regulations imposed on occupants of commercial facilities in your community or the local area to which you plan to relocate.

See the discussion of public agencies in **PART I, Chapter 3**, Public Officials.

Consider these typical areas of public agency concern:

■ Commercial zoning
■ Construction and building codes
■ Food preparation and handling
■ Workman's compensation
■ Employee safety / fire safety
■ Provisions for the disabled
■ Toxic and hazardous materials
■ Airborne pathogens
■ Environmental air and water contamination
■ Vehicular traffic control
■ Interior workplace (VDT) environment

Obtain officially printed copies of guidelines, statutes, ordinances, etc. Where appropriate, start the process for appeals to especially costly regulations.

Notify concerned agencies of your plans to move. Put them on notice to provide you with pertinent agency regulations and guidelines.

Call and visit, where possible, local agency offices to receive printed instructions and interpretations, review maps, etc.

Anticipate regulatory pipeline delay, the probable lead time to approval, and estimated cost, or other complication, of post-move-in compliance.

VENDORS, F F & E

P19

Inventory your existing furniture and equipment, and evaluate its current condition and suitability for continued use.

Collect information regarding loose furniture (chairs, desks, tables, file cabinets, etc.), workstation or systems furniture, floor-standing equipment, portable (work-top) equipment, etc.

Depending on the nature and use of the items being inventoried and/or evaluated, information on the following characteristics will be useful:

- Type
- Manufacturer and model number
- Size, (height, width, depth)
- Age
- Color, finish, fabric, pattern, etc.,
- Power or utility required
- Access space required,
- Condition, appearance, serviceability

Check with local dealers for used office furniture and equipment, and with local repair and refinishing shops for items which can be restored. (See the discussion of *Furniture & Equipment* in **PART I, Chapter 3,** Vendors.)

VENDORS, PRODUCTS AND SERVICES

P20

Identify and collect information on products and services related to your relocation that have not yet been discussed.

Consider your need for the following:

- Design professional
- Broker
- Personnel consultant and/or agency.
- Residential moving and transfer agent,
- Residential real estate agents
- Storage and warehousing
- Commercial mover
- Printing, stationery and supplies, etc.
- Graphic designer

Describe the needs of your organization in these and other areas specified by you. Search for available resources, solicit product, service and cost information, distribute (internally), and evaluate the information received.

See the discussion of the *Players* in **PART I, Chapter 3**.

Contact the local Chamber of Commerce for names and contact information on resources serving commercial users. For cross-referencing and checking of background data on these resources, contact:

- Your industry organization
- Any local utility company
- Owners of or agents for major buildings
- Administrators for large local users
- The SBA (Small Business Administration)
- The Building Owners & Managers Association
- Your fraternal order (Masons, BPOE, etc.)

Prepare a brief, written description of the product and/or service you need and submit this to two or three vendors, with a request for a statement of competence, and delivery and price guidelines.

COST
ESTIMATES

P21

Identify all areas of study, relocation activities, resources, products and services, etc., that have cost implications. Prepare a budget outline.

See our discussion of relocation *Costs and Budgets* in **PART I, Chapter 4**. Make the best estimate you can at this time of the probable new Cost of Occupancy, including:

■ Rent, including operating expenses
■ Tenant improvements
■ Personnel
■ F F & E
■ Moving

FURTHER PLANNING REVIEW

You have reached another **GO/NO-GO** point in your relocation planning process. It is time to look at the results of Further Planning, compare them with your last checklist and see if you are still on track. Are the indications for a relocation still the same? Stop now and look at your situation before you commit to further expense.

Our questions are much the same, but different. Review them and check your response to each. Add the numerical values of each answer you checked to arrive at a total value, as you did before.

Are anticipated relocation costs still within reason?

(1) They are well within reason.
(2) They are manageable.
(3) With luck, they'll fit in our budget.
(4) Estimates are in excess of our budget.
(5) Some severe budget cuts will be necessary.

Are probable rents still manageable?

(1) We can make some substantial savings.
(2) They are well within our budget.
(3) They will meet our budget.
(4) They will probably exceed our budget.
(5) They are much higher than we expected.

Do prospective locations look better that your present location?

(1) Several locations appear much better.
(2) There are a couple of better locations.
(3) There may be one better location.
(4) There isn't anything better out there.
(5) We can't improve what we have.

Can you meet preliminary project goals and timetables?

(1) We can achieve all our goals.
(2) We can achieve most of our goals on schedule.
(3) We can achieve many of our goals.
(4) We'll give up some goals, but we'll make it.
(5) We'll have problems with goals and schedules.

Can your needs for major operating systems be met?

(1) Operations and systems will greatly improve.
(2) We can install the operating systems we need.
(3) We can function about the same.
(4) We may not be able to function quite as well.
(5) We'll definitely lose some efficiency.

Can you get the professional help you need, on time?

(1) We can get good professional help anytime.
(2) If we plan well, we can get what we need.
(3) We can make do with what is available.
(4) Professional help will be hard to get.
(5) Key professionals are not available.

Can you meet your telecommunication and utility needs?	(1) We can get everything we need. (2) With some effort we can get what we need. (3) We can duplicate what we have. (4) We'll be missing some features we enjoy now. (5) We can not meet our minimum level of need.
Can you meet personnel problems and needs?	(1) We'll be able to improve in this area. (2) We expect few problems and manageable costs. (3) Personnel losses and costs will be as expected. (4) Personnel losses and costs will exceed budget. (5) We will have major personnel problems.
Can you meet public agency requirements?	(1) This area will be much improved. (2) Public agencies will not be a problem. (3) We can probably meet these requirements. (4) Some of these requirements could be costly. (5) These requirements will penalize us heavily.
Do Internal or External Factors greatly alter your plans?	(1) These are encouraging to all our plans. (2) No problems are anticipated. (3) All these factors are manageable. (4) Some factors could give us problems. (5) Several factors present major problems.

TOTAL   ( )   TOTAL

SCORECARD

If the total of the answers you have checked is in the range of:

40 to 50   You don't **have** to move. There is little to gain, and the move would be costly in many ways.

30 to 40   Gains may not equal losses if you relocate, but you may want to continue planning until you get a better sense of direction.

20 to 30   The probable gains seem to outweigh the negatives. You're on the right track and should continue the planning process.

10 to 20   The signs seem to be clear that a relocation is in order.

COMMITMENT PLANNING

PROJECT
CRITERIA

P22

Prepare a list of characteristics and features that can be used as criteria for selecting a new facility.

> *Such a list would represent a combination of your Want List, the facility evaluation you prepared for an existing facility, goals information, and cost estimate and budget information.*

SITE
SEARCH

P23

Contact a commercial real estate broker of your choice to assist you with a search for a new facility location.

Provide the broker with your project criteria and review it with him/her in detail.

Review the broker's market information and provide guidance with respect to candidate site characteristics.

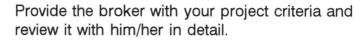

Establish time guidelines and broker reporting procedures. Conclude an arrangement for payment of the broker's fees for services.

(See *The Broker* in **PART I, Chapter 3**.)

> *For the names of commercial real estate brokers active in the area where you plan to relocate and in your facility type, call the nearest office of the Society of Industrial and Office Realtors (SIOR), the Chamber of Commerce, the local city or school district property management group, the local office of BOMA (Building Owners and Managers Association), or the local office of a brokerage firm you know.*

SITE
REVIEW
PROCESS

P24

Contact a design professional of your choice to assist you with a review and update of your Program, a technical evaluation of prospective site information, and trial space layouts, (see below).

Prepare a Request for Proposal (see *Requests for Proposal* in **PART I, Chapter 4**.) of limited design professional services. Solicit a statement of capabilities.

> *For the names of candidate design professionals in your area, call the nearest office of the American Institute of Architects (AIA), the Institute of Business Designers (IBD) or the facility manager with a local college or large corporation.*

Provide the design professional with all data related to your physical facility requirements, including your Program and Want List and broker-provided information concerning candidate sites. Establish contract terms, reporting procedures and schedules.

EXAMINE
SITES

P25

Identify a number of prospective sites in the area where you might relocate and make an informal and preliminary evaluation of each.

Keep the following in mind.

- Select as many sites to look at as appear to fit your needs description.
- Do site drive-bys at your leisure, evenings and weekends.
- Drive and/or walk the site(s).
- Look through building public areas when they are open.
- Pick up standard leasing brochures.

> *This is a first look-through, to be done with or without a broker and without formal notice of your interest to an owner. Use your Want List, Program, and/or site-selection criteria to guide you.*

See *Evaluations & Analyses*, **PART I, Chapter 4**.

| SITE DATA | **P26** | **Review the site information collected in the informal site examination of the previous step.** |

Within your staff or project management group, exclusive of outsiders, discuss User first impressions of facility sites.

Review the results of your staff or project management group discussion of prospective sites with your broker and architect or design professional.

Request corresponding site information from your broker, along with additional building and ownership details, and rental or purchase information.

| SHORT LIST | **P27** | **Create a list of candidate relocation sites to be examined in detail.** |

From your information-gathering and reviews and discussions above, eliminate, if appropriate, unsuitable sites from consideration. Generate a list of approximately three sites that are available and otherwise generally suitable for your occupancy.

Examine the Short List by means of a guided walk-through of the selected projects.

Arrange with each landlord or landlord agent to be conducted through their building and be shown the premises they might make available.

> *This is a landlord show. User questions in this environment may not elicit useful answers and should be kept to a minimum. No User commitments, or indications of preference of any kind should be made.*

> *Careful observations should be made and notes taken of any observed condition that might require correction. Follow up site visits should be made, as needed, to answer all User questions.*

R F P

P28

Prepare and transmit to the owners of the Short List properties a Request for Proposal to lease and/or to buy their facilities at the location indicated.

See the discussion of the *Request for Proposal* in **PART I, Chapter 4**, and the Landlord's RFP form in the Appendix. Allow ten days to two weeks for the Owner's initial response.

EVALUATE
SITE DATA

P29

Evaluate each proposal submitted in response to your RFP.

Using the guidelines in External Change Factors, Deterioration Change Factors, and the instructions for Measurement, evaluate the site data provided.

(See *Evaluation* at the start of this Part; also see **PART I, Chapter 4** for the Quicklist.)

> *In evaluating site data provided by those responding to your RFP, include your own personal response to items you noted during your informal site visits.*

Determine what areas, if any, in the Short List of projects, require examination by a qualified technician or professional.

Request a brief report on the condition of each of the specified area(s) (e.g., conditions of structure, hazardous materials, mechanical equipment, acoustics), and an estimate of the time and costs involved in bringing the condition in question up to an acceptable level.

Hire third-party professionals or technicians, not connected with the owners of the properties in question or with brokers or design professionals previously hired.

Request a commitment for reimbursement of the costs of these services from the appropriate property owner.

EVALUATE FINANCIAL TERMS

P30 Abstract all cost information from the proposals received and submit this data to a rigorous comparative examination.

Check for completeness of financial information. (See *Costs & Budgets*, **PART I, Chapter 4**).

If your organization already employs a system of financial analysis suitable for discount rates and simple future value calculations over a term as long as the fixed portion of a proposed lease, use the system for this purpose.

> *Use all figures consistently. Choose a conservatively high median of the variable expense figures proposed for your analysis of all proposals (e.g., CPI, interest rates, operating expense estimates), and a conservatively low figure for discount rates.*

Review our discussion in **PART I, Chapter 4**, *Costs & Budget Estimates*.

EVALUATE SPACE LAYOUTS

P31 Ask your design professional to prepare a single-line drawing space plan of your requirements in each of the (two or three) projects under consideration.

> *The drawing should be to a 1/4 or 1/8th inch scale, developed strictly according to previously approved User space standards*

> *Only critical, clarifying detail and dimensions need to be shown.*

> *Furniture and/or equipment should be shown where it is important to an understanding of space use.*

> *Design professional's space planning strategy, organizing elements (like corridors), "soft" space, etc., should be the same for all trials.*

EVALUATE
LEASE
FORMS

P32

Examine the lease or purchase agreement form submitted by the proposing Short List project owners.

Study the form for organization and completeness, extent of landlord bias, clarity, etc.

If appropriate, request a review by your attorney.

Review *The Lease Agreement* in **PART I, Chapter 4**.

RANK
PROPOSALS

P33

Review and score each Owner proposal received and rank them in terms of their suitability for your organization's use.

Establish an order of priority or order of relative importance among your building selection criteria (above). Rank the candidate projects initially on the basis of grades received for the first ten of these priority criteria.

If this process does not produce a clear preference, or limit the preferences to no more than two, review information submitted concerning the balance of your selection criteria. Develop an additional ranking. If this fails to produce a clear choice, continue with your examination of candidate project detail until you have exhausted available and important information. If necessary, ask your broker to contact the owner for additional information.

If necessary, arrange for another walk-through of the site, or sites, selected for final consideration.

SITE
SELECTION

P34 **Notify the preferred-site owner of your intent to proceed with the work necessary to relocate your organization into the owner's project or building.**

This notice should be given as soon as possible after the decision is made. It should be made informally and preferably not in writing. Competing projects should be notified, preferably in writing, of the status of your choice at this time.

Letters-of-intent should be avoided. Lease execution can take place following Documenting and the start of the Execution phase of the work.

Step D

DOCUMENTING

DOCUMENTING

Understanding the Step

You have made some more key, critical decisions and passed another **GO/NO-GO** point. It is time to move on!

You are ready to begin documenting those decisions preparatory to starting construction on your new space. You are almost halfway to the end of the path to relocation, and still very much in control of the process, your budget and your future commitments—which is where you want to be. There are still opportunities for Murphy's Law to halt the project or slow it down—which is why it is wise to guard your commitments. Keep your contractors and your future landlord in check, but don't let them lose their enthusiasm!

In this next set of steps, your outside team, architect, attorney, broker, etc.—if allowed—can be of great help in implementing the tough decisions you had to make in **Planning**. This is a period when you can diminish your own input and get the most from the skills of others.

In **Documenting**, use your good common sense with regard to the sequence of work. Many of the tasks described can be accomplished concurrently—and should be. Your attorney can work on your lease independently from the balance of the team, as can vendors processing orders. The contractor must wait for the completion of construction documents before submitting a firm bid, but he can familiarize himself with the site and plan well before bidding, and he should be encouraged to do so.

STARTING UP **D1** **Bring the User Project Team together to establish administrative procedures and protocols, schedules, task assignments, etc., to facilitate the progress of the Documenting phase of the work.**

Discuss roles, tasks, working relationships, reporting procedures, etc. Establish guidelines prior to meeting with the new outside team members.

> *When meeting with outside team members, reaffirm User leadership and control of the project.*
>
> *Be clear about duties, relationships, performance quality and timing. Emphasize economy of time and expense if that is appropriate; emphasize detail, thoroughness, and quality of presentation if that is of principal concern.*

Establish clear limits, if desired, of outside team members' access to facilities or User personnel.

Establish a project team work space, or a War Room, and identify User administrative support staff.

Prepare a space adequate for small internal conferences (provided large meeting space is available when required), and storage and mounting of project materials. A secured room that is well-lighted, conducive to clutter, paste-up, pin-up, and away from mainstream traffic, is preferred.

Bring all schedules, Code and Permit material, documents, research reports, study materials, plans and drawings, etc., together into the War Room. If appropriate, establish a checkout system for these materials.

Establish a manned project communications center within or adjacent to the War Room.

> *The Documenting and Execution phases will require substantial support in the nature of telephone work (initiating and receiving), word*

processing and document maintenance, etc. The assignment of a User staff person on a part-time or full time basis for this activity is recommended.

**RFP FOR
DESIGN
PROFESSIONAL**

PROFESSIONAL CONTRACTS

Review your requirements and take the steps necessary to bring on to your team the professional assistance you need in the areas of real estate, space planning, design and construction.

Prepare a short list of candidates in each area.

Prepare and transmit a written Request For Proposal to each candidate.

D2 **Review and discuss the nature and extent of the space planning and design work that needs to be done to prepare your premises and to move your organization into new quarters.**

Review the discussion of architects and the design professional in **PART I, Chapter 4**.

Describe the project in writing (or update the previously written project description) and itemize the tasks to be performed, eg:

- Program update
- Space plan
- Interior design
- Bidding documents
- Supervision of the work, etc.

List the background, training and experience required. in your own terms, define the kind of look or appearance design you seek.

From your work in **P24**, prepare a short list of candidate professionals. Seek an informal expression of interest from each and, if practical, hold a preliminary interview to probe methodology and preferred fee structure.

Selecting a design professional on a fee basis is not a recommended procedure, so soliciting a fee estimate at this time is unnecessary. The nature of the practice and its practitioners is such that a satisfactorily competitive fee may be negotiated following selection.

Incorporate all of the above in a Request for Proposal. Transmit this to each candidate professional being invited to bid. If appropriate, include the design professional who prepared your program of facility requirements.

RFP FOR
BROKER

D3 **Review your organization's requirements for a real estate broker, develop a short list of candidate brokers and prepare and transmit a Request for Proposal of Services to each.**

Review and discuss the nature and extent of the work to be done to select your new quarters and enter into a new lease or purchase agreement.

Review the discussion of brokers in **PART I, Chapter 4**, and your work in **P23**.

Use the project description prepared previously (see above), and itemize the tasks required from this point forward:

- Broker rent analysis
- Broker lease analysis
- Mediation and negotiation

If you have been satisfied with their earlier services and fee arrangements, include the Broker who assisted you in **P23,** above in your list of candidates.

Prepare a Request for Proposal of Broker Services, develop a short list of candidate brokers, and invite the professionals on that list to respond.

SELECT
BROKER

D4 **Enter into an agreement with the broker of your choice for the services indicated, or for extended services in the case of the broker used earlier in the project.**

There is no standard or typical form for such an agreement, except that it contain the ingredients of an enforceable contract, such as a statement of work to be done, consideration, a defined time period, and signatures, etc.

The rent and the lease analyses prepared by the broker should supplement and not substitute for those your organization does internally.

The functions of mediation and negotiation are variable in content and duration. They are best defined by a number of hours on a weekly basis that the User/tenant is willing to pay for, and the broker is willing to commit for, the fee asked.

The broker functions of mediation and negotiation can extend beyond the User/tenant/landlord relationship, to include interaction with design professionals, contractors, consultants, etc.

(See the discussion of broker fees and commissions in **PART I, Chapter 4**).

EVALUATE
THE DESIGN
PROFESSIONAL

D5

Review and discuss their written submittals with proposing design professionals and inspect samples of their work.

The extent of your evaluation will depend on the extent to which appearance design considerations are a part of your project, since examples of the latter should be viewed first hand, if possible.

Evaluate planning capabilities through the professional's two-dimensional work.

On-site evaluations of plan effectiveness alone can be distorted by the poor housekeeping of the host-client.

(See the discussion of the subject in **PART I, Chapter 3**, *Design Professional Selection*)

Look for contractor and sub-contractor references who can inform the User about the ability of the design professional to generate contractor-friendly drawings and specifications.

Establish a set of selection criteria and a ranking method, using the five-point system, to evaluate and rank the competing design professionals.

SELECT
THE DESIGN
PROFESSIONAL

D6 **Review available contract forms, determine the scope of services required, negotiate fees and costs, etc., and execute a contract for services with the selected design professional.**

Review the selected proposal and preferred fee structure in terms of the AIA contract for services.

> *The **AIA** document for Interior Design Services is recommended for most design and construction of commercial tenant premises. This form is available through the local office of the AIA, or by writing the American Institute of Architects, 1735 New York Ave., N.W., Washington, D.C., 20006.*

Select a fee structure and payment method that accommodates the nature of the project and your organization's systems, keeping in mind these general characteristics:

- An **Hourly rate multiple** (multiple of direct personnel expense or **DPE**) are preferable for brief assignments, some Additional Services and supervision of the work.
- A **fixed fee** or **stipulated sum** is difficult to evaluate unless it is accompanied by an hourly rate schedule, and an estimate of task hours.
- A **percentage fee** can be acceptable when the scope of work is very large and the risks to the provider are known to be greater than with the typical interior construction project. Conflicts of interest are easily generated by this fee structure.
- A **fee based on square footage** has the same inherent conflicts, since the design professional

is critical to the process of increasing or decreasing User square footage.

Review all services described for the nature and extent of their limits, (e.g., where does a service become extended, overtime, or additional, and become billable at a hourly rate?)

Review the list of Additional Services for tasks that fall outside the scope of your fee agreement, but appear to be a logical part of it.

The obligation of the agreement should be predicated on User need--that is it should be cancelable upon reasonable notice.

The AIA contract agreement typically does not extend to matters of liability, indemnification, insurance, etc. Professional liability insurance should be requested. Errors and Omissions insurance in the amounts popularized by the lawsuits of recent years has become prohibitively expensive for many architectural practitioners, and the User may have to accommodate the professional in some way in this matter.

SELECT TECHNICAL SPECIALISTS AND CONSULTANTS

D7 **Review your requirements for outside technical assistance with your staff, your broker and your design professional, solicit the services of competing providers, and select and contract those needed.**

Review the technical reports you obtained in **Planning**. General guidelines for determining the need for such providers:

■ The Uniform Building Code or local statutes may require data, analyses or tests, etc., prior to issuing approvals for special structural or electrical loads, hazardous waste disposal methods, etc.

■ User/tenant functions may require a level of technical input not available through the relocation project team (e.g., acoustics, lighting, security).

Commercial product vendors often employ fully trained professionals, who can be made available at little or no cost when the sale of a product appears possible.

In contrast to our advice on this matter concerning design professionals, above, check for proof of professional liability insurance coverage prior to finalizing contractual arrangements with needed technical consultants.

DOCUMENT
THE PROGRAM

D8

Update your Facility Requirements Program and prepare a complete and final draft for distribution to all interested parties.

Consult with your staff and your design professional on the work necessary to put this document into final, fully useable form.

Submit abstracts of departmental portions of the program to department heads for their review, comment and written approval.

Review, confirm and alter as necessary, all earlier selections of planning standards, modules, and sizes, etc.

Incorporate updated furniture and equipment inventories.

Review, confirm and/or establish furniture standards for item size, type, style, color and pattern, etc. Identify items to be newly purchased or leased.

Incorporate all additions, deletions and changes made by staff and others. Review the updated document.

Print, compile and durably bind sufficient numbers of the new program for use by team members and selected vendors, staff and service providers.

(Review the discussion of *The Program* in **PART I, Chapter 4.**)

DOCUMENT PLANS AND DESIGNS

Instruct your design professional to prepare a space plan based on the organization's needs, as described in the approved program.

Discuss and establish an informal protocol for review, change and approval of the design professional's work.

Review the schedule of work outlined in the design professional's contract. Confirm the work to be done in this step along with anticipated completion and review dates.

BUILDING
CODES

D9 **Review applicable segments of the local municipal building code with your design professional to determine those that are most likely to affect your plan.**

Acquire a copy of your Municipal Building Code at the office of your city's Building Department or its equivalent. If your construction is outside city lines, contact the appropriate county office.

A personal visit to that office is recommended.

Since the local Code will incorporate the Uniform Building Code by reference, you will need a copy of the UBC. If it is not sold locally, contact the offices of the International Conference of Building Officials at 5360 South Workman Rd., Whittier, CA 90601

BLOCK PLANS

D10 **Instruct the design professional to prepare a block plan study, based on your most recent program information.**

If block plans or comparative plans have already been drawn for the space in question, the design professional should proceed with his/her work based on these.

(See the discussion of Space Plans and Designs in **PART I, Chapter 4**.)

If more than one planning scheme or concept has been recommended for study, a plan based on each concept should be prepared in sufficient detail that there is no doubt about the outcome of its development.

Initial versions of the plan should consist of single line drawings, to scale and freehand, if the design professional so chooses.

Distribute, review, study and comment on the block plans and/or space plans that have been submitted.

Prepare sufficient copies for your review so that each User team member has a copy to read and mark up.

Review the comments from Team-member copies. Compile and resubmit these to the design professional.

The User should retain a copy of each plan, as altered by the User Team, for future reference.

Each Department Head and Team member is well advised to maintain a record of each plan change submitted or recommendation made by them.

Avoid submitting originals of marked or annotated plans or drawings to persons outside the User organization or the User Project Team. Do not allow current annotated drawings outside of the War Room.

SPACE PLANS AND DRAWINGS **D11** **When a block plan has been approved, instruct your design professional to proceed with a full space plan.**

In the case of multi-floor or multi-building projects, the first space plan should include the development of all areas.

Avoid requests to approve space plans in which floor areas are marked as "typical" or "same as..." other floor areas.

Adjustments and refinements to the space plan, even of a "minor" nature, should always be shown in the context of the entire plan, or a complete floor.

Review the space plan submitted by the design professional and check it for:

- General readability and completeness
- Conformance with the Program
- Conformance with Code
- Conformance with approved space standards
- Traffic flow (corridor configuration)
- The relationship of user functions, etc.

Review elevations, details, sketches, models and other materials submitted in conjunction with the space plan, to describe designed features of the project. Check for:

- Accuracy and completeness
- Impact, if any, on plan function
- Efficiency
- Compatibility with User design guidelines
- Probable cost/budget relationship
- Need for additional descriptive materials
- Need for color samples, etc.

Approve a space plan, and design concept. Distribute copies or portions of the approved plan to group or department leaders for review, comments, approval and signature.

Maintain a file of signed space plans in the War Room.

Request a reproducible copy of the approved space plan from your design professional to print and distribute copies internally and for requesting consultants and vendors, etc.

DOCUMENT CONSTRUCTION

STRATEGIES **D12** **Instruct your design professional to start preparation of construction documents based on the approved space plan and design concept material.**

With your project team and your design professional, discuss the desired approach to constructing your premises from the point of view of economy, quality and on-time performance.

Consult your lease agreement and its workletter, to determine the arrangements for construction that it permits. If the lease permits Tenant hiring of the contractor, explore the pros and cons of a negotiated contract vs. bidding.

With your design professional, discuss the time and cost implications of each approach on production of your construction documents.

Discuss the recommended approach to development of an accurate construction cost estimate.

Discuss and review the Owner/contractor agreements best suited to your work.

Discuss and review the design professional's planned approach to the preparation of construction documents, including:

- The nature and number of sheets to be drawn
- The subcontractors to be involved
- The nature and extent of written specifications required, etc.

PRELIMINARY **D13** **Distribute a space plan, including telephone and**
CONSTRUCTION **electrical information, and an outline specification,**
COST ESTIMATE **to construction contractors interested in preparing a preliminary construction cost estimate.**

> *The outline specification should include written instructions that are critical to estimating the cost of materials and labor.*

Assemble a list of area contractors. Send each a brief description of your project and request a statement of interest and qualifications.

Describe your current need and explain that, to be useful, the estimate you seek must be as detailed as the information you have provided will permit. It should provide, at a minimum, estimates of all significant line items. Ask for:

- A description of each item
- Unit cost of each item
- Contractor's overhead and profit structure
- The contractor's bonding level
- Normal amounts of insurance carried
- Contractor's role with respect to permits and agency approvals.

REGULATORY AGENCIES

D14 **Seek preliminary approval from regulatory agencies:**

- Building Department
- Fire Marshall (state and local);
- EPA
- OSHA
- Department of Health
- Zoning Commission
- Planning Commission
- Design Review Board
- Other agencies with approval authority.

Review the discussion of public agencies and public officials in **PART I, Chapter 3**.

SECONDARY SYSTEMS

D15 **Provide your design professional with a checklist of secondary systems required, e.g.:**

- Time (clock) systems
- Paging, intercom
- Security, building protection
- LAN systems
- Cable TV, (satellite dish)

- Gas,oxygen, and other gases
- Vacuum, and/or compressed air
- Distilled water and/or steam
- Pneumatic tube
- Raised floor
- Robotics systems.

Contact all utility companies and public authorities regarding all utility services. Get written approval for service connections.

Check conformance with all local public and utility regulations.

PREPARE DOCUMENTS FOR CONSTRUCTION   D16

Prepare all documents necessary to fix and describe the project, to include:

- Bidding Requirements: Notice to Bidders, Advertisement or invitation, Instructions to Bidders, Sample Bid Form
- Plans and drawings
- Owner/Contractor Agreement
- General Conditions
- Supplemental Conditions, if any
- Technical Specifications

Ask engineers and consultants to prepare layouts and drawings required to illustrate and describe their portion of the work.

- Structural
- Mechanical
- Electrical, and others.

Check document preparation progress against the design professionals' schedules.

Review and update schedules of completion dates and check compliance of drawings with your User program.

As pertinent documents are completed, seek and get approval from the Public Agencies noted above.

Check with agencies for submittal and review procedures and schedules.

Discuss and determine alternates and substitutions to be allowed in construction methods and materials.

Determine installations that are to be made by User personnel and are not to be included in the construction contract.

Provide the design professional with the schedules for the delivery of all owner-furnished materials, equipment, installations, etc.

Determine your requirements for phased occupancy.

Advise the design professional so that drawings and construction can proceed accordingly.

CHECK DOCUMENTS	**D17**	**Review, correct and alter the finished documents as required, check them against the program, approved space plans and designs, consultants and engineers work, etc.**

Request copies of General Conditions of construction contract for review and approval.

Check the documents for Architect's and Engineer's seals.

PERMITS	**D18**	**File the required documents for approvals and permits.**

Review the discussion of public agencies and public officials in **PART I, Chapter 3.**

PREPARE TO BID CONSTRUCTION	**D19**	**If the construction contract is to be bid, instruct the architect to publish the advertisement to bid, and/or distribute invitations, and/or issue documents to plan rooms to solicit bids.**

Follow a similar procedure to distribute invitations for separate prime contracts, (e.g., carpet, millwork, cabling, raised floor.)

Instruct the architect to collect deposits against the cost of printing, etc.

Hold a pre-bidding conference.

Receive, tabulate and analyze bids; evaluate proposed substitutions and note selection of alternates.

NEGOTIATED CONTRACT **D20** **Negotiate the terms of contract with the selected contractor.**

If the construction contract is not to be bid, discuss the selection process with the architect.

Review and evaluate the responses of interested contractors to your earlier request for qualifying data; arrange personal interviews with two or three of them.

Provide each with the plans you have developed. Explain the nature of your project, and discuss the pros and cons of the negotiated contract versus the bidding process with each.

Select a contractor with whom you wish to continue detailed discussions; negotiate the terms of a construction agreement.

VENDOR CONTRACTS

Initiate actions necessary to issue purchase orders for major items of Furniture and Equipment.

Review actions taken in **Planning.** Review the status of inventory and equipment descriptions.

(Review the discussion of *Vendors* in **PART I, Chapter 4.)**

Review lists of available resources: manufacturers, dealers, distributors, suppliers, etc. Contact a limited number of these to determine general availability and lead time information on the products you seek.

Review the availability and relative advantages, if any, of leasing the type of equipment you require.

MAJOR
EQUIPMENT

D21

Prepare a detailed draft specification of the equipment needed for review by the User person most concerned; request a draft specification from that person.

Transmit the draft specification, for information purposes only, to selected resources for a confirmation of availability of the item in the detail, form and finish, etc., desired.

Determine the conditions, if any, attached to the delivery, assembly, installation and placement in operation of the items in question.

Identify points of interface between the building and the equipment or system to be installed. Bring these to the attention of your design professional and contractor.

See the checklist in **PART I, Chapter 3**, under *Furniture & Equipment Vendors*.

Request that all parties concerned notify the UPM of the lead time and additional costs, if any, required by each in preparing for installation of the item.

Discuss with equipment operators, supervisors, department heads and your design professional, the feasibility/advisability of consolidating equipment utilities and supplies, and how this might be done.

Identify features of the equipment and its installation that might be subject to public agency regulation and contact those agencies for information regarding required approvals.

Interview agency personnel, if possible. Determine test data, specifications and other information they may require. Determine the nature form and cost of any permits required.

Determine the lead time required for Agency inspection and approval.

Convey the above information to your design professional, contractor and other concerned parties.

Identify the utilities (electricity, water, gas, telephone and data lines, etc.) required for the equipment you plan to install.

Contact local utility companies for information concerning availabilities, rates and installation.

Request information regarding utility installation lead time, and inspections and approvals required.

Use utility technicians and experts to assist you in detailing equipment placement and utility connections, recommended power, features, etc.

Where more than one utility is involved in the same installation, provide each with information concerning the involvement of the other.

Advise your design professional and contractor, in writing, of all of the above.

Review and redraft your equipment specification to include all of the information developed above, prepare a Request for Proposal and transmit this to selected manufacturers and suppliers.

> *Follow your organization's normal purchasing procedures.*

Request manufacturer/dealer recommendations regarding warehousing, shipping, receipt, assembly, installation, testing, and start-up. With certain equipment, the nominal additional cost of these services from the source is well worth the risk involved in assuming responsibility for equipment too early, or at all.

Provide each respondent with the project description you developed earlier and a schedule of completion dates, including the anticipated installation of the equipment in question.

> *Allow sufficient time in your required delivery date for manufacturer's delays and equipment testing and repair (or replacement) on-site.*

Request references and the location of the nearest installation of a unit identical or most similar to that being proposed to your organization.

Review and evaluate each response to your request for proposal and cost estimate, select a resource for each item and issue purchase orders.

Confer with your operating and technical staff regarding the review of references and a site visit to the equipment installation recommended by the preferred vendor.

> *Make this visit at your expense to avoid future misunderstanding; send only those members of User staff most qualified to perform a detailed technical evaluation.*

Select and specify optional features, colors, finishes, fabrics, trim, etc., and coordinate these choices with your design professional.

If appropriate, submit an approved contract to your attorney for comment

TELECOM **D22** **Contact a business representative of your local telephone company, describe the size and nature of your organization, and any inadequacies of your present system.**

Request an evaluation and recommendation by the local telephone company representative concerning required upgrades in the existing system or proposed configuration of a new system.

Contact independent telephone system service and equipment providers; request a similar evaluation and recommendations.

Try your Chamber of Commerce or the business reporter of your local newspaper for alternative telephone companies and telephone equipment and systems dealers.

Determine the number of lines you require for the type and volume of traffic you generate (include fax, modems, data lines, etc.); anticipate and verify their availability with the local telephone company.

Review the recommendations and informal proposals made by telecommunications equipment and service providers and prepare and transmit a Request for Proposal to selected providers.

Establish clear User performance guidelines for the system, equipment or service (e.g., cabling) based on requirements over the term of your new lease or longer.

Provide respondents with a copy of your program and a telephone plan based on your space plan, and a schedule of critical project dates.

Establish a delivery date for installation, substantially in advance of the date planned for rollover from your current system to provide for delivery delays and system testing.

Coordinate all dates closely with your local telephone company, your design professional and your contractor.

Discuss and coordinate your plans for cabling service with your Contractor

Review and evaluate each response to your request for proposal for telecommunications

systems and equipment, select one or more resources, as appropriate, issue purchase orders and enter into contracts.

Review your preferred sources with representatives of your local and long distance services, your rate wholesaler, rate accountant, telecommunications consultant, etc., to resolve any perceived conflicts in installation or service.

If appropriate, submit approved contracts to your attorney for comment.

THE MOVER   **D23**   **Select three commercial moving companies in your area to visit your premises and discuss their recommendations regarding the relocation of your organization, its furniture and equipment.**

Review the discussion of the Mover in **PART I, Chapter 3**.

Request information regarding marking, tagging and packing system, moving equipment and supplies, personnel, availability (work schedule), security, insurance, etc., and rate structure.

If appropriate to your needs, discuss the implications of a staged move.

Request a meeting with and interview the individual proposed as each mover's move coordinator.

Evaluate the interview data and select three moving companies to submit proposals for services.

Provide each with a project description, a copy of the facility program, a schedule of critical dates and hours, and addresses, locations and maps, etc., of existing and new locations involved in the move.

Indicate probable hazards, narrow passageways and routes, delicate or oversize equipment, unusually costly items (artwork, etc.) and other factors that might not be uncovered by reasonable due diligence by the mover.

Discuss and identify optional proposals to exclude or include certain specified furniture and equipment (systems furniture, laboratory or warehouse equipment, etc.) that could be relocated and installed by others.

Clearly state the levels of moving personnel performance, behavior and dress that are acceptable to your organization.

Request written confirmation of the presence on your project of the move coordinator previously approved by you.

Evaluate the proposals received, select a moving company, and execute a contract for services.

If appropriate, submit an approved contract to your attorney for comment.

THE LEASE

DOCUMENT
THE LEASE

D24

Review the lease document submitted by the selected project Owner/landlord and determine your organization's preferred approach to it.

Submit a copy of the entire agreement to your attorney and to your broker, and of those portions of it pertaining to their areas of expertise, to your architect and other consultants, for an overview and preliminary opinion.

Request an opinion from your consultants, and determine the advisability of:

Developing your own lease agreement to submit to the landlord for approval; or refining your organization's standard lease form for the purpose of this project and submitting this lease to your landlord for review and approval.

> *In most instances, use of the landlord's lease can be recommended.*

Look back over your lease review procedures and specific comments regarding this landlord's lease if it came up during **Planning**.

(Review our discussion of the Lease Agreement in **PART I, Chapter 4**.)

If you elect to work with the landlord's lease, meet with your team to structure a detailed review of the lease and establish procedures, schedules, areas of emphasis, negotiating strategies, etc.

Determine reading and review assignments (see below) and the additional fees required for this activity, if any. Set limits to the time and fees involved.

Provide your review group with guidance regarding special emphases, concerns and non-concerns of your organization.

Determine the most efficient format for recording the organization's lease comments, and for annotating the lease.

Designate a lease secretary or lease compiler who is to be solely responsible for maintaining the necessary record of lease comments, and/or reducing them to acceptable language.

Establish a lease-review liaison with the landlord or a landlord representative to deal with administrative and procedural matters during the lease review period.

> *Landlord-tenant dialogue seldom takes place on a principal-to-principal basis; costly misunderstandings can develop regarding the authority of those acting in their behalf.*

Maintain the tenant-landlord relationship through communication at comparable personal-comfort levels, if possible: agent to agent; attorney to attorney; professional to professional; principal to principal; etc.

For purposes of review and analysis, approach the lease through its distinctive parts, e.g., business terms, workletter, operating expenses, contingencies, etc.

Limit the time spent in discussing any single segment.

Develop substitute solutions and/or language; do not stop at the establishment of objections.

Establish and confirm a rationale for your position, and/or need to alter language; and note it in writing for future discussion.

Develop an informal method of valuing your positions on various questions, in terms of degree of importance to the User organization.

Do not release original User comments or notes to the landlord representative for study or review.

Arrange for and enter into discussions of the lease with the landlord until an agreement is concluded or it is clear to all concerned that an agreement cannot be reached.

Evaluate the probable nature and climate of these discussions; select a representative for the User organization who can best promote your interests in the circumstances you describe.

> *If lease discussions extend beyond a reasonable period of time, best determined by User organization judgment, or they encounter substantial difficulties that continue to resist resolution, the User organization should re-establish contact with the next-preferred project on their Short List.*

Once an agreement has been reached and the appropriate documents have been executed, request signed originals in a quantity not to exceed those required for your files.

Maintain a copy of the last pre-execution lease draft in your files.

When you receive leases to be signed from the landlord, compare each with your latest pre-execution lease draft.

> *The content of each "original" should represent all details of your draft agreement. Note and report discrepancies to the landlord.*

Execute the lease originals and transmit them to your landlord.

Lease signing protocol requires tenant execution before that of the landlord.

Photocopy and file one of the lease originals you signed

Upon receipt of the landlord-executed originals, compare these with your photocopy. Note any discrepancies and report these to your landlord and/or your attorney. To minimize future confusion, destroy all draft copies of the lease agreement; maintain notes that can provide future historical perspective.

Step X

EXECUTION

Step X   EXECUTION

EXECUTION

**Understanding
the Step**

You completed your part of the **Execution** of the relocation process at the end of the last step, when you signed all of those contracts with design professionals, brokers, landlords, lawyers, contractors, etc. Now you are entering the period, very often a long one, when you must watch while others fulfill their obligations to you.

But this is not an idle period, because the watching you will do is critical to the success of your project, and because there are still move-preparations to be accomplished within the organization.

This is also the period when the quality of planning and documenting becomes most apparent and when you must face the awful reality of the weaknesses that are inherent in this process for everyone who attempts it. We mention this because, whether it's called process management or crisis management, you will want to control the finger-pointing that invariably accompanies a facility relocation.

Two aspects of relocation are often overlooked in the euphoria of arriving in your new home. The matter of *housekeeping* gets passing attention, when it deserves major mention for being the one activity that, more than any other, will demonstrate how successful your move was.

When it is set in motion in your new home, *Evaluation* will complete the cycle you started many months, perhaps years before.

STRATEGIES

PROJECT
COMPLETION
PROCEDURES

X1 **Discuss and fix procedures for fully utilizing your contracted resources and completing the project.**

Meet with your Project Team, minus outsiders, to review and discuss the current status of the project.

Update, review and discuss project budgets and schedules. Review this entire step, including MOVE PREPARATIONS at the end of it; make any necessary adjustments to your schedule.

Review and discus the need, desirability, and implications of a staged move, or one that requires an interruption in the moving process of several days or weeks.

Schedule budget review checkpoints through the balance of the project, since there will be changes as the work progresses that will result in altered budgets.

Establish a priority level project review meeting to take place weekly through completion of the project, and more frequently as needed.

Establish staff responsibilities in key areas: construction, regulatory agencies, telecommunications/MIS, equipment and systems, furniture, moving, etc.

Discuss follow-up procedures, techniques, tools, strategies, etc.; develop an agenda and schedule for the Pre-Construction Conference.

Discuss and make note of special User emphases in attention to the work or workmanship that should be conveyed to the General Contractor.

Arrange with your contractor or design professional for an accompanied practice walk-through of a site currently under construction.

Do this walk-through in the company of someone thoroughly familiar with commercial construction.

Discuss strategies and procedures with your design professional and General Contractor.

Discuss your plan for the Pre-Construction Conference and request input.

Review the General Contractor's schedule; discuss your plan for User site inspections and walk-throughs and request input and cooperation.

Arrange for a three-way discussion of expected workmanship levels on an item-by-item basis.

(See **PART I, Chapter 2**, and the discussion of the site inspection in *Execution*.)

Arrange weekly sit-down project review meetings with the General Contractor and others, as required. Arrange more frequent informal and telephone contact to discuss the work as it proceeds.

Take care of outstanding contract business such as insurance and bond certificates.

PRE **X2** CONSTRUCTION CONFERENCE

Arrange to meet with your General Contractor, your design professional, your new landlord, and key subcontractors and vendors in preparation for the start of construction.

Schedule this meeting at least one week prior to the scheduled start of construction to allow for final adjustments that result from the meeting.

Review our discussion of the Pre-Construction Conference in **PART I, Chapter 2**, *Execution*. The UPM should plan to chair this meeting.

Be prepared to distribute complete sets of drawings to those who need them. Have a supply of single sheets for those with limited needs (sub-contractors and vendors). Reduce key drawings, for convenience; distribute them in 8.5 by 11 inch format.

Provide ample written and telephone notification of the meeting to all invitees.

There will be some reluctance to attend. Choose a comfortable, neutral venue and provide appropriate refreshment. The meeting will not be short.

Prepare an agenda and bring your file material on permits, hazards, and other due diligence.

WORK PERMITS **X3** **Closely monitor schedules for securing work permits at your site.**

In most jurisdictions, work is not supposed to begin until a permit has been issued for the trade in question and is on display at the site.

Work of an approved trade that is dependent on one that is not yet permitted may not be able to proceed until the missing permit is obtained.

Ask to see the required permit once it is obtained by the trade in question; photocopy it for your records; see that the original (or copy if so allowed) is securely fastened at the location required by local law.

Ask to be advised by beeper or phone when an inspector has appeared at the site; accompany that inspector along with the appropriate contractor on his tour of the work in question.

Make periodic checks of work permit inspection schedules and stay current with the status of work approvals by responsible agencies.

Most local law requires that work remain uncovered, or easily visible, for inspection. This can often mean that other work cannot proceed until an inspection has been made and an approval given.

When a contractor feels that an inspector's rejection of his work has been made capriciously--or maliciously--the contractor may ignore the required correction and prejudice the progress of the project.)

CONSTRUCTION PROCEDURES

CONSTRUCTION
SITE
INSPECTIONS

X4

Familiarize yourself with the construction site, its general environment and key personnel, like security guards and the project superintendent.

See **PART I, Chapter 2**, and the discussion, in *Execution* of the **Site Inspection**.

Observe the Work.

Use the **Quicklist** in **PART I, Chapter 4**; note your observations alongside items in the list that correspond to an area of concern in your project.

Add subjects that are not covered in this list.

Schedule visits for stages of activity in each area until the activity is complete.

Review the results of your observations with the contractor's Project Manager on a daily basis, if appropriate.

If your approval is requested for the start of an activity, provide that approval at or by the time requested.

> *Your contractor will often seek your approval of activities like the placement of walls or panel boards, etc.*

Provide your contractor with an immediate follow up, in writing, of verbal reports of all key observations.

Observe completed work before it is closed up or built on and submit any comments to the contractor.

> *These observations constitute a preliminary punch-list of the work in question. (See the Punch List, Step X9.) Since the labor and materials involved are about to be hidden from view, they cannot benefit from the final punch list for construction.*

Observe and check the leveling of floors prior to the start of interior construction.

All poured floors, especially those above grade, are subject to sag and unevenness. Floor leveling is critical in spaces where equipment and/or furniture performance (and appearance) requires aligning and/or leveling with little or no need for shimming.

Observe above the ceiling work (duct work, electrical and telecom cabling, light fixtures, acoustical material, etc.) before the placing of ceiling tile.

Observe acoustic material placement, electrical and telecom wiring, electrical outlets, plumbing pipe, etc., before the closure or completion of sheet-rock partitions.

Observe coring of the floor for electrical outlets or waste water drains, etc., prior to installation of the finished flooring material.

INDEPENDENT CONTRACTORS

X5 Provide necessary on-site guidance and assistance to independent contractors, as they require.

If you have employed contractors independent of the contract for general construction (for mechanical systems, carpet, millwork, etc.), you will be responsible for certain logistical and/or administrative assistance, like providing access, electrical power, etc., when they need it.

Verify, check and follow up on construction site requirements for Other Systems installations.

Most systems contractors will be operating independently of the General Contractor but will require a certain amount of site preparation to install their equipment properly. These requirements should become a part of the documents for general construction, but are frequently overlooked.

Here are a few typical requirements:

Telephone: Telephone equipment room and/or wall-mounted panel boards, utility risers, and conduit for running wire, outlets with jacks and pull-strings, etc.

DP/MIS/LAN: Space and conduit above the ceiling and/or below the (raised) floor, with separate raceways for voice, data, signal and electrical power. Extra (isolated) air ducts and/or dedicated AC equipment for a dust free environment for main-frames, power surge protectors, a fire-protection device (other than sprinklers) for main frames, static-free floor covering for equipment rooms.

Security: Panel board space. Above the ceiling space and dedicated raceways for wiring, dedicated locations for TV monitors with blocking for equipment attachments, electronically operated door locks, etc.

Intercom: A speaker connected system for music, paging, white sound, alarms, etc., requires counter and/or shelf space for tape and control cabinets, and above the ceiling space for wire in dedicated raceways. Ceiling tiles in which speakers are to be mounted should be set to one side.

Gas: Lines for natural gas need to be brought, from the utility's point of supply, to a convenient and accessible location in the building for a meter and from which pipe can be run to your premises. An adequate pipe-chase must be made available. The installation will require municipal inspection.

Bottled gas: Propane, oxygen, acetylene, etc. should be located off-premises (outside a fire-wall or in a fire-rated enclosure) in accordance with local Fire code. Space should be provided for above the ceiling routing of gas pipe, or corridors of sufficient width for carting bottles.

Exhaust: Requirements may be determined from equipment manufacturers' specifications, and/or local health code, or OSHA regulations pertaining to the release of toxic gases. Exhaust air and gases must exit outside (if allowed) and generally at the top of a building.

Water: For other than city water (distilled, ionized, etc.) and other process liquids, sufficient space will be required for storage of containers near freight elevators and/or loading docks. Piped water will require space and power for a code approved pumping system. Gravity feed systems will require structural bracing and reinforcing

Others: Other systematized distribution of materials or services, like robot carts, dumb waiters, pneumatic tubes, etc., will require some degree of building preparation prior to their installation Their manufacturers should be consulted for particulars.

WORK SITE CONDITIONS

X6 Make periodic checks of general work site conditions for which contractors may not have responsibility and/or are being ignored.

See that construction trash is removed periodically and is not obstructing, or endangering, general traffic on sidewalks and streets or other tenants or public in a building.

Arrange for traffic police when circumstances suggest.

Arrange for portable toilets and/or on-site food vendors as appropriate.

CHANGES IN THE WORK

X7 Review requests for changes in the work as they arise and approve work changes as appropriate.

Request unit costs and total costs for the work; compare these to costs for the original item.

Review the specifications, and/or request an explanation of the performance specifications of any item being added or substituted.

Evaluate the impact of the recommended change, addition or substitution, etc., on other work and other related components.

Ask for, and verify the reasons for, substantial disparities between new and original quantities or costs when these will add to your total project cost.

In the interest of the progress of the project, act to review and approve requested changes as quickly as possible.

> *Changes in the work will occur with some frequency and precise cost information will be lacking or ignored in the rush to complete something. Track the costs of these changes carefully and frequently, in accordance with the schedule you established earlier.*

APPROVALS
& PAYMENTS

X8 **Review Shop Drawings, materials samples and mock-ups, etc., as required.**

Review this material as soon after its presentation as possible to advance the work that depends on it as quickly as possible.

Be sure the information provided is sufficient to make a reasonably informed decision.

> *Shop drawings originate in fabrication shops which often do not have trained draftspersons or a clear idea of the information needed.*

> *Similarly, mock-ups will often lack key elements, because of excessive cost or lack of availability, which are important to the function of the whole.*

Review requests and authorize payments for work as required by your various contracts.

Review your contracts for the conditions and amounts of periodic payments and retainage.

The actual extent of completion at intermediate stages of the work is approximated on the basis of observation and good faith. The retained amount of the contract, negotiated at the outset, should be adequate to provide incentive for the contractor to complete a quality job.

Final payment is normally due upon substantial completion of the work as specified in the contract. The definition of the latter is agreed upon at the time of contract negotiation. An agreed upon portion of the final payment may be held by the User for punchlist items that remain unfinished.

Completion and approval of the remaining items must occur within a specified time for the balance of retainage to become due.

Request a release of liens from contractors and sub-contractors.

CONSTRUCTION PUNCH LISTS **X9** **Prepare, and/or review punch lists to be prepared for authorization of final payment for the contractors' work, and for identifying items to be corrected.**

The final punch list is a tedious and exacting task and one wisely assigned to an architect or design professional.

Perform the punch list based on your observations of the work to date, preliminary conversations with the contractor concerning levels of acceptable workmanship, your understanding of the construction documents, etc.

The interior architectural punch list is organized by space or room number, by compass direction, (North, South, etc.) and by surface (wall, ceiling, floor, etc.)

Since the punch list is prepared while walking and looking, the most efficient means of recording it are by voice-recorder. A hand-held dictating machine is excellent; one with a hands-free microphone is even better.

Submit the punch list to the contractor so that listed deficiencies may be corrected.

If the punch list has been prepared by an architect or design professional, review it carefully before submittal and incorporate (but do not duplicate) findings from your own observations.

Review and approve corrections of deficiencies as requested by the contractor, when a significant amount of work has been done--that is, limit the amount of time which you have to spend making follow-up punch lists.

INSTALLATIONS

SYSTEMS **X10** **Observe the installation of the components of Telecommunications and Other Systems, listed above, under INDEPENDENT CONTRACTORS.**

Review purchase agreements and documents to identify the system components contracted and to verify those delivered and waiting for installation.

> *Installers are often unfamiliar with detailed order information and will proceed to install a component which may fit but which may not be of the capacity or type, etc., ordered.*

If it is not specified in drawings or other documents and instructions, advise the contractor/installer regarding the on-site location and manner of the component's installation.

After the equipment provider verifies that the installation is complete, prepare an installation punch list for submittal to the provider/contractor.

In evaluating the installation of systems components, consider:

- Ease of their operation by your staff
- Security
- Ventilation
- Obstruction of other activities or equipment
- Noise
- Appearance
- Housekeeping problems.

EQUIPMENT
INSTALLATION **X11** **Observe the installation of Equipment.**

Review the notes above about verifying the equipment awaiting installation.

> *Motivated by a contract to complete an installation, contract installers will sometimes proceed with the wrong equipment in order to fulfill their limited obligation.*

If moving the equipment into place will be costly and time consuming, you should arrange to check it before installation at the distributor's, shipper's or installer's location. If you fail to do this, you may suffer from the results to a far greater extent than the parties responsible for any errors.

Prepare the site for delivery.

See that off-street access, loading dock and platform space, building entry, freight elevator, corridor floor and wall protectors, doors and door removal, ceiling, floor and wall obstructions, etc., are ready.

See that the installation area is free of debris, well lighted and that installation and assembly crews have the information necessary to locate washroom and waste disposal facilities, common tools and hardware, telephone, food service, personal transportation, etc.

Prepare and submit punchlists of installed equipment to their providers.

Review your purchase order documents for guidance with respect to specifications, warranties, operating instructions, start-up conditions, etc.

Prepare your punch list after the equipment installer verifies that the installation is complete, all power and utility hook-ups have been made, and an observed test-run or start has been made.

Check for and report equipment installation deficiencies in the following areas:

> **Operation:** The equipment satisfies agreed upon specifications and functions properly.
>
> **Human engineering:** Controls and equipment functions are conveniently placed and comfortable to work.
>
> **Fixturing:** Sufficient and proper supports and attachments have been made to secure the equipment.
>
> **Appearance:** All exposed surfaces are finished or treated in the material and color,

etc., specified. Places where construction is joined, drilled, cut, blocked, fastened, etc., are satisfactorily repaired, sealed and finished.

SYSTEMS
FURNITURE
INSTALLATION

X12 **Observe the installation of (panel) systems furniture**

See the comments above regarding preparation of the site for equipment installation.

Measure the site (space or room) and verify actual dimensions for workstation placement.

Where these are slightly at variance with the dimensions shown on your furniture plan or partition plan, differences may be divided (added to or subtracted from) among aisle or corridor spaces. Substantial subtractions of space from code corridors can cause safety problems or unwanted encounters with building inspectors.

Verify locations and alignment of overhead light fixtures, especially for free-standing (floating) work stations.

Verify locations of power, data and telephone outlets, especially for free-standing work stations.

Power poles, for free-standing work stations, should abut workstation walls. They will be best located where two or more work stations meet. Floor mounted or under-carpet outlets or junction boxes should fall directly under the workstation wall or immediately inside it.

Where the space plan allows for dimensional flexibility in the layout of workstations, move them as necessary to cover floor outlets or abut power poles.

Avoid the use of work station panels with stabilizing floor supports which intrude into aisle space.

Firmly fasten work station panels to one another in strict accordance with the manufacturers' instructions.

Fixtures hung on workstation wall interiors (and the things put on them) should not exceed the load limit established by the manufacturer. They should be hung in accordance with the manufacturers' suggested layouts of work surfaces, storage, task lighting, etc.

(See the discussion of work station design in connection with the ADA and pending VDT legislation in **PART I, Chapter 3**, *Public Officials*).

Prepare and submit a punchlist for the work station system installation.

Work station furniture systems can be evaluated on the basis of the following:

- Conformance of the product with the manufacturer's specifications

- Your reasonable expectations concerning furniture function and appearance

- The quality of the installation.

Where the manufacturer, vendor and installer are distinct and independent enterprises, send the punchlist to each.

COMPLETION PROCEDURES

NOTIFICATION **X13**
OF PROJECT
STATUS

Inform concerned parties of the status of your project and its stage of completion so that they may take action to facilitate your relocation.

If local public agencies require a certificate of occupancy and/or a final inspection before approval for occupancy, request that action or certificate, based on the various inspections, corrections and approvals made during the construction of your premises.

Request utility company approvals of your installations at your new location, and request a date for the initiation of services.

Notify your Mover of the completion status of your new premises. Ask that their team inspect the new installation in preparation for the move.

Notify your existing landlord of the date and time of your planned move-out. Discuss any landlord arrangements and procedures for existing building access, hours, air conditioning or heating, security, freight elevators and loading docks, etc.

Notify your insurers of the coming move. Verify the adequacy of property damage and liability coverage that may be required during the move period, notwithstanding the mover's insurance.

Notify equipment manufacturers and lenders who have an interest in your equipment or furniture of your move. Determine the extent of any change in status, payments, warranties, etc., as a result of the change in your location.

Notify utility companies and others providing regular or long-term contract services at your existing location of your planned move-out date.

Arrange for your relocation project team members to tour the newly completed premises.

WORKLETTER
COMPLETION

X14 **Notify your landlord of the status of construction and your plans to occupy the premises, in accordance with the terms of your lease and your workletter.**

Whether or not it is explicitly required by your lease, ask your landlord to inspect your premises and new construction and to approve them for your occupancy.

If your lease provides for a fixed rent start date with the landlord sharing responsibility for construction, and you were not able to move in on or before that date, settle responsibility for the time delay under the terms of the workletter, prior to move-in.

Inspect your completed premises.

> *If your lease start is dependent on satisfactory landlord completion of the premises, you will be asked to inspect the premises immediately upon completion by the landlord contractor and to notify the landlord of your acceptance of them.*

> *You may have agreed already to terms for a conditional acceptance--based on substantial completion--that is, no work remains that, by its omission or by being performed while you occupy the premises, would interfere with your use of the premises. Such allowable conditions are referred to as minor punch list items.*

If you are moving in under the terms of a building standard workletter, settle (identify and agree on) any outstanding construction costs accounts with the landlord before move-in and taking occupancy.

If you are moving in under the terms of a tenant improvement allowance agreement with the landlord, request final reimbursement under the terms of that agreement before you move-in.

MOVE AND POST-MOVE

MOVE
PREPARATIONS **X15**

Review preparations that will be necessary for a successful and trouble-free move.

Review the checklists printed below at least one week to ten days prior to your scheduled move day. What items that are not there does it remind you to take care of?

Walk and/or drive the move route. Check for hazardous or unusual characteristics that will require special attention and care.

Prepare a move-in schedule for general distribution among User personnel. Request personnel not having specific move-day assignments to stay out of the workplace that day; give them a day off if that is appropriate to your schedule.

Convene the User project team with the mover team and rehearse the activities of move day.

Go over those activities in discussion and on paper, in step-by-step fashion, until all questions have been clarified.

Outline your plan for move-day communication among team members and plan to rent or make available whatever equipment is most appropriate (phones, cellular phones, beepers, walkie-talkies, etc.) for quick communication at each site and between sites.

Whether the move is local or long-distance, assign User team personnel at each end of the move in numbers at least equal to those recommended by the mover.

> *Whether the move is local or long-distance, overnight accommodations near the new site should be arranged for User Team personnel who will be required to start early and stay late.*

Prepare a layout of existing quarters, graphically indicating the new location of the contents of existing spaces.

Reproduce this in sufficient quantities to post in existing quarters and to distribute to user team and mover personnel.

Verify the arrangements that are being made to meet your requirements for the shut down and start up of critical User equipment such as telecommunications and data processing equipment.

Make a schedule of follow-up telephone calls to be made periodically through the evening prior to your move to verify that:

- Vendors, installers and providers will have sufficient technicians on hand at both locations to disconnect and to start up.

- If needed, back-up equipment is available and ready to be installed.

- On-line data services have been notified of the transfer.

- New telephone and extension numbers have been assigned and handsets have been tagged.

YOUR LIST   **Use the balance of this page for YOUR checklist**

X16 PRE-MOVE CHECKLIST, EXISTING QUARTERS

PAPERS/FILES
☐ Loose papers, books, files, documents, etc., are boxed, labeled and ready to move.

PERSONAL BELONGINGS
☐ Employee/staff personal belongings are boxed, labeled and ready to move.

FURNITURE
☐ Private office and work station furniture is labeled and ready to move.

LOCKS/KEYS
☐ Lockable file cabinets, cabinets and desks, etc., are locked and keys are tagged and safely stored.

ACCESSORIES
☐ Non-breakable, low-value accessories are packed, labeled and ready to move.

VALUABLES/ BREAKABLES
☐ Valuable and breakable accessories are safely arranged, labeled, and ready for mover packing.

CASH AND SECURITIES
☐ Arrangements have been made to transfer cash, gems, negotiable paper, securities and other vault contents by a security service or other insured carrier.

UTILITIES
☐ Equipment is disconnected from utilities, and loose parts and attachments are packed and labeled.

SCATTERED ITEMS
☐ Items presently widely dispersed, but destined for the same space in the new location have been brought together and labeled.

DRY ICE
☐ Dry-ice has been ordered and is on hand for the packing of perishables.

LEASE EQUIPMENT
☐ Cranes and/or materials handling equipment has been leased and is on hand for lifting and loading large and/or cumbersome and heavy equipment items.

ITEMS NOT MOVING
☐ Loose items which are not to be moved are clearly marked as such.

INVENTORY
☐ Large quantities of product inventory, parts, supplies, etc., have been inventoried, boxed, binned or bagged, etc., and taped off in groups clearly coded with their new destination information.

HAZARDOUS MATERIALS
☐ Hazardous and/or toxic materials have been properly packaged, boxed and stored in appropriate

sealed containers, labeled for separate shipment in appropriately designated and marked vehicles.

RACKS & SHELVES ☐ Racking and shelving to be moved for use in the new location are unloaded and ready for shipping and immediate assembly in the new location.

HAND TOOLS ☐ Sufficient common hand tools (hammer, screw driver, pliers, etc.) are on hand to assist as needed.

YOUR LIST **Use the balance of this page for YOUR checklist**

X17   MOVE CHECKLIST, NEW LOCATION

SIGNS
☐ Adequate numbers of temporary signs are mounted (with landlord permission as appropriate) at strategic locations to assist mover and user team personnel in locating and accessing the new site.

ROOM NUMBERS
☐ Door frames or the walls adjacent to doors (but not doors) are clearly and securely tagged with the space numbers corresponding to the space plan given to your mover.

CLOTHING
☐ Tags, caps, T-shirts, or other clearly identifying clothing are available to be worn by User personnel on move day.

TRASH
☐ The premises are clean and there is no trash or construction debris that has not been placed in appropriate containers.

CLEANING
☐ Ceilings, walls and floor covering, are clean and unblemished.

EVERYTHING WORKS
☐ All required building systems are in operation, including elevators, heating or air conditioning, as appropriate, water, lavatories, general lighting in all areas, and electrical power at convenience outlets.

WORK IS FINISHED
☐ There is no construction or installation work being done, except for that allowed by the punchlist and the workletter agreement.

LAYOUTS POSTED
☐ Layouts of the premises are both wall mounted and placed loose at any and all locations where they can be easily seen by mover and user team personnel.

HAND TOOLS
☐ Common hand tools (pliers, hammer, screw driver, etc.) are available in sufficient numbers, in various locations around the site.

KEYS/LOCKS
☐ Keys, cards and other unlocking devices for building entries and interior doors have been tested and are available in sufficient quantities in several secured locations.

STATIONERY
☐ New stationery and printing supplies have been shipped and are on hand in sufficient quantities to allow for immediate start-up.

PRODUCTION
SUPPLIES

☐ A sufficient quantity of production supplies and parts have been delivered to the new location, to allow for immediate production start-up.

YOUR LIST

Use the balance of this page for YOUR list.

X18   MOVE DAY CHECKLIST

TRAFFIC COPS	☐ Contract traffic police are in place, if required.
DOORS/GATES	☐ Security stations and security guards are alerted to your requirements, and barricades, gates, entries, loading dock doors and other doors that are to be used by your mover are unlocked and/or propped open.
RAMPS	☐ Ramps are in place where required.
CRANES AND FORKLIFTS	☐ Materials handling equipment and operators are on hand.
SCUFF PROTECTION	☐ Wall, door and floor protectors are in place, and are adjusted from time to time.
TELECOM	☐ Phones and/or walkie-talkies are in place, tested and operating.
TEAM IN PLACE	☐ User team personnel are in their assigned locations.
COFFEE & DONUTS	☐ Plenty of refreshments are on hand for the project team and movers.
YOUR LIST	**Use the balance of this page for YOUR own checklist.**

X19   FIRST WORK DAY CHECKLIST

SIGNS

☐ Adequate temporary signs are placed about the site, access drives and building interior to orient and direct your personnel to their new quarters.

POSTED LAYOUTS

☐ Copies of the layout of the new premises are well posted and are also available for distribution to each employee.

HOT-LINE

☐ An internal telephone hot-line is established and monitored during the first week to answer employees' move-related questions and to find strayed items.

WELCOME

☐ A time is set aside for formal welcoming and introduction, questions and celebration.

USER PUNCH-LIST

☐ All User organization personnel are invited to complete their own punch-list of the facility, on a form prepared by you, and to submit it for action to the UPM.

YOUR LIST

Use the balance of this page for YOUR own checklist.

X20   HOUSEKEEPING RULES

Move quickly to establish some guidelines for keeping your new quarters looking new.

SPILLOVER

■ Limit the spillover of paper, furniture and personal belongings into aisle and corridor spaces.

TACK-UPS

■ Eliminate tack-ups (ad hoc notices, posters, etc.) in specified areas; restrict them to designated locations.

GREENERY

■ Keep cabinet tops clear of anything that is not green plants or fresh flowers.

COMMON AREAS USAGE

■ Establish rules and guidelines for the use of shared areas, like waiting rooms, conference rooms, open work space, shops and laboratories, corridors, etc.

CLEAN AIR

■ If smoking is permitted at all, limit this to fully enclosed private (not shared) work spaces. Call your local Health Department for recommended clean air guidelines and methods for testing for other air contaminants. Test regularly for interior air pollution.

SOUND POLLUTION

■ Follow the guidelines you established above for clean air to the control of unwanted noise in the workplace, from any source.

WORKPLACE ART

■ Augment your public-area fine art with art for the workplace. Solicit displays of works from local artists in media suitable for showing in open work areas, shops, laboratories, etc. Local gallery owners can be encouraged to provide a gratis curatorial service in this connection. Rotate the work with some frequency.

FACILITY DEFICIENCIES

■ Establish guidelines for reporting facility deficiencies of any kind. Establish permanent facility responsibility in your organization and start your program of FACILITY EVALUATION.

APPENDIX

Construction Checklist
RFP for Architects
RFP for Brokers
RFP for Developers & Landlords

SELECTED BIBLIOGRAPHY

CONSTRUCTION CHECKLIST

Make your own checklist from the list below, adding and deleting items as appropriate for your premises and your construction. Expand each item to include conditions and characteristics of each that you want to look for.

CONSTRUCTION SITE	**Storage of materials and equipment** **Security enclosure for storage** **Command post with telephone and work table**
BUILDING SITE	**Walkways, driveways, loading docks** **Parking garage** **Parking area striping** **Exterior lighting** **Exterior signage** **Landscaping and drainage** **Handicapped provisions**
BUILDING STRUCTURE AND CORE	**Exterior doors and windows** **Loading dock** **Roof, roof parapet and downspouts** **Seismic reinforcement** **Exterior siding** **Stairs** **Elevators, passenger and freight** **Floor leveling** **Fireproofing**
MECHANICAL SYSTEM	**Building equipment room** **Furnace & chillers** **Local (floor) equipment room** **Fans and soundproofing** **Ducting and mixing system** **Thermostats** **Return air and supply air registers**

ELECTRICAL SYSTEM	**Building equipment room**
	Panel, available incoming power
	Risers, power distribution
	Transformers
	Local (floor) equipment room
	Available power
	Distribution system
	Power protection devices
	Electrical outlets
PLUMBING SYSTEM	**Water supply metering**
	Sprinkler system
	Standpipes
	Waste water system
	Lavatories and handicapped provisions
	Wet counters and water heaters
	Drinking fountains and handicapped provisions
	Emergency eyewash
	Showers
TELECOM/MIS	**Switch and cabinet equipment room**
	Cabling system, telephone and LAN
	Raised floor
	Conductive floor covering
	Jacks, telephone and data line
OTHER SYSTEMS	**Intercom**
	Gas, natural and bottled
	Exhaust
	Security
	Liquids other than city water
	TV with satellite dish
	Pneumatic tube, robotics, etc.

PARTITIONS
AND WALLS

Chalkline layout for partitions
Semi-partitions and slab-to-slab partitions
Pre-fabricated panels
Studs and sheetrock
Architectural detail
Sound batt insulation
Lead lined walls and doors
Wall caps, trim and base
Furred walls and chase walls
Structural or shear walls
Door frames and doors
Door openers, locks and closers
Door glass and sidelights
Signage, numbering and graphics

CEILINGS

Plaster ceilings
Architectural detail
Exposed, finished or unfinished ceilings
Hung ceiling grid system
Acoustic and fissured ceiling tiles
Lay-in light fixtures
Return and supply air grills
Speaker and exhaust fan grills

FLOORS

Sealed concrete slab
Raised cellular floor, removable tiles
Vinyl surfaced, roll or tiles
Carpet and carpet tiles
Wood
Stone or ceramic tile
Rubber or metal

MILLWORK

Wet counters
Shelving
Cabinets
Built-in seating
Built-in workstations
Architectural detail

FINISHES

Wall paint
Wall base, wood metal, plastic
Wall fabric
Acoustic or tackable surfaces
Architectural detail
Wood and metal doors
Plastic laminate doors
Door frames and hardware
Interior glass
Counters, shelves and cabinets
Ceilings and ceiling tiles
Wood floors
Stone or ceramic tile floors
Vinyl flooring
Carpet and/or carpet tiles

LIFE SAFETY

Exit signs
Fire doors and panic bar openers
Standpipes
Sprinklers
Fire suppression system (DP room)
Night lights
Stair and Elevator security
Ramps
Wide entry doors
Lowered drinking fountains
Lavatories for the handicapped
Elevator doors and controls

RFP TO ARCHITECTS

FROM   : Candid Corporation
TO   : Yale & Russell
RE   : Request For Proposal
DATE   : October 9, 1999

We are pleased to forward this Request for Proposal for services, in connection with the relocation of our Macro-Processing Division to new quarters in Wanona. Attached you will find a description of our company, the building or type of building we plan to move to, and our detailed facility requirements, including a statement regarding our desired level of design and finish of new tenant improvements. We are now seeking the assistance of a local design professional in the planning, design and interior construction of our new quarters. This work will be divided into two parts, as follows:

- **Part I** will consist of refining our program of requirements, the development of block plans, and the preparation of trial layouts in no more than three different locations.

- **Part II** will consist of plans and designs of our work space, preparation of construction documents, coordination of construction, and punchlists.

Your answers to the questions below will help us determine the firm or individuals best suited for this project. Please review the information attached to familiarize yourself with the nature of our project; then answer all of the questions that follow. Please key your response to the appropriate question number.

(1)   How long have you been in practice? As it is presently constituted, how long has your firm been in practice.

(2)   Please estimate the percentage of your firm's work to date in commercial projects versus other kinds of work. In the commercial area, how much has been in retail versus office versus industrial? In building type, how much of your work has been in single story buildings? Low rise buildings? High rise buildings? Identify projects in your experience that might have been similar to ours.

(3)   Please estimate how much of your work has been in building planning and design versus interior planning and design? How much in planning and design versus preparation of construction documents and construction management?

(4)   How many disciplines (architecture, engineering, interior design, construction management, etc.) are represented by your staff, and how many persons are degreed in each?

(5)   How many architects on your staff are currently licensed to practice in your state? How many are authorized to stamp drawings? How many of your engineers are so licensed?

(6)   How would you characterize your familiarity with the Uniform Building Code; Fire Code; local regulations modifying these codes; planning and zoning ordinances; regulations regarding waste and energy management, and worker health and safety; local agency personnel?

(7)   Please provide a statement regarding your professional practice liability insurance coverage. (You would be asked to submit copies of pertinent policies at the appropriate time.)

(8)   Do you sub-contract professional work? If so, what kind? Do you do your own material and finish selections? Architectural detail? Construction and/or bidding documents?

(9)   How many persons from your office do you estimate would be required to complete the work described in Part 1?

(10)   Please describe the professional background of a person from your office who might be assigned responsibility for the work in Part 1.

(11)   Please identify recent programming projects in which the person who might be responsible for this project was a significant, active participant; provide a short client contact list.

(12)   Please identify recent space planning projects in which the person who might be responsible for this project was a significant active participant, and provide a short client contact list.

(13)   Are you willing to work with a standard AIA contract form?

(14)   Please provide a brief statement describing the way you would go about completing the work outlined in Part 1.

(15)   Please estimate the total fee, or range of fee, you might charge for the work outlined in Part 1 using an AIA contract form for a fee-maximum agreement.

(16)   Please state your hourly rate charges for professional personnel. Identify those rates that would apply to persons assigned to this project.

(17)   Please indicate your current work load and availability.

We would like you to be as specific as possible in your proposal, with respect to work required in the Part I; be brief in your description of the basis on which you would work in completing the Part II. Any evaluation by us of your design capability will be accomplished at a later date. If you would like to be considered for this project, please have your response to this request in our hands no later than ten days from the date of this RFP.

Thank you for your response to this Request. Please do not hesitate to call with any questions. Feel free to submit any brochures or other supporting data that might help us evaluate your work.

By   : I.M. Upatre
Title   : Vice President
For   : Candid Corporation

RFP TO BROKERS

FROM   : Candid Corporation
TO   : Husselnrun Commercial Brokerage
RE   : Request for Proposal
DATE   : October 9, 1999

We are pleased to invite you to submit your proposal for real estate services in connection with the relocation of our Macro-Processing Division to new quarters in Wanona, in approximately 9 to 12 months. In the material attached, you will find a detailed description of our facility requirements, including the characteristics of the area where we prefer to locate.

We are familiar in a general way with the commercial property market in Wanona. We need assistance, however, in identifying the facility that will best suit our needs and meet our budget requirements. This assistance would consist of the following:

- Research properties that are available in our area of interest.

- Provide physical descriptions and rental rate data on selected properties along with your evaluation of this information.

- Facilitate exchanges of information and mediate discussions with landlords and their agents.

- Review and comment on our RFP for landlords, as well as the proposals and lease forms received from them.

Answers to the questions below will help us determine the individual broker best suited for this project. Please review the information attached to familiarize yourself with the nature of our project. Then answer all of the questions that follow. *Please key each response to the appropriate question number.* Unless otherwise indicated, each question is directed to the individual broker responding to this Request and answers should only reflect that person's experience.

(1)   Do you have a valid license to practice real estate brokerage in this state? As a broker? As a salesperson or broker associate?

(2)   Do you have an equity interest in any commercial property in this area? Please specify.

(3)   Do you presently practice as a representative of a state licensed real estate brokerage firm? Are you contracted to, or have an equity position in, the firm? Please specify.

(4) How long have you practiced real estate brokerage? How many months in the past two years have you worked exclusively in real estate brokerage? Do you support yourself from other occupations as well as real estate ?

(5) Please estimate the percentage of your time currently spent in the practice of real estate. How long have you worked in commercial real estate in this community?

(6) Please estimate the percentage of your experience in residential brokerage versus commercial brokerage. In commercial brokerage, estimate the percentage in retail versus office versus industrial. How much of your work in commercial brokerage has involved multi-tenant buildings?

(7) In approximately how many commercial projects were you directly responsible for the tasks listed above? In the past 12 months? In the past 24 months?

(8) Approximately how many square feet of commercial space have you leased ? Of the type of space we are probably looking for? In the past 12 months? In the past 24 months?

(9) Do you currently act as a landlord agent for commercial property in the area? Do you currently represent properties that might fit the description of the facility we are looking for? Please specify.

(10) Do you practice law or architecture? Do you presently work in commercial construction? In what capacity? Do you presently own an equity interest in a local firm operating in any of these areas?

(11) Please give us a brief statement characterizing your familiarity with the each of the following: commercial construction practices; interior architectural planning and design; local planning and zoning ordinances; the UBC, local Fire and Health Codes, environmental and other laws affecting commercial building in your community; commercial lease agreements.

(12) Without revealing proprietary information, tell us the types of resources you normally use in searching for a property of the type we describe.

(13) Please give us a brief statement of how you would provide the kind of assistance we have outlined above, how you would be reimbursed for your services, and an estimate of the fees involved. Please include a reference list of clients; indicate those with whom you would like us to make contact.

If you would like to be considered for this project, please have your response to this request in our hands no later than ten days from the date of this RFP. If a personal interview is suggested, we will arrange that at your convenience after a review of your submittal.

Thank you for your response to this Request. Please do not hesitate to call with any questions. Feel free to submit any brochures or other supporting data that might help us evaluate your work.

By   : I.M. Upatre
Title   : Vice President
For   : Candid Corporation

RFP TO DEVELOPERS & LANDLORDS

FROM   : Candid Corporation
TO   : Sure Management & Leasing Company
RE   : Request for Proposal (Part 4)
DATE   : October 9, 1999

This is one of five parts of our RFP of this date concerning the proposed rental of workspace in Wanona for our Company's Macro-Processing Division. The other four parts describe our company and our facility needs. In this part we ask questions concerning your company and your property at the following location which will help us determine its suitability for our operations:

Russell Business Park
Building S
1234 Corporate Blvd

Please respond to all of the following questions. You may do so in the space provided below, or in your own attachment. Please identify the name and title or position in your company of the preparer. We are familiar with this property, but you may feel free to forward any additional information explaining its features.

(1) Please review our statement of facility requirements in Part 3. Other than tenant improvements, are there any items in this statement that could not be economically provided by your facility? Please specify.

(2) Are there any items of tenant improvements noted in our statement of requirements that could not be provided economically? Please specify.

(3) Are there any items noted in our statement of requirements that would be offered by your facility, but in a substantially modified form? (Different quantities, sizes, capacities, etc.) Please specify.

(4) State the rentable area you propose based on the useable area noted in our statement of requirements. Please attach a diagram identifying the part of the site, building or floor you propose to lease.

(5) State the rent you propose, per square foot of rentable area, per year.

(6) State the lease term for which this rent would apply.

(7) State the amounts you propose for the following components of rent. Indicate whether they are included in the rental proposed above:
- Building load or add-on factor
- Taxes
- Insurance
- Operating expenses, actual or estimated.

- Allowance for tenant improvements
- Allowance for architectural services
- Abatement of rent

(8)   Describe the method you propose for distributing the tenant's share of expenses.

(9)   Describe the method you propose for increasing or escalating the tenant's share of expenses.

(10)   State the amount and basis for proposed parking charges, if any.

(11)   How do you propose tenant improvements be made? If you have a standard workletter, please enclose a copy. If your workletter lists standard improvement items, please include the current unit prices of the items listed.

(12)   Please indicate the terms you propose for the expansion and/or renewal options we have requested.

(13)   Please indicate the earliest date on which the proposed premises may be made available.

(14)   Please attach to this submittal a reference list of tenants now leasing in this or other similar properties you own or operate, and a list, with locations, of such other properties.

(15)   Please attach a copy of a typical lease, in use by your company at this property.

If you would like us to consider tenancy in your property, please have your response to this request in our hands within ten days from the date of this RFP. If an additional visit to the property seems appropriate, we will contact you at a later date to arrange such a visit.

Thank you for your response to this request. Please do not hesitate to call with any questions. Feel free to submit any brochures or other supporting data that might help us evaluate your project.

```
By      : I.M. Upatre
Title   : Vice President
For     : Candid Corporation
```

SELECTED BIBLIOGRAPHY

Ambrose, James, *Building Construction: Interior Systems*, New York, Van Nostrand, 1991.

Architecture California, a periodical published by the California Council, American Institute of Architects, Sacramento, CA., Dec 1991.

Arnold/Wurtzebach/Miles, *Modern Real Estate*, Boston, Warren, Gorham, & Lamont, 1980.

Bailey, Stephen, *Offices*, London, Butterworth, 1990.

Barna, Joel Warren, *The See-Through Years*, Houston, Rice University Press, 1992.

Becker, Franklin, *The Total Workplace*, New York, Van Nostrand, 1990.

Binder, Stephen, *Corporate Facility Planning*, New York, McGraw Hill, 1989.

Boorstin, Daniel J., *The Discoverers*, New York, Random House, 1985.

Bowman, Arthur G., and Milligan, W. Denny, *Real Estate Law in California,* Englewood Cliffs, New Jersey, Prentice-Hall, 1986.

Brandt, Peter, *Office Design*, New York, Whitney Library of Design, 1992.

Brauer, Roger L., *Facilities Planning*, New York, AMACOM, 1986.

Building, U.S.A., New York, McGraw-Hill, by the editors of Architectural Forum magazine, 1957.

Drexler, Arthur, *Transformations in Modern Architecture*, New York, The Museum of Modern Art, 1979.

Drucker, Peter, *Managing in Turbulent Times*, New York, Harper & Row, 1980.

Ergonomic Design for People at Work, Vol I, Health, Safety and Human Factors Laboratory of Eastman Kodak Co., Belmont, Ca., Lifetime Learning Publications, 1983.

Galer, Ian, *Applied Ergonomics Handbook*, London, Butterworths, 1987.

Garson, Barbara, *The Electronic Sweatshop*, New York, Simon & Schuster, 1988.

Goldberger, Paul, *The Skyscraper*, New York, Knopf, 1982.

Goumain, Pierre, *High Technology Workplaces*, New York, Van Nostrand, 1989.

Gutman, Robert, *Architectural Practice: A Critical View*, Princeton, Princeton Architectural Press, 1988.

Handbook of Facility Planning, Volume I, Laboratory Facilities, ed by Theodorus Ruys, New York, Van Nostrand, 1990.

Huxtable, Ada Louise, *Architecture, Anyone* ? New York, Random House, 1986.

Jones, Frederic H., *The Concise Dictionary of Architecture*, Los Altos, CA, Crisp, 1990.

Lacey, Dan, *Your Rights in the Workplace*, Berkeley, Nolo Press, 1991.

Magee, Gregory, *Facilities Maintenance Management*, Boston, R.S. Means, 1988.

Michelson, William, *Man and His Urban Environment*, Reading, MA, Addison-Wesley, 1976.

Molnar, John, *Facilities Management Handbook*, New York, Van Nostrand, 1983.

Mumford, Lewis, *Sticks & Stones*, New York, Dover, 2d rev ed, 1955.

Olin, H.B.; Schmidt, J.L.; Lewis, W.H., *Construction Materials, Principles and Methods*, Chicago, Institute of Financial Education, 1980.

Office Planning and Design Desk Reference, James E. Rappoport, Robert F. Cushman, Karen Daroff, ed. New York, Wiley, 1992.

Peters, Thomas J., and Waterman, Robert H., *In Search of Excellence*, New York, Harper & Row, 1982.

Rasmussen, Steen Eiler, *Experiencing Architecture*, Cambridge, MIT Press, 1959.

Scully, Vincent, *American Architecture and Urbanism*, New York, Praeger, 1969.

Stein, Reynolds, McGuiness, *Mechanical and Electrical Equipment for Buildings,* 7th Edition, New York, Wiley, 1986.

The Physical Environment at Work, D.J. Osborne and M.M. Gruneberg ed. Chichester, England, 1989.

Vischer, Jaqueline C., *Environmental Quality in Offices*, New York, Van Nostrand, 1989.

Ward, Sharon Kaye and William Gary, *Company Relocation Handbook*, Grants Pass, OR, The Oasis Press, 1991.

Whiton, Sherrill, *Interior Design and Decoration*, Philadelphia, J.B. Lippincott, 1974.

Wolfe, Tom, *From Bauhaus to Our House*, New York, Farrar Straus Giroux, 1981.

NOTES

NOTES

NOTES

NOTES

NOTES